Modern ERP

Select, Implement & Use
Today's Advanced Business Systems

Modern ERP

Select, Implement & Use
Today's Advanced Business Systems

Marianne Bradford, Ph.D., CPA

College of Management
North Carolina State University
Raleigh, NC

© 2008

Contributing Editor:	John Keadle, MBA
Editorial Assistants:	Charlotte Brewer, Jill Crook, Emily Etter, Callie Grubbs, Charmaine Lau, and Jennifer Weurding
	North Carolina State University Master of Accounting Program

Special thanks to the Jenkins Graduate College of Management Enterprise Systems class, summer 2008

Trademark Acknowledgements:

Business Objects

Cisco

COBIT

Cognos

Hyperion

IBM

ISACA

Microsoft

NetSuite

Oracle

SAP

SAS70

SPSS

These are registered trademarks in the U.S.A. and other countries. This book is not sponsored or endorsed by or affiliated with any of the above companies.

ISBN: 978-0-557-01291-6

To my brother Hudson,
who never got to write his own book
You were the money

Table of Contents

Preface

For a moment, consider the gap between what you learned in college and what you needed to know when you began your first job. If you have yet to complete your education, or are still hoping to land your first job afterwards, maybe you have acquaintances that can help you measure that gap.

On the one hand, our instruction in business academia covers the topics of management, accounting and finance in often vivid detail. On the other, our first weeks with a new employer will doubtlessly include system training. How can it be that we spend years studying business and are yet so poorly prepared to use our new knowledge to contribute to our new employer's mission?

We needn't focus our blame on our educators. The fact is that modern businesses run on modern business systems and those systems can be both sophisticated and complicated. Sophistication empowers the business system to bring more information to more employees exactly when and where it is needed to help the employee execute tasks in favorable ways. Complications allow the system to adapt to a company's unique and peculiar business needs allowing it to extend its competitive advantages further into the market.

Yet, while complication implies a need for custom training, this book seeks to close the gap between a traditional business education and the sophisticated and rapidly evolving technologies on which modern business systems rely. When we have mastered the topics covered in this book, we may still need an introduction to our employer's "system," but we need not be disadvantaged by a lack of understanding of the sophisticated technologies these systems employ.

In many ways, an evolving, dynamic company also needs its employees to "graduate," taking the knowledge gained from years of experience and embarking on a new endeavor that may include the introduction of new technologies. Perhaps you need a plan to rehabilitate a struggling firm. Perhaps, to gain some competitive advantage, your firm needs to boost efficiency in the way it interacts with customers and suppliers. Perhaps your company needs but one final boost to completely squash the competition. In each of these cases, embracing modern business systems and the accompanying benefits in business processes, business intelligence and accountability, is often the wisest move.

Whether you still anticipate your first encounter with business systems or you need to deploy, update or rework an existing system, Dr. Bradford has outlined the tasks ahead of you using three Roman numerals:

I.   Buy it - We will begin by studying the market place for modern business systems, how they work, and how to choose the best system for our needs today and in the future.

II. Deploy it - Next, we will map the effort to bring our system to life and ensure that our stakeholders quickly gain the advantages it offers.

III. Use it - Last, we will look at the advantages we gain when we've executed the first two steps appropriately and explore the new power we have over the valuable information that drives our success.

We believe our book includes the best, most current coverage of these topics. We want you to appreciate how the topics we cover will prepare you for your encounters with modern business systems that lie in your future. Whether you are currently situated in academia or in a company that relies on outdated technology, if you will work to gain a command of this subject matter, you will find that the gap between your current state and one that is more technologically empowered has closed considerably.

John Keadle, MBA
Contributing Editor

Acknowledgements

I would like to thank the following professionals for their invaluable feedback:

Gabriele Bauman, Manager
Technology SAP Center of Excellence
Talecris Biotherapeutics

Barry Delves, SAP Consultant
Plant Maintenance
GlaxoSmithKline

Lisa Dion, Manager
ISV Business Development
Microsoft Dynamics

Jill Eddy, Senior SAP Analyst
Smithfield Packing

Donald Frazier, Principal
Deloitte Consulting

Linda Hayes, Founder
Worksoft, Inc.

George Holland, Partner
Camblin and Holland Consulting, LLC

Jon Hornby
Worldwide Marketing Performance
Management
SAS Institute

Ken King, Director
Telco and Media Convergence
SAS Institute

Geoff Lewis, Regional Vice President
mcaConnect

Hiel Lindquist, Consultant

Rick Lombana
Navy ERP Project

Rufus Lohmueller, Managing Partner
LS Technologies, LLC

Cara Ridenhour, Consultant
Clarkston Consulting

Craig Sullivan, Vice President
International Products
NetSuite, Inc.

Ed Thomas, Partner
Enterprise Risk Services
Deloitte and Touche

Sharon Ward, Strategy Director
Global Manufacturing ERP and SCM
Microsoft

About the Author

Marianne Bradford is an Associate Professor at North Carolina State University, where she teaches graduate and undergraduate ERP systems in the College of Management. She holds a Ph.D. in Accounting with a concentration in Information Systems from The University of Tennessee and is also a CPA. Dr. Bradford has been published in numerous journals including:

- *Journal of Information Systems,*

- *Issues in Accounting Education*

- *Communications of the Association of Information Systems*

- *Journal of Cost Management*

- *International Journal of Accounting Information Systems*

- *Strategic Finance*

Her research interests include ERP systems, IT outsourcing, systems diagramming methods, business process reengineering, and costs and benefits of the Sarbanes Oxley Act of 2002, Section 404. Her professional experience includes auditor with KPMG and Rhea and Ivy, CPAs in Memphis, and she recently worked in Ernst and Young's Technology and Security Risk Services (TSRS) division in Raleigh, NC while on sabbatical.

Chapter

1

Introduction to Enterprise Resource Planning Systems

Objectives

- Understand the essentials of ERP Systems.

- Be familiar with the different ways in which business professionals interact with ERP systems.

- Recognize the advantages and disadvantages of ERP systems.

- Understand the ERP Marketplace.

Introduction

The introduction of desktop computers to the business environment initially led to many information systems that were narrowly focused to serve a specific, single function. In contrast, **Enterprise Resource Planning (ERP) systems** seek to broaden that focus and ensure that information entered in one information system can be shared with other systems used elsewhere in the organization. When information is shared by systems throughout the organization, the enterprise becomes more efficient. For example, a payroll system requires an employee's social security number and the number of hours the employee worked. ERP systems would gather the list of current employees and their social security numbers from the Human Resources system that tracks employee hiring and terminations. The system would gather the number of hours from the production system where the employee logged into work and logged out to go home. This enterprise solution would be more efficient than having payroll staff enter the employee and time information into a payroll system that cannot share the information generated by those other systems. Such a payroll system would be considered a **legacy system**, an older stand-alone system that does not "talk" to other systems. ERP systems gain efficiencies by reducing or eliminating legacy systems and integrating data across the enterprise. They often serve as the most important part of an enterprise's systems because they support the information associated with the organization's primary inputs of materials and labor, its production and value-adding processes, and finally, its distribution and sales. While these functions may be at the core of an **enterprise system (ES),** the two terms are not synonymous; ES can include systems not directly associated with the organization's resources and plans for their use. Such other ES include systems that manage the organization's customer relations, vendor quality assessments, organizational intelligence and so on. By managing the information associated with inbound logistics, production, and outbound logistics, ERP systems form the core of the organization's systems

ERP Essentials

With the goal of eliminating many if not all isolated data stores, an ERP system integrates all of the organization's purchasing, human resources, production and sales information that may have previously been contained in separate systems. The typical legacy application serves the needs of a single department. Such systems can be considered functional because they gather input and provide output relevant to a single function such as payroll or purchasing. In contrast, ERP systems are considered **cross-functional** and **process-centered** because the data they contain serves the needs of the entire enterprise as it processes inputs into outputs often serving the information needs of many departments. Rather than isolating pieces of business processes into departmental areas, organizations can improve communication and collaboration across all departments and business units by using cross-functional business processes.

Business processes can span multiple departments and in many cases they can escape the boundaries of an organization to share information with partners, suppliers, and customers. These extranet functionalities, like Supply Chain Management (SCM) and Customer Relationship Management (CRM) allow the organization to further streamline the purchasing, production and sales operations. Because ERP systems seek to commit all of the organization's information to a common, well-structured database, an implementation involves far more than just a simple installation of an off-the-shelf software program. Each ERP system is uniquely installed in its host company and is designed to accommodate the company's many business processes.

An ERP system may be the most costly IT investment a company will ever make, costing in many cases millions of dollars and taking several years to implement. Department members may be quite comfortable with their existing systems and the autonomy and control they have over their own stove-pipes. Department leadership may resist the need to conform to a common data structure for enterprise-wide use because of the additional training or process modifications compliance may require as well as loss of control. Successful implementations require that executives, department heads, super users, and IT leadership be motivated to work closely together to advance the organization's mission. Thus, companies should not take the decision to implement an ERP system lightly.

Figure 1 - 1 presents functionality of a typical ERP system. ERP systems are sold in **modules**, or separate software components; one module may support financials, while others would support production planning, material management or vendor management. **Core ERP** is considered the Financials, including accounts receivable and accounts payable, Human Resources, and Operations modules. Organizations do not have to purchase and implement all modules, but more modules leads to greater integration, which in turn, can lead to a greater return on investment (ROI.) Having an ERP system in an organization is more effective the more comprehensively it is used to support an organization's operations; otherwise, we are back to systems that do not seamlessly share data.

Manufacturing		
· Engineering	· Bills of Material	· Scheduling
· Capacity	· Workflow Management	· Quality Control
· Cost Management	· Process Management	· Projects
Supply Chain Management		
· Inventory	· Order Entry	· Purchasing
· Product Configuration	· Supply Chain Planning	· Supplier Scheduling
· Inspection of goods	· Claim Processing	· Commissions
Financials		
· General Ledger	· Cash Management	· Accounts Payable
· Accounts Receivable	· Fixed Assets	
Projects		
· Costing	· Billing	· Time and Expense
· Activity Management	· Availability	
Human Resources		
· Human Resources	· Payroll	· Training
· Time & Attendance	· Benefits	
Customer Relationship Management		
· Sales and Marketing	· Commissions	· Service
· Customer Contact	· Call Center Support	
Plus: Various Self-Service Interfaces for Customers, Suppliers, and Employees		

Figure 1 - 1: Typical ERP Modules

Why Learn About ERP Systems?

Business professionals interact with ERP systems in many different contexts, including as end user, decision maker, auditor, implementation partner, and consultant. End users interact on a daily basis in their business context. For example, shipping personnel will use the ERP system to view logistics information; purchasing personnel will manage vendor data; accounting will book cash receipts and adjusting journals, finance will view cash requirements; and human resources will enter W-4 information for processing payroll. Even those employees whose jobs do not require them to enter or view company data may use the ERP system for self-service activities such as changing their exemption status for payroll, requesting time off, or signing up for training classes.

Financial statement auditors will need to understand their client's ERP system for the annual audit and the Sarbanes Oxley audit. They will collect reports such as the Trial Balance and General Ledger and other relevant data such as customer account balances used to substantiate balances in the financial statements from their client's ERP system. IT auditors will need to work with financial statement auditors to identify the ERP system's **application controls.** These are the program controls embedded in the ERP software that maintain segregation of duties and track transaction activity in order to provide adequate security and maintain the integrity of the data.

Given the widespread adoption of ERP systems by businesses, and the size and scope of implementations, professionals with business and IT experience can expect to be involved with the implementation of these systems on an internal project team, as an external consultant, or implementation partner. All of the Big 4 and other large accounting and consulting firms employ specialists who assist organizations in implementing and maintaining ERP systems. In addition, these companies also offer design alternatives, customization, ancillary components, maintenance, and hosting services, enabling their clients to enhance and upgrade their ERP system performance. Skills in project management, ERP system logic, process flows, as well as software design and engineering are all pertinent to the ERP system consultant's job requirements.

ERP has changed the nature of IT and business functions. The basic nature of the IT function has been changing from that of analyst and designer to that of ERP system specialist. There is a huge demand for users or line-of-business personnel who also have professional-level IT skills. Because these systems are so highly specialized and extremely structured to support information requirements throughout the enterprise, traditional software developers and programmers who know mostly about technology and little about business are not as valuable as they once were. Understanding a company's business operations is the most critical expertise necessary for a successful ERP implementation and life cycle support. An understanding of an organization's processes and how they work is a more valuable skill than programming and IT-specific services such as database and network administration except for the few places where the ERP system needs to be customized to add extra functionality.

ERP Systems and Best Practices

As industries mature, certain techniques, processes and methodologies become generally recognized as more effective and/or efficient and are known as industry **best practices**. ERP system vendors enable enterprises to take advantage of industry best practices by embedding programming into their applications that will support the techniques, strategies, processes, actions, and methodologies that are proven most effective. When management of a company chooses an ERP package, they are "buying into" the ERP vendor's view of these best practices and will rely on the system to support their efforts to embrace these practices.

Of course, ERP vendors vary by level of industry expertise and the priorities their systems place on the various best practices recognized in a particular industry; this is one of the major differences between the many ERP systems available. Consequently, matching a company's needs to the best practices built into an ERP system is a key contributor to the ultimate success of the ERP implementation.

The larger ERP vendors, such as SAP and Oracle, have literally thousands of best practices programmed into their software. These vendors support enormous research and development efforts to identify industry best practices and embed them into their applications. As new best practices are recognized, they become available for inclusion in new versions and upgrades of ERP software. As a result, the cycle of finding best practices, codifying, and delivering those applications to customers, allows the ERP customer to maintain the advantages associated with these high value business methods. Often, this commitment to best practice research and development has enabled many vendors to offer industry specific **vertical solution**.

Other Advantages of ERP Systems

From the onset of heavy desktop computer use in business until the arrival of ERP systems, companies would typically create and maintain several sets of the same customer data in several different departmental databases. And while these stand-alone systems obviously thwart efforts to integrate and aggregate information, another problem with this approach was the time lags incurred as information was moved from one system to another. Often this involved printing output from one system and handing it off to an employee in another department who would read the printed output and enter the same data or parts of the data into their department's stand-alone system. With ERP systems, once the data is entered, it is visible to all users in all departments (of course with the authority to view/edit the data) and the information is online and real-time.

> "Total ERP revenue grew to more than $25B in 2005 based on strong customer demand and a number of acquisitions of smaller, niche vendors"
>
> *Source: AMR research 2006*

For example, in a firm with a horizontally integrated, interdepartmental ERP system, suppose a member of the purchasing department processed a purchase order. Once that event is committed, since it shares a common General Ledger with both Accounts Payable and Receiving, the record of that purchase order would be immediately available to those departments. The time lag that used to arise when documents sat in in-baskets waiting to be re-keyed into another system is eliminated, along with all the paper documents involved. The heavy dependence on paper begins to diminish as ERP systems take over. The single point of entry reduces the risk of inaccuracies in transactions, and employees spend less time checking, rechecking, and reconciling output from the disparate systems involved.

ERP systems are great tools for preventing human error. Obviously, each time a re-keying requirement is eliminated, each time a document need not be routed to another department, each time a record update is used immediately by another user elsewhere in the enterprise, the likelihood of information-based error is diminished. ERP systems even simplify the error correction process; if a mistake is detected, it only has to be edited and saved in one location and every department will have access to the updated, corrected information.

Additionally, with a single-point of data entry, there is universal access to that data throughout the company, and the data is immediately updated as business processes occur. Therefore, single-point entry gives stakeholders the ability to gain an accurate and consistent view of the business as it runs. Stakeholders could be customers who will be able to see the real-time status of their orders and the balances of their accounts. They could be customer service representatives who, in contact with a customer, will have complete and accurate information needed to provide intelligent account support. The stakeholder could be management, who can be notified in real time about bottlenecks and performance problems as they occur, possibly quickly enough to avert large scale process failures. The enterprise has one set of data and everyone benefits because they share access to, and responsibility for, information that is current, complete and accurate.

Finally, ERP systems demand standardization of business processes. A **business process** is a collection of activities that together add value to the company. ERP systems provide companies with a template to standardize business processes across the company, leading to the advantages we have discussed. Different business units, external partners, suppliers and customers will encounter less friction and greater ease in collaborating and conducting their affairs. This real-time, immediate access to enterprise information can help improve financial management, corporate governance, and management of enterprise risk and creates a horizontally "joined up" company, ultimately improving productivity, insight, and optimized business processes.

Disadvantages of Implementing ERP Systems

One of the main criticisms of ERP systems is that they impose a standardized way of conducting business processes. While this structure is presumably dictated by thoughtfulness and best practices, if this structure is different or runs counter to the firm's culture or expectations, difficulties in implementation or operation can arise. For example, employees can find the systems difficult to use. Some find the systems too restrictive and rigid, not allowing for much flexibility. They can blame the system for problems that are really cultural or caused by lack of user acceptance.

Employee resistance can be a major obstacle for a successful ERP implementation particularly if employees have not been educated in the organization's motivation for undertaking the ERP initiative. Resistance also arises when employees do not receive sufficient training on the system. This can often lead to employees developing counter-productive work-arounds where they elect not to use the system as intended perhaps reverting back into their old ways of doing work. At times, frustrated or fearful of organizational change, they may even attempt to sabotage the implementation process, creating problems where none need exist, intentionally interjecting errors, or make excessively complicated demands of the system in order to hinder the system's implementation or operation. An example of sabotage during an implementation was the SAP install at FoxMeyer Drug Co. in the 1990's. Warehouse workers, threatened with a loss of their jobs due to the closing of old warehouses, damaged inventory being transferred to new inventory centers. Most of these situations arise from inadequate pre-implementation communication, education, and motivation. Companies should not only educate their employees (the "why") but also train their employees (the "how") in order to ensure smooth transition from the legacy systems to the ERP system. Organizations that successfully implement and use ERP systems oftentimes employ **change agents** to assist in transformation. Change agents bring to the table **change management** skills, or the systematic approach to dealing with change, both from the perspective of an organization and on the individual level. Change management will be discussed more in-depth in Chapter 6.

In addition, ERP systems are sophisticated and complex. This complexity often requires, in many cases, hiring expensive consultants and implementation partners to assist in the implementation. Companies often struggle to take command of the technology and to leverage that technology into consistent and measurable business process improvements. ERP systems are often expensive; the sheer magnitude of the cash outlay required for an ERP system is a major downside to many companies.

ERP Evolution

The roots of ERP systems are in discrete manufacturing and in particular **Manufacturing Resource Planning (MRP II)** systems. MRP systems were developed in the 1970s to address issues such as frequent changes in sales forecasts which require continual readjustments in production. Where MRP systems once managed the computing needs of the manufacturing environment, ERP systems now manage the resources of the *entire* enterprise. For many companies, the year 2000 (Y2K) issue was the initial driver behind ERP adoption. Now, ERP systems have become a "must have" for all types of organizations that need to gain the advantages of greater information management in order to remain competitive in this fast-changing global landscape. As this evolution continues more and more ERP functions are being refined and reworked so that they are becoming more accessible to mid-sized and small firms as well as a greater variety of industries.

ERP Today

Today the use of ERP systems has a much broader scope than just manufacturing. ERP systems today support service companies, research organizations, distribution companies, non-profit, government and many others. These systems continue to embrace more and more functions of an organization, regardless of the organization's business or charter. In doing so, they begin to approach the status of a complete ES blurring the distinctions between the two. ERP vendors often fine-tune their software by offering multiple versions of their software to suit particular industries or market segments. Other vendors specialize in a single industry or market. When a vendor targets a single, specific industry and seeks to provide solutions for all the information management requirements that can be expected to arise by players in that market, the solution is known as a vertical solution. As an example, SAP, the largest ERP vendor in the world, currently offers vertical solutions for financial and public service, manufacturing, and a wide range of service industries. Figure 1 - 2 shows a more complete listing of the industries currently supported by SAP's vertical solutions. The relative size of the major providers in this market is shown in Figure 1 – 3.

Industry		Revenue ($M)	
	Year:	2004	2005
Manufacturing	Total:	**$3,799**	**$4,045**
Textiles		$135	$156
Apparel		$111	$120
Wood Products, Paper, Printing		$155	$179
Petro Products, Chemicals, Plastics		$355	$312
Pharmaceuticals/Biotechnology		$247	$273
Primary/Fabricated Metal		$186	$156
Machinery		$258	$266
Computers and Electronics		$705	$810
Automotive and Auto Parts		$567	$624
Aerospace and Defense		$336	$382
Food, Beverages, Consumer Goods		$463	$496
Other Manufacturing		$282	$270
Non-Manufacturing	Total:	**$3,492**	**$3,756**
Resource Extraction (Mining, Oil and Gas)		$104	$117
Utilities		$309	$304
Telecommunication Services		$202	$234
Wholesale Trade		$275	$312
Retail Trade		$397	$476
Transportation and Warehousing		$180	$172
Information and Media (excluding Telecom)		$286	$320
Finance and Insurance		$425	$499
Healthcare and Social Assistance		$256	$242
Education		$182	$156
Public Administration		$400	$421
Other Services		$476	$503
Total		**$7,291**	**$7,801**

Figure 1 - 2: SAP license revenue and share by vertical industry, 2004-2005

Source: AMR Research, 2006

The ERP Market

The market for ERP system customers can be divided into three categories:

- First Tier – Companies with over 1000 employees. Tier one ERP suppliers usually include Fortune 500 companies and other companies with sales over $250 million including large government and other national operations.

- Second Tier – Medium sized companies with 100-999 employees. Sales for these companies range from $2-$250 million with most of the companies between $5 and $50 million.

- Third Tier – Companies with sales under $2 million and with less than 100 employees.

Collectively, the second and third tiers are known as **small-to-medium sized enterprises (SME)**.

2005 Rank	Company	Revenue ($M)	
	Year:	2005	2006
1	SAP	$10,542	$12,334
2	Oracle	$5,155	$6,664
3	Sage Group	$1,438	$1,582
4	Microsoft	$891	$1,051
5	SSA Global	$733	$755

Figure 1 - 3: ERP vendors ranked by 2005 application revenue
(incl. estimated 2006 growth)

Source: AMR Research, 2006

First Tier ERP Vendors

Also known as the Enterprise Space, the first tier has been captured by two software giants, SAP and Oracle. They are compared with other large vendors in Figure 1 - 3.

In 2008, SAP is the world's 4th largest software supplier and the largest European software enterprise with over 105,000 installations. Systems, Application, and Products in Data Processing (SAP), was founded in 1972 and the company's headquarters is located in Walldorf, Germany. SAP employs more than 39,300 people in more than 50 countries, and serves more than 41,200 customers in 120 countries. They are the recognized leader in providing collaborative business solutions for all types of industries and in every major market.

Oracle is known for their expertise in databases; however, Oracle also sells a suite of business applications (ERP systems and more.) Oracle E-Business Suite includes software for financials, manufacturing, and human resources. Like the majority of ERP systems, users access the software through a web browser interface over the Internet or through the corporate intranet. Beginning in 2003, Oracle aggressively acquired a number of high-value ES companies including PeopleSoft, JD Edwards (previously acquired by PeopleSoft), Hyperion and Siebel. The first two companies produced sophisticated and successful ERP software of their own. The latter two are ES companies specializing in business intelligence and customer relationship management, respectively. By integrating these products into their offerings, Oracle is able to offer a highly competitive product under the umbrella term Oracle Fusion. Projected market share for SAP, Oracle and other ERP vendors is shown in Figure 1 - 4.

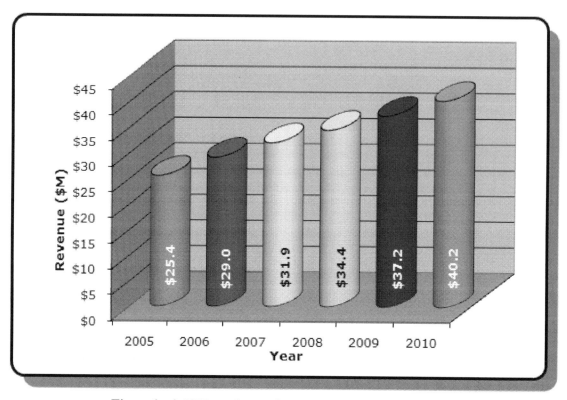

Figure 1 - 4: ERP market total revenue, 2005-2010 (estimated)

Source: AMR Research, 2006

Second and Third-Tier ERP Vendors

Also known as mid-market and small business vendors, NetSuite, Sage, and Microsoft are just a few of the competitors in this space. Many of these vendors offer vertical solutions as well. Others offer advanced or unique technical solutions that represent a departure from the top-tier vendors' typical client server or multi-tier solutions. The 2005 market share for the top ERP vendors regardless of what tier they specialize in is shown in Figure 1- 5.

ERP Vendors	
Vendor	Market Share
SAP	42%
Oracle	20%
Sage Group	6%
Microsoft	4%
SSA Global	3%
Infor	2%
Geac	2%
Intentia	2%
Epicor	1%
Lawson	1%
Other	18%

Figure 1 – 5: ERP market share based on license company revenue, 2005

Source: AMR Research, 2006

Summary

By supporting the requirements of a number of departments, ERP systems are a departure from legacy systems that support a single function or department. They broaden this traditional single function business environment to ensure that information entered in one system can be shared by other information systems used elsewhere in the organization. They support the information associated with the organization's primary inputs of materials and labor, its production and value-adding processes, and finally, its distribution and sales. It is important to understand how ERP systems operate, as many business professionals will be using them in their organizations, working on their implementation, auditing them, or engaging in ERP systems consulting and integration. ERP systems have multiple advantages, such as providing industry best practices and data integration we well as disadvantages, including high cost and employee resistance; these are benefits and costs an organization should weigh prior to implementation.

Keywords

Application controls

Best practices

Business process

Change agents

Change management

Core ERP

Cross-functional

Enterprise Resource Planning (ERP) systems

Enterprise system (ES)

Legacy system

Manufacturing Resource Planning (MRP II)

Modules

Process-centered

Small-to-medium sized enterprises (SME)

Vertical solution

Quick Review

1. True/False: Best practices are techniques, processes and methodologies that are generally recognized as more effective and efficient.

2. True/False: ERP systems evolved from Business Intelligence systems.

3. True/False: A vertical process is a collection of activities that together add value to the company.

4. Information is online and _____ when it is entered and visible to all users at once.

5. A(n) _____ system supports the information associated with an organization's primary inputs of materials and labor, its production and value-adding processes, and its distribution and sales.

Questions to Consider

1. What are ERP systems?

2. How are ERP systems different than traditional enterprise systems used in organizations?

3. What are advantages and disadvantages of ERP systems?

4. How do ERP systems support industry best practices?

5. What is the difference between Tier 1, 2, and 3 ERP vendors?

References

Data Guidance Group, Inc. (2007). *Top 10 Accounting and ERP Systems*. Retrieved August 7, 2007, from http://www.4dgg.com/web/Financial_Management/ TopTenERPSoftwarePackages/Accounting_Software_ERP_Top_10.htm

Franke, J. (2007). *ERP Market Strong Through 2011, SaaS Products Gain Share*. Retrieved August 30, 2007, from
http://searchsap.techtarget.com/news/article/0,289142,sid21_gci1264010,00.html

Institute of Management Accountants. (2006). *Content Specification Outline for CMA exam*. Retrieved from http://www.imanet.org

Kimberling, E. (2007). *ERP's Big Bang Theory*. Retrieved August 30, 2007, from
http://blogs.ittoolbox.com/erp/roi/archives/erps-big-bang-theory-11954

Koch, C., & Wailgum, T. (2007). *ABC: An Introduction to ERP*. Retrieved August 10, 2007, from
http://www.cio.com/article/print/40323

Markus, M., Lynne, C. & van Fenema, P. (2007). Multisite ERP Implementations. *Communications of the ACM, 43*(4), 42-46.

O'Leary, D. (2000). *Enterprise Resource Planning Systems*. Cambridge, UK : Cambridge University Press.

Chapter

2

ERP Technology

Objectives

- Understand ERP system technology.

- Understand the types of database relationships.

- Differentiate between customization and configuration of ERP software.

- Provide examples of configuration and customization.

- Provide examples of ERP bolt-on software.

Introduction

In Chapter 1 we discussed legacy systems, which are older information systems in organizations that do not easily "talk" to each other. This creates inefficiencies in the organization such as duplicate data entry and fragmentation of business processes. Most of these legacy systems are built on **mainframe architecture**, which means that all computing intelligence is within the central host computer. Users interact with the host through a terminal that captures keystrokes and sends that information to the host.

In the 1990's as desktop computing grew, organizations set up **local area networks (LANs)** to share files among computers. **File sharing** allowed users to download a file and use the computational power of their personal computer to perform a job. The file was then stored back on the file server. As LANs grew in size, file sharing was no longer optimal as the speed of processing was too slow.

In the 1990's a new architecture emerged, **client server,** which reduced network traffic by providing a query response rather than total file transfer. Instead of downloading a file from a **file server**, the "client" computer accesses data provided by a more robust machine, a **database server.** In the 1990's, ERP system vendors began taking advantage of this newer **two-tier** technology, and began developing client server versions of their systems.

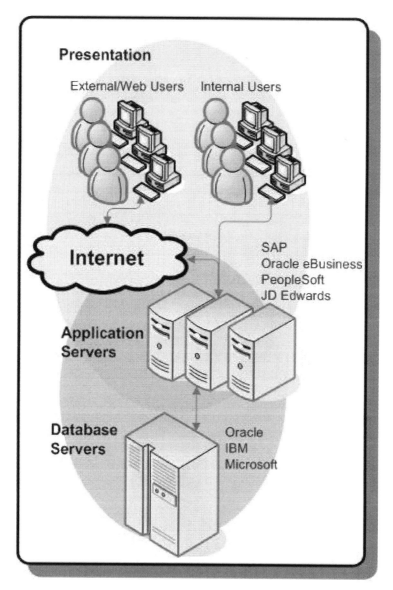

Figure 2 - 1: Three-Tier Application

ERP Hardware and Software Configuration

As ERP systems have continued to evolve, many now employ **three-tier** (often referred to as **multi-tier**) **architecture**. In the three-tier architecture, a middle tier was added between the user system interface client environment and the database server environment. In these cases, client computers may access programming on one server while data may be stored on another. Programs may use components and data that is stored and served to clients by any number of other computers. Figure

2 – 1 provides an example of three-tier architecture and some of the software vendors that support them.

Business logic (the ERP application) is maintained on the **application server(s),** which is the middle tier. While internal users can interact with the applications on these servers using a dedicated software client, most of the major ERP vendors support the use of **web browsers.** Users can interact with these applications using web browsers connected to the Internet or through the company Intranet.

The bottom tier of this structure is the database server. This is a computer (or computers) optimized for database operation and provide for data input and output from any number of application servers. While the data may take many forms when presented to users, the databases provide an **authoritative data source** where the business logic between the applications and databases are programmed to maintain verifiable and valid data that is current, complete, and accurate. These data files may be **master files** that are relatively permanent data files of records that reflect current status of business items such as inventory, fixed assets, customers, and employees. Master data does not change often and usually represents resources (e.g., inventory) and agents (e.g., employees, suppliers) of the organization. The files may also be event or transaction files, which capture financial and non-financial chronological records.

Because these servers interact with both the users and the databases, the software these servers use is an example of middleware. **Middleware** on the application servers is able to route these interactions from users to databases to provide the users with a seamless user experience. While one purpose of middleware is to route data between users and the database, it is also able to interact with one another and with other computers to which they can connect. For example, a company's ERP system may include a customer relationship management application that gathers information from a legacy system that stores a customer's order history. When a salesman looks up the customer, the history information appears on a single page. By combining information from any number of sources, this seamlessness is an example of **enterprise application integration (EAI),** a form of middleware that connects applications together.

As networks grow more sophisticated, additional tiers can be added. These tiers could add greater capacity for data input and output, data analysis and storage. In addition, other tiers might provide security and network monitoring or other support to allow the network's capacity to grow larger, more stable, and more robust. A multi-tier architecture would describe one where more than three tiers are integrated in support of the applications and their users.

In modern ERP systems, the client uses a **graphical user interface (GUI)** to request information from a server connected to the **relational database**, or a type of database where data is stored in tables connected with attributes in common. Historically, as businesses adopted the use of desktop computers, the software programs they used were installed on those computers, and as internal networks grew, those programs would be configured to connect to the other computers that were designated as database or application servers in the classic client server fashion. These programs were often large and required a great deal of configuration on each desktop computer. Because of this size and complexity, these programs were considered **fat client** applications. More recently, these programs on the server have provided an interface to a generic web browser, a **thin client**, that can connect or browse to web pages supporting any number of software applications. By using a common, generic web browser, computer programs eliminate the need to install or configure large programs on all the desktop clients that they are intended to support.

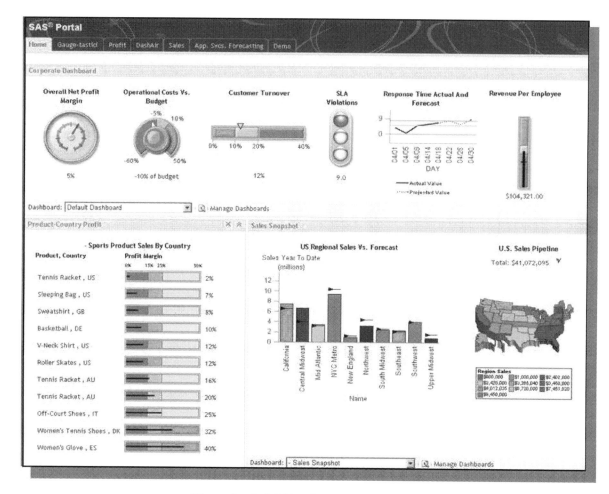

Figure 2 – 2: SAS Institute Dashboard

Source: SAS Institute, Inc.

ERP Interfaces

With ERP software, the GUI usually takes the form of a **dashboard** that graphically presents many different types of information in any number of visual presentations. These web pages are generally customized to suit the needs and preferences of a set of users or a specific user. For example, dashboards can be tailored according to an employee's role to provide information relevant to that role. Dashboards can display reports, charts and graphs as shown in Figure 2 – 2. They can also include any number of other visual elements to provide the user with information about:

- Business process activity based on production or logistics information.

- Tasks, reminders and other notifications.

- Calendaring and scheduling resources.

- Messaging including email, instant messaging and telephone traffic.

- Official communications from designated sources.

When a web page is intended to provide a starting point used to navigate to the information and applications needed by a group or team of employees, it can be considered a **home page**. Often, when that home page provides intuitive navigation that helps employees navigate to more specific information and functionality, that home page can be referred to as a **portal**.

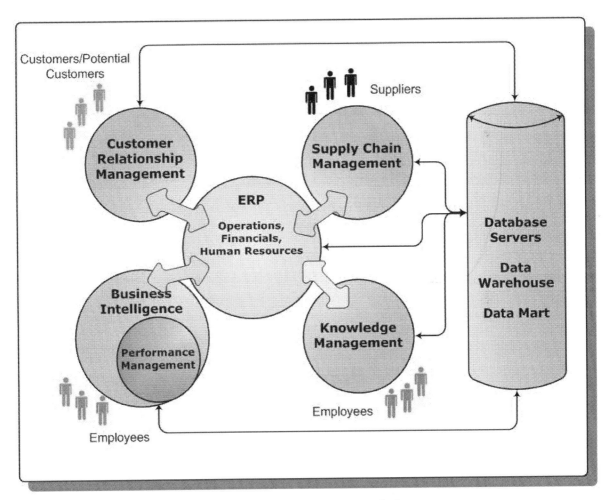

Figure 2 – 3: Core ERP and ERP Bolt-Ons

ERP Modules

Vendors bundle their software into **modules,** which group applications into certain business functions. This provides the flexibility for a company to select some functions and solutions but not others. Often, companies may "mix and match" purchasing modules from different ERP vendors, connecting the modules using enterprise application integration. Some common modules, such as finance and accounting are adopted by nearly all companies implementing enterprise systems. For example, service companies will not likely need a module for manufacturing, and companies with a few fixed assets may not need an asset management module. Other times companies will not adopt a module because they already have their own proprietary system they believe to be superior. Core ERP and common ERP bolt-ons are shown in Figure 2 – 3.

Vendors use modules as pricing units. Aside from providing price advantages as the number of modules grow, generally speaking, the greater number of modules selected, the greater the integration benefits. These benefits as well as the costs, risks, and changes involved are considered to determine which modules should be implemented.

ERP Technology

Databases

An ERP system stores data in one or more highly structured **relational databases** where it can be accessed by the program to respond to user actions. Relational databases are collections of **tables** in which data is stored in rows and columns. The columns, called **fields or attributes**, define the data such as "Customer Name" or "Zip Code" while the rows, called **records**, amount to instances of the data such as "Joe Customer" and all his related information.

Database designers employ a sophisticated process of structuring these tables known as **database normalization**. While the intricacies of database normalization are beyond the scope of this discussion, the objectives are to:

- Eliminate the duplication of data in multiple tables. For example a customer's address is entered in a single table, and that table can be accessed by any process that needs the customer's address.

- Identify a key, known as a **primary key,** for each row of a table that uniquely identifies the data in that row. For example, a Customer ID number will uniquely identify a customer and the data associated with that customer, such as name, street and zip code. The Invoice table will include a column for the customer ID number, and the database programmer will see that whenever an invoice is needed, the values associated with the Customer ID number will be gathered with the invoice.

- Connect the tables using relationships. For example, the Invoice table and the Customer table can be connected by adding the Customer ID number attribute to the records in the Invoice table. When one table, such as the Invoice table, includes an attribute that points back to a primary key in another table, such as the Customer ID number in the Customer table, that attribute is known as a **foreign key** because it points to a key in a different, or "foreign", table.

Table Relationships

A relational database consists of many tables of data that can be connected through the common data elements of primary and foreign keys in the tables. Where the database designer identifies a relationship between and among tables, the common keys will be connected by the database software's internal programming. In database classes, students learn about the different relationships that exist between tables. These relationships are:

- One-to-One – The primary key of one table is associated with only one record in another table. These relationships are not nearly as common as one-to many relationships, but do occur. Consider the relationship between Invoice and Shipment in which a system creates an invoice every time a shipment is made. Thus, one shipment goes with one invoice. The relationship is represented as (1, 1).

- One-to-Many – The primary key of one table is associated with several different records in another table. These relationships are very common in databases. Consider a Customer table and an Order table. Over time, a customer can have many different orders, but a particular order only comes from one customer. Thus, the relationship is represented as (1, N), with the 1 being Customer and the N being Orders.

- Many-to-Many – Technically, a very complicated relationship where the primary key in one table is associated with several different records in another table and the primary key in the other table is associated with more than one record in the first table. Consider the relationship between Inventory and Orders. A type of inventory can be on many different orders, and an order can have many different types of inventory on it. Thus, the relationship is (M, N). This type of relationship requires a separate table to be established that converts the many-to-many into two one-to-many relationships.

By normalizing data into appropriately structured tables, the database can become cross-functional. For example, sales, marketing and shipping personnel need to access customer data. Requests for this data may take forms such as:

- A sales representative looking up a customer's credit limit.

- A marketing representative aggregating the previous month's sales by zip code.

- A shipping clerk looking up a customer's address.

Before ERP systems, all of this data would be supported by single-function, stand-alone systems; each department would use their system to store the customer's name, address and zip code. This situation gives rise to any number of complications in the face of certain events such as a change of address, and in addition, multiplies potential points of failure as each system requires its own data entry and maintenance. In such a case, one can easily see how customers can submit a change of address to their sales representative who, in turn, can ring up a sale and have shipping send the order to the old address. With a single data entry point these errors are eliminated and users share a common view of the data, a condition known as **data symmetry**. Data asymmetry results from the same information getting entered into more than one system; these fields run the chance then of being keyed in differently, although they represent the same data.

Configuring and Customizing ERP Software

Given the complexities of ERP software, its installation will, by necessity, require configuration and customization to best fit a company's processes, or the new processes they desire. **Configuration** amounts to the process of "setting software switches." These switches are stored in **configuration**

tables that enable a company to tailor a particular aspect of the system to the way it chooses to do business. **Customization** requires that programmers rewrite the underlying code or develop extra code to make the software perform in ways the software vendor had not originally intended.

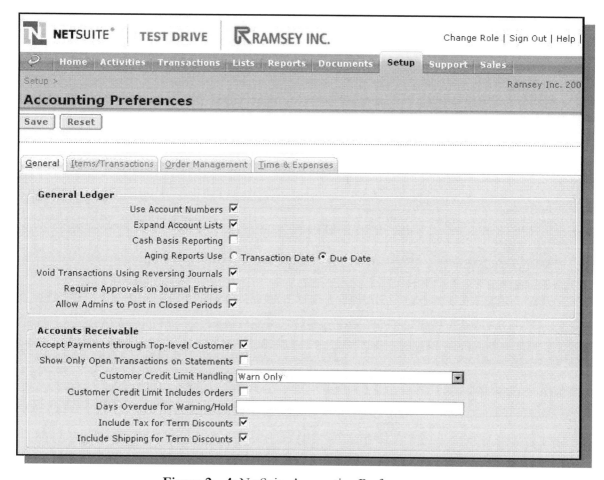

Figure 2 – 4: NetSuite Accounting Preferences

Source: NetSuite

Configuring options allow ERP vendors to sell the same package to different companies by accommodating slight variations in approaches to the operations the software is intended to support. This allows vendors to expand their market, thereby cutting unit costs. They can then pass those savings along to their customers. These settings include:

- **Technical configuration** - These settings allow the software to operate on the company's hardware and network and to gain access to the data and other resources available.

- **Functional configuration** - ERP software comes shipped with a default process configuration. The software allows the project team to make changes to these defaults, enabling, disabling, or otherwise modifying the way the functions behave to better match the company's processes.

For example, as an ERP system is installed, it can be directed to access databases on one or more servers. It could be designed to provide for connection from certain users while barring other users from access. It could be provided access to servers that would allow it to generate reports or messages. These are examples of technical configuration.

On the other hand, the software may be support for business processes that allow for a merge in transit during shipping as well as for drop shipments. While both processes may come standard in the ERP system, a company may choose not to allow one or the other; the software could be configured to disable functions accordingly. These are examples of functional configuration. Figure 2 - 4 shows a NetSuite screen shot of the Controller Role. In this screen, the Controller can configure accounting preferences. For example, for audit trail purposes, reversing entries might be used instead of voiding entries and holds may be enforced when customers reach their credit limit.

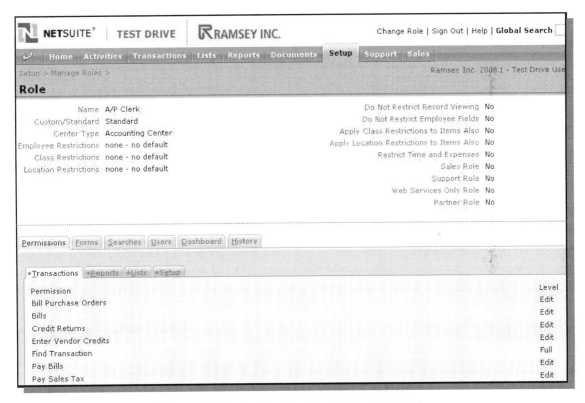

Figure 2 – 5: Configuring User Roles in NetSuite

Source: NetSuite

One primary set of functional configurations are those that support security. Typically, ERP systems use roles to designate levels of access to data and functionality. Users assigned to those roles will have certain levels of access and privileges to certain data. Those privileges often define permission to **create, read, update or delete (CRUD)** the data. The ERP software will include configurable options to assign CRUD permissions to roles and then populate these roles with users based on their log in identities. Figure 2 - 5 shows a NetSuite screen shot of the Administrator Role, which has the authority to define permissions for various roles. In this case, the "Custom A/P Clerk" role, a standard role within NetSuite, is being configured. Other roles may be added and configured as well.

Configuration options provide for a number of other settings as well. They can be used to optimize the software for individual sites, offices or departments. A global company might configure their U.S. division differently than their Chinese division to accommodate different languages or currency. These last settings are called regional settings and also include arcane details such as date formats, thousands separators and time zones. All of these settings are examples of functional configurations because they change the way the software behaves.

Often, when a company is widely dispersed geographically or operates as a number of distinctly autonomous departments, divisions, or entities, the company will need to use separate instances of the ERP software. An **instance** is an installation of ERP software and related components and it is defined by the boundaries set on the business processes it supports. The global company we just spoke of may use one ERP instance in the US and second instance in China; the software may support the same processes and the same roles, but may use different regional settings and run on different servers on different continents. While organizations would benefit from the simplicity of having just one ERP instance, the reality is often quite different. Many organizations find themselves licensing and implementing multiple instances of a vendor's ERP software in different divisions or geographic locations of the organization.

While some amount of configuration is required in every case, customization implies more dramatic changes to the software. The company may want to change the software in ways not supported by the configuration options built into the software. It may want to substantially alter or add functionality to the system or connect the software to data sources that had not been contemplated by the software publisher. Often, an ERP system will not include support for a process a company needs or wants. Modifications may be required to meet these specific needs or fit with the company's other IT resources, political realities, or operational culture.

When the ERP system is installed and the configuration options remain set to their default values, the system is considered **vanilla,** or out-of-the-box. Configuration options are typically changes to these default settings and can be expected to be completed in short order. Customization, on the other hand, requires a great deal more technical sophistication and begins to increase the expenses and risks associated with the implementation. The experienced ERP professional will warn against this approach to ERP implementation. Customizations can have far reaching effects; since ERP systems are so tightly linked together, a customization can affect many different users and processes. Customization also complicates efforts to upgrade the ERP software later. While such upgrades are no walk in the park under the best of circumstances, they can become a nightmare of conflicts where the software, the customization or both may require substantial reprogramming to retain the pre-upgrade level of functionality. Because of the customization, the software publisher or vendor may decline to support the installation. Customization also increases the costs associated with the additional programming labor and the recurring costs to maintain the added code. Finally, customization can be expected to increase deployment cycle time; such efforts may cause an ERP implementation to run longer than expected. Because of this, companies should seriously weigh the advantages customization may bring against these added costs and risks, only customizing their ERP system if absolutely necessary to gain demonstrable competitive advantage.

Unlocking ERP Value with "Bolt-Ons"

ERP systems have historically been seen as **back office** systems, meaning they are used to integrate back office functionality such as financials, operations and human resources. Now, ERP systems encompass more **front office** aspects such as supply chain management (SCM) and customer relationship management (CRM.) In cases where a core ERP system is in place, these additional functions can be added to the existing system using **bolt-on software**, or software that is "bolted on" to the core ERP system. Bolt-on software can be provided by the core system vendors or purchased from third party vendors. Adopting bolt-ons is another opportunity for a company to integrate more functionality into a common data source. For instance, Siebel is a CRM application now owned and sold by Oracle. Previously, Siebel offered its software under its own brand. Despite Siebel's acquisition by Oracle, companies can still implement the Siebel CRM software even if they are not using the Oracle E-Business Suite. Customers of SAP and other ERP vendors can even implement Siebel CRM as a bolt-on.

Summary

ERP system technology has evolved from mainframe to client server over the years. A typical ERP environment would consist of three tiers: the database, the application, and the user interface. The environment would also consist of core ERP modules of Human Resources, Accounting and Finance, and Operations. Bolt-ons to core ERP deliver even more value for the enterprise. All ERP systems reside on top of one or more database servers that include relational tables which store data. Tables are connected with relationships including one-to-one, one-to-many (or many-to-one), and many-to-many. Given the complexity of the software, teams should consider many things when implementing an ERP system including hardware and software configurations and possible customization needed to best fit the organization's processes.

Keywords

Application server

Attributes

Authoritative data source

Back office

Bolt-on software

Client server

Configuration

Configuration Tables

Create, Read, Update or Delete (CRUD)

Customization

Dashboard

Data symmetry

Database normalization

Database server

Enterprise application integration (EAI)

Fat client

File server

File sharing

Foreign key

Front office

Functional configuration

Graphical user interface (GUI)

Home page

Instance

Local area networks (LANS)

Mainframe architecture

Master file

Middleware

Module

Multi-tier architecture

Portal

Primary key

Record

Relational database

Technical configuration

Thin client

Three-tier architecture

Two-tier

Vanilla

Web browser

Quick Review

1. True/False: Data asymmetry refers to users sharing a common view of the data.

2. True/False: Dashboards can display lists, charts, graphs and other visual and audible elements to users.

3. A _____ consists of many tables of data that can be connected through common data elements using the primary and foreign keys.

4. _____ requires that programmers rewrite the underlying code or develop extra code to make the software perform in ways the publisher had not originally intended.

5. Adopting _____, such as CRM, gives companies an opportunity to integrate more functionality into a common data source.

Questions to Consider

1. What is the role of databases in an ERP system?

2. What business concepts might be considered a one–to–many relationship; many-to-many?

3. In what circumstances are customizations unavoidable?

4. Describe the purpose of each tier in three-tier architecture.

References

Koch, C., & Wailgum, T. (2007). *ABC: An Introduction to ERP*. Retrieved August 10, 2007, from http://www.cio.com/article/print/40323

O'Leary, D. (2000). *Enterprise Resource Planning Systems*. Cambridge, UK: Cambridge University Press.

Chapter

3

ERP and Business Process Reengineering

Objectives

- Define business process reengineering.

- Understand the benefits of reengineering.

- Differentiate between clean slate and technology-enabled reengineering.

- Explain how reengineering is linked to ERP.

- Know the reengineering principles.

- Be able to recognize processes that are good candidates for reengineering.

Introduction

Modern businesses face the challenge of making their business processes more efficient and value-added. Increased competition, technology and globalization have forced organizations to rework their traditional business methods in pursuit of greater efficiency and value. This chapter discusses **Business Process Reengineering (BPR)**, which consists of the methods used to develop changes to processes, implement them, and gain efficiencies and new values. According to Michael Hammer, the "father of reengineering," ERP systems are disruptive technology that essentially forces companies to reengineer their processes in order to retain their competitiveness. His assertion is that ERP systems force organizations to change their processes to best practices inherent in the software. Doing this requires radical changes in the way employees do their work and the way the company interacts with its customers and suppliers.

Business Process Reengineering

Since ERP systems are based on a solid set of business processes, an ERP implementation often serves as the catalyst for a BPR effort. Implementing an ERP system requires (in many cases) a drastic departure from the way an organization used to work. Business processes are changed to match the best practices built into the ERP software. The definition of BPR is the fundamental, radical redesign in business processes to achieve dramatic improvements in key measures of performance, such as cost, quality, speed, and service. Processes can be reengineered without deploying an ERP system, but in many cases, the two go hand in hand.

Dr. Michael Hammer coined the term "reengineering" and has written numerous books on the topic over the last two decades. He began developing his managerial techniques in the 1980's when he noticed that a few high profile global companies, such as IBM and John Deere, had drastically improved their performance. With further research, he found that these companies were not changing their core competencies (i.e., the services they provided or the products they

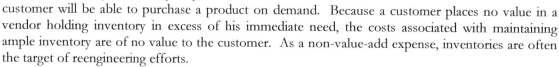

manufactured), but were transforming their business processes in order to make them more efficient and customer-oriented. These organizations had revamped their activities and reduced or eliminated processes that the customer would not consider valuable. Tasks that only served to meet the internal demands of the business process were ideal candidates for reengineering. In Hammer's book, *Reengineering the Corporation*, he promulgated managerial techniques (also known as **reengineering principles**) he saw in these companies that made them world-class.

A perfect example of a non-value-added cost in a traditional firm is that of inventory. Inventory only increases the likelihood that a customer will be able to purchase a product on demand. Because a customer places no value in a vendor holding inventory in excess of his immediate need, the costs associated with maintaining ample inventory are of no value to the customer. As a non-value-add expense, inventories are often the target of reengineering efforts.

Unfortunately, in the 1990s, many BPR projects resulted in wide scale layoffs, and the term "reengineering" fell out of favor. New terms, **business process improvement** and **business process redesign**, have surfaced, which refer to more of a slow, systematic approach to help optimize processes versus a radical reengineering approach.

How do we define radical changes in business processes? One research study gives a context for the meaning of radical changes over current ways of conducting work:

- Radical changes are those that result in excess of 60% improvement.

- Major changes are those that result in between 30-60% improvement.

- Incremental changes are those that result in less than 30% improvement.

The study looked at 79 cases of what companies announced were "reengineering" initiatives and found that only 69% could be considered radical improvements, while 28% were major and 3% were incremental. This way of determining what radical means is somewhat arbitrary, but the meaning is clear. To be considered true reengineering, an organization must experience a transformation. As the breadth of transformation decreases and changes become less radical, they become more incremental. An example of an incremental approach is a **Total Quality Management (TQM)** initiative, in which processes are studied in an attempt to identify opportunities to gain minor, small-scale improvements that are expected to accumulate and build on one another over time. Given the advantages of ERP technology over legacy systems, the ERP systems and the business processes they support offer opportunities far greater than you might expect from a TQM project. Consequently, the ERP implementation is often used as a keystone for more radical reengineering efforts.

What Business Process Reengineering is Not

Oftentimes BPR is confused with software reengineering. Software reengineering simply implies modifications to software - changing the way a company uses a particular software product. Companies will regularly adopt new uses for existing software, improving the users' communication, knowledge and skills all the while. In more technical terms, software is constantly being updated, upgraded with patches and bug-fixes. While the goal of BPR is efficiency in the business processes of the company, the goal of software reengineering is to make sure that the software is becoming even more understandable to users, supporting more efficient business processes and keeping technically current.

Also, BPR is not TQM, the incremental approach to improving business processes. An example of TQM might be changing the verbiage on a purchase requisition form to eliminate a common error; this is an example of an incremental change. Reengineering the purchase requisition process might entail deploying a self-service software application that eliminates paper purchase requisitions entirely. This is an example of where a process is completely revamped, end to end, to make it more efficient.

Benefits of Business Process Reengineering

BPR can provide a number of benefits including:

- Cost reductions - BPR should enable people, money, and equipment to get more accomplished more quickly. This reduces the overall cost of products and services, improving the firm's competitive advantage as well as the customer's perception of value.

- Improved customer satisfaction - BPR can quickly provide clear and visible differentiation in the marketplace, protecting profit margins and pricing power.

- Improved agility - Reengineering begins with standardizing wherever and whenever possible. Standardization makes it easier for new employees to learn and adapt to specific environments and tasks. Well developed standards allow systems to interact easily including the systems of business partners and customers. Standards also reduce risk of error in new activities, making it faster and easier for companies to adopt new practices.

- Increased profitability and reputation – If the BPR project is handled effectively, increased profitability and reputation will result. However, if handled badly, cascading consequences could mean a temporary improvement that is totally wiped away in the medium to long term. Many CEOs have been hired to "transform" a company and seek to improve short term performance by quickly reducing headcount. In such cases, these CEOs have tried to gain cover for these headcount reduction efforts by calling them "reengineering." This tends to give BPR a bad name and makes it harder to gain acceptance and support for those projects that will truly transform an organization.

Every organization that implements an ERP system is, in effect, reengineering. There are two main types of reengineering: clean slate and technology-enabled.

Clean Slate Reengineering

Clean slate reengineering involves starting over from scratch, essentially a blank slate, and overhauling a process design. Clean slate reengineering tends to foster innovation and creativity because the reengineering project team is typically burdened with fewer bounds and constraints. Asking "if we had no limitations, what would this process look like?" encourages a free flow of ideas and can result in unique and competitively novel processes that will be extremely difficult for competitors to match. Thus, the benefit of clean slate reengineering is that this creativity can result in a sustainable competitive advantage.

However, clean slate is not without its drawbacks. This approach to reengineering can be costly, requiring substantial time and resources. Usually first movers in an industry and large companies with plenty of money to spare can afford to embrace a clean slate reengineering effort. Sometimes, these new processes will end up in ERP software as vendor and customer work together to create new best practices for an industry. This is beneficial to both parties because the ERP vendor embeds the new processes into their software and, in turn, the company will save on the cost of the system and implementation.

Technology-Enabled Reengineering

One of the key concepts of BPR is that information technology is an enabler of business processes. When ERP systems experienced wide-scale acceptance in the late 1990s, organizations began to seek ways to improve their operations without the risk and overhead associated with 100% "clean-slating." ERP technology benefited from the vendors' energetic industry research and more and more proven best practices showed in the products. To gain the advantages of these best practices, organizations began to modify their strategies, people and processes specifically to adapt them to the particular ERP technology they had chosen to implement. This new type of BPR was defined as **technology-enabled reengineering** because it involves the use of technology to facilitate the reengineering process; the company's processes are reengineered to match best practices in the software.

In these cases, because the technology imposes constraints on the resulting business operations, this type of reengineering is also known as **constrained reengineering**. In technology-enabled reengineering, the ERP system constrains the ultimate operations to those that are consistent with the best practices; the software drives the reengineering effort and gives companies the roadmap to get there. Figure 3 – 1 graphically presents the difference between clean slate and technology-enabled reengineering.

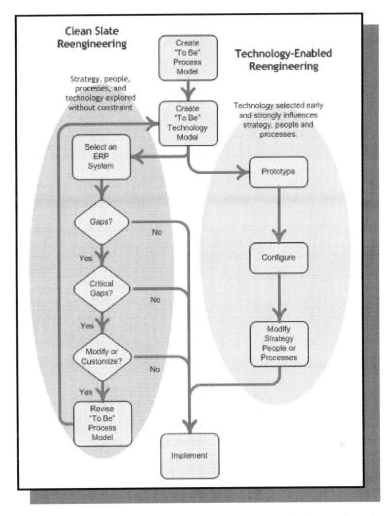

Figure 3 – 1: Clean Slate versus Technology-Enabled Reengineering

Advantages of technology-enabled reengineering include:

- The process design is bounded by the software chosen eliminating many difficult decisions and allowing quicker implementation than a clean slate design where decisions regarding process design are often complicated.

- Process designs previously may have been adopted by other organizations reducing the uncertainty of adopting new processes.

- Process designs can be more focused on those specific processes addressed by the technology and therefore may be more cost effective than clean slate designs.

- The software selected will support proven industry best practices.

Real World Reengineering Projects

John Deere & Company:

The company reengineered various parts of the business including the insurance office and the leadership process. The effort gained its biggest success when the engineering, supply management, and manufacturing departments were unified into a single "product delivery" process.

Duke Power:

Duke turned to reengineering to solidify its position as an established leader in their industry. With a great attitude and intense training, Duke successfully reengineered customer operations in the electric utility industry.

Cisco Systems:

Cisco used five disparate systems in various locations to support their currency exchange operation. Adopting FXall, a currency transaction platform, this technology-enabled reengineering effort completely automated the firm's currency exchange processes, eliminated re-keying, and provided real-time information to any location.

IBM:

Starting with a charismatic leader, IBM reengineered both its customer relationship management and product development processes, making them more customer-focused and integrated.

Kamaz:

This heavy duty truck manufacturer undertook a large reengineering project to improve logistics, free under-utilized production space, and renovate a range of products. As the project is completed, the company expects a six-fold increase in labor, a significant reduction in required production facilities, and substantial reductions in energy use.

Business Process Reengineering in Business

We can learn a great deal about BPR through research of real world cases. One study analyzed the experiences of organizations undertaking reengineering and found that, although BPR was viewed in the early 1990's mostly as an American concept, these ideas have been exported to other parts of the world. Of the 79 cases, 59% were from the US and 41% from other countries. The study also found that BPR has been applied in all types of organizations – public, private, non-profit, and government. These cases included a nearly equal number of manufacturing and service firms. Clearly, BPR can provide benefits to all types of organizations.

Business Process Reengineering and ERP

BPR and ERP share a central philosophy; both aim to reduce costs and improve customer satisfaction while increasing profits and stakeholder value. Both require changes to the way people work and in the processes employed to achieve business goals. Whether deploying an ERP system (technology-enabled reengineering) or undertaking a complete redesign of business processes (clean slate reengineering), the main goal is to move the focus from functions to processes. When a system supports a function, the input, the output, and methods used to connect the two are specifically tailored to the function without regard to other functions in the organization. These functional silos are the target of the reengineering effort.

This effort will shift the focus to organizational goals and shared processes; system inputs and outputs are designed to provide value throughout the organization, eliminate duplicated effort, and boost organizational goals. When the processes involved must support a number of departments and functions, the organizational goals must be agreed upon across the company; the sharing of cross-functional processes must be at the forefront of management's strategy. In pursuit of this strategy, eliminating functional silos will boost efficiency, communications, customer service, and overall profitability.

Neither BPR nor ERP have a perfect record. These efforts have a few drawbacks that should be studied and considered as companies approach projects to implement them. Employee resistance arising from expectations of headcount reductions, unwelcome job modifications and increased visibility and accountability can make the effort politically challenging. For example, a process could be reengineered to replace the four clerks that entered data into separate systems and reconciled that data with one because of the automation and integration of the systems involved. Optimally, companies can relocate or retrain employees to do other jobs.

Business Process Reengineering Principles

Through case studies, interviews, and observations certain BPR principles emerged. While many of these principles were developed before ERP systems became popular, they can also be applied to enterprise systems in general. These principles include:

- Organize around outcomes not tasks - Design processes with the end in mind, eliminating unnecessary steps. Examine processes step by step to make sure every step is essential and no step is repeated.

- Have those who use the output of the process, perform the process – When members of a department use information, they should also execute the processes that produce the information. When processes are organized such that an employee depends on someone else to process information so they can do their job, this handoff becomes a point of delay and a potential point of failure. The information processor becomes a middleman that adds time and overhead to the operation without actually adding anything a customer might find valuable, anything for which a customer might be willing to pay. Eliminate the handoff, for example by having the information user support the process themselves, and these delays, these failures, these non-value activities can be eliminated.

- Empower workers – Many companies have found that empowering workers with decision-making responsibilities leads to a higher quality product and service, faster response times to problems, and fewer levels of management. Some companies, such as Mutual Benefit Life, have streamlined their processes by reducing the number of employees involved in a process. For instance, it used to take 19 people in five different departments to perform a 31 step insurance process. Now, a case manager has the power to grant approval and performs the entire process. Several layers of supervision were also eliminated and the remaining supervisors are responsible for facilitating the work of case managers. As a result of this reengineering, Mutual Life was able to cut 100 jobs.

- Treat geographically dispersed resources as though they were centralized – Geographical dispersion does not have to equate to logical dispersion. Although a company may be global, it can still share a common database for shared services. The problem with decentralized resources is that they are redundant and repetitive. Centralized resources, however, are not tailored to the individual needs of separate geographical needs. For some processes or services independence from the corporation as a whole may make more sense. This is where separate instances of ERP begin to emerge in a company.

- Link parallel activities instead of integrating their results - Sometimes different parts of a company perform the tasks that merge together at the end. It would be better if the functional units worked together throughout the process instead of merging results of their separate work on the process at the end. For example, concurrent engineering teams participate in new product design and engineering at Xerox. This allows for collaborative efforts throughout the process and a reduction in process cycle time.

- Put the decision point where the work is performed and build control into the process - Most of the time, people doing the work have a better idea than a higher level manager when it comes to decisions regarding their process. They should be able to make the day to day technical decisions regarding the needs of the process while they do the work, allowing managers to work on strategic improvements for the process. With suitable controls, this responsibility can be moved off of management onto the worker.

- Capture information once and at the source - Data should be entered one time where it originates and then dispersed to all who need it. At Mutual Benefit Life, customer service representatives enter insurance application information into a central database. Once this data is entered, anyone in the company that helps process a policy has access to the customer and property data. This increases data visibility and reduces errors and redundancy in information throughout the company.

Selecting Processes to Reengineer

The primary focus of the reengineering effort is customer value. When selecting a process to reengineer, organizations should consider its impact on value as perceived by the customer. To measure this value, companies should compare current levels of performance to customer perceptions and expectations. For example, an IT manager could require that programmers add customer satisfaction surveys to their existing applications. By gathering customer satisfaction data on all of the customers, not just the squeaky-wheel customers, the manager can make a more informed decision about which processes to redesign. Employees throughout the organization must see their work product as a contribution to this customer value rather than as valuable only to their own functional area.

Expanding this focus a bit, we should allow the Three Cs (customers, competition and change) to help us target our reengineering projects. We have seen that we should streamline our processes around those that support customer value. In addition, we must reengineer processes to enhance those processes that make our companies more competitive. Finally, we should embrace those technologies that disrupt the *status quo* by generating value from changes in processes.

With the Three Cs in mind, suitable targets for reengineering include the following:

Process as Part of a Core Competency

Core competencies are those processes that a company employs that transform generic inputs into uniquely developed products or services that provide the company with its competitive advantage. These core competencies must yield returns in line with stakeholder expectations. Core competencies may be:

- An area of specialization where the company possesses unique equipment or knowledge that allows them to differentiate themselves from their competition.

- A large operation with sufficient economies of scale that provides a competitive advantage and the magnitude of the capital required to become competitive act as an entry barrier for competitors.

- A brand that sends universally favorable messages throughout the market.

The study of these core competencies and others form the core of business strategy. While they vary by company, industry and location, they are considered the company's bread and butter.

Examples of focusing BPR on core competencies are those efforts targeting customer service or quality management. Often, these efforts include a set of **key performance indicators (KPI)** that allow the company to compare its performance to industry best practices and standards. This measuring process is known as **benchmarking**. With these measurements in hand, a company can determine which processes and practices they can change in order to realize the greatest return.

High Volume, Low Margin Activities

High volume, low margin activities are usually a symptom of operating in a highly competitive market with substantial price pressure. Usually suppliers are poorly differentiated offering a commodity product. Commodity processing might include these characteristics:

- High Revenue - The high volume generates a lot of revenue and therefore may be extremely important to the company's cash flow. This revenue does not, however, necessarily translate to high profit and certainly not high profit margins.

- Efficient and Controlled - The low margin increases the need for efficiency and magnifies the detrimental impact of defects.

- Capital Intensive – The need for efficiency can require a lot of dedicated capital equipment such as automated processing equipment or sophisticated production facilities. Likewise, high inventory costs might be high because of the high volume and the need to maintain production levels.

Together, these characteristics combine to drive up operational leverage; with sufficient volume, BPR needs to generate only tiny improvements to result in remarkable gains.

An example of this kind of process is manufacturing potato chips. Manufacturers must attain sufficient scale to turn train-car loads of potatoes into chips and deliver them to stores fresh. A moldy potato, a defect in a cooking batch, or a faulty packaging system may ruin tons of products. If those defects are not identified before a customer is hospitalized for food poisoning, the remediation costs can be staggering.

High Defect/Reward Activities

Each time a process produces an error or defect; costly material and labor are wasted or are consumed reworking the defect, material and labor that would otherwise be committed to other revenue-generating activities. **Quality controls** can be implemented to reduce this error rate but controls can be costly too, such as when they slow production to allow time for quality checks or when a form must be filled out noting some activity has been completed successfully. The challenge is balancing the costs of implementing these controls with the value saved reducing the defects; a company could conceivably eliminate all errors, but the cost of doing so would far outweigh the benefit. Quality impacts costs and revenue in several ways such as:

- Reduced defects during manufacturing, packaging and distribution that lead to customer dissatisfaction and waste.

- Costs of controls in place to monitor process quality and drive continuous process improvements.

- Reduced inbound material flaws and receiving errors that may lead to errors later in processing.

- Reduced outbound shipping errors that lead to customer dissatisfaction and costly rework.

Because quality is such a major driver of costs and revenue, a major BPR effort should consider opportunities to make quality controls more cost effective.

Many manufacturing processes are of this type and manufacturing firms such as Toyota and General Electric have been instrumental in the evolution of BPR efforts that target high defect, high reward processes. For example, an automobile consists of many subcomponents, assemblies, and parts, each of which is capable of ruining the entire effort. With adequate focus on quality, manufacturers are able to avoid these pitfalls.

High Skill, Time Intensive Activities

Not surprisingly, time intensive processes that consume highly skilled workers are expensive. Companies will seek to control these processes aggressively to assure themselves that they are deployed effectively and, as a result, customers are often burdened with processes that provide little or no value. These controls can make it harder for customers to do business with the company leading to customer disenchantment and lost sales opportunities. In these cases BPR may seek one of two objectives: reengineer to empower the same people to perform the job faster or reengineer to allow lower paid workers to perform the activity or part of the activity.

Home mortgages are a common example of this type of activity. Mortgage officers are highly skilled, detail oriented financial analysts. Their firms may require scheduling an interview, gathering a number of documents, ordering credit reports, inspections, and any number of other requirements for a customer to "jump through hoops." Historically, approval could have taken over a week. Using the first method noted, mortgage officers could end up with a software application that tracks and arranges all of these details automatically. Using the second, their firm could hire customer service representatives to tend to the customers and all their application details. In this industry the turnaround time from application to approval has been reduced to as little as a few minutes.

High Complexity, Specialized Resource Activities

Everyone has heard of KISS, which stands for the saying, "keep it simple, stupid." Another similar mantra is "less is more." Businesses and inventors tend to embrace complexity and the market advantages complex solutions gain. A firm's marketing message may take the form of "We are very clever and have dreamed up this complex solution to your complex challenges." The difficulty here is one of escalating complexities. When a customer's need is complex, the solution may become more complex, and the processes that produce the solution may also become more complex. As a result of this complexity:

- Processes may require highly paid specialists.

- Pools of suitable specialists may be small making recruitment, training, and succession planning difficult and expensive.

- Growth may be difficult as complex processes may involve diseconomies of scale.

- Errors and defect rates may climb unacceptably.

One further manifestation of this tendency toward complexity is the way companies often seek to differentiate their product by adding features and components to existing products because, otherwise, the product would seem too ordinary. By moving away from KISS, businesses move toward riskier activities that threaten the likelihood of success.

BPR can focus on all of these tendencies in an effort to replace complex activities with more simple ones. An example of this type of activity is computer programming. As complexity rises, the costs and defect rates increase quickly. Programmers are always adopting methodologies, such as rapid application development and object oriented programming that enables them to reduce technical complexity and reduce the level of skill required to produce quality programs.

Obsolete or Changing Technology

Oftentimes legacy systems are built, designed, and implemented for a different or outdated, perhaps obsolete business model. Companies need to evaluate their current business model and define where they want to be in the future. Most likely, their legacy systems will not be efficient in supporting a new business model. Companies should look to designing a new business process model around their strategic value proposition as perceived from their customers' points of view. These new models can then be automated around those processes into the new customer-focused architecture. Perhaps adoptable systems are available that closely match those models. Perhaps a complete customization of all systems is warranted. Either way, the objective is to use the opportunity to upgrade systems as an opportunity to gain the advantages of BPR. These advantages include:

- The advanced flexibility of modern ERP systems.

- Standardization of features and interfaces between and within companies.

- Enterprise-wide adoption of common information management practices including common, normalized data structures compliant with standards adopted by business partners or other software.

- Widely predictable interaction with systems across the enterprise makes enterprise-wide functions, such as security and administration, simpler.

- Simpler and more effective governance as structures and processes become more standardized and widely available and shared flowcharts and advanced business rule engines.

- Solid change management opportunities allow more efficient, secure, and controlled updates as well as a simplified process change life cycle.

- Predictable localization processes to adapt systems to different cultures and languages.

Older technologies suffer from these disadvantages due to the state of their core software code. Changing the code creates costs, risks and burdens associated with testing, integrating, and deployment. These costs, risks and burdens may outweigh the potential advantage that the change would have achieved. Instead, companies can implement modern software and gain the advantages of the associated BPR.

Lessons Learned

Despite the sound theoretical background and often striking results, reengineering has not always led to success. The study discussed earlier suggests that approximately 70% of BPR projects fail because of a lack of sustained management commitment and leadership, unrealistic scope and expectations, resistance to change, and non-alignment of rewards and recognition with the new business processes. Not surprisingly, these factors are similar to factors leading to ERP implementation failures. Other BPR lessons learned by organizations include:

- Low Cost Labor - Oftentimes, processes can be supported by low cost labor at less expense than the cost of implementing a new ERP system.

- Scalability – Includes both scaling up and scaling down. Companies need to be aware of processes which may suit a larger organization's processes but then burden to a smaller division or business unit. If a company has a small division off-shore and implements a system that supports their largest division, they may indeed burden the small division with license and operational support costs to the extent that the advantages of the system are lost. In addition, local regulatory requirements must be planned for, sometimes on a country by country basis.

- Think outside the functional box - If a company reengineers in silos, it tends to harden those silos hindering subsequent BPR efforts and creating risks problems up or downstream. ERP analysis presumes an understanding of the various systems that business processes involve and the ways those systems are connected. Connecting them typically creates value and BPR opportunities. This value should be quantified and considered in cost-benefit analyses.

- Look at other companies for similar solutions to similar processes - The technical communities that support ERP implementations are often eager to share knowledge about various deployment experiences. With outsourced implementations common, a firm may gladly provide case histories with their marketing material, often with references to the specific host company eliminated. This way a potential customer can see a first-hand account of the implementation. Lessons learned from another company could save time and money and help with setting budgets, plans and expectations. While companies should not expect that they can copy another company's process and get identical results, proven processes often eliminate a number of risks and uncertainties. Many have tried to copy Dell and Toyota, with varying results.

- Recognize that a process is just one aspect of success – Other influences include culture, both corporate & geographical, incentives, people and their capabilities, experience, adaptability, motivation and values, and marketplace realities and perceptions.

- Deliver sooner rather than later - Too many times companies have attempted massive BPR implementations that have taken years to complete. Despite delivering on time and within budget, people have lost their jobs because the market had changed and made the enhancements irrelevant. Second, it is rare to get 100% support for any project; "fence sitters" will wait to see how things turn out before giving their support. Others will object or, worse, try to undermine the project's credibility and success. Setting and meeting more short-term goals helps to overcome this behavior by providing more visibility for more successes earlier. Each delivery builds credibility and momentum, converting "fence sitters" and making it harder for those who oppose the changes or seek to undermine success. Finally, short-term or interim deliverables provide a great opportunity for feedback and refinement.

Constituents for Reengineering

Businesses operate for the sake of stakeholders. From the smallest stock holder to the last customer and out to the ends of the supply chain, these stakeholders each have an interest in BPR.

Employees

Some employees fill a day no matter how much or how little they have to do. If that time is not dedicated to value added activity, then companies gain less output with the same "fixed" employee cost. This reduces margins, profitability and the company's ability to meet customers' expectations. Some people are "self starters" that will invent and create new things to do or new, more effective ways to do things. This can add value both financially and strategically. When given more time to think, some people will perform at higher levels. Others will get wrapped up in "pet projects" that add little or no value. In fact, some of these projects could detract value. If the reengineering frees up time for employees, what will be the response?

If the reengineering project was designed as part of a cost cutting initiative, there is a high probability that it will result in headcount reductions. According to research, BPR failures often are due to paying insufficient attention to the "human factor." Many projects have neglected this and the companies involved have paid dearly for this neglect. Few BPR projects are perfect. Questions to think about regarding employees include:

- If staff must be let go, will there still be the experience and capacity to deal with those potential errors or flaws? Will they carry valuable corporate knowledge to competitors?

- If employees must be hired back, will they be available? Will they want to come back? Will they come back for the same money, or expect more? Will they be loyal and put their heart and soul into the work again, or will they do the minimum to get by?

- Experience can be priceless - so can loyalty. Headcount reductions should be the last choice after considering opportunities to reallocate employees to other parts of the organization, retrain them to work other positions within the company, or enable their transition to a supplier or business partner. This is where understanding employee capabilities, experience, adaptability, motivation and values becomes so important. Mishandling these issues will negatively impact morale, support and performance across an entire organization.

All these issues are risks a company must explore and quantify at the outset. When measured against these risks, costs savings can begin to look less desirable; saving $1 million per year does not look good if, as a consequence, top employees depart because of the way excess employee capacity was managed. This is more of an issue for companies that have not historically let go of large numbers of people before. Employees will question whether they are next and begin to explore other options to protect their finances and their families. This will reduce performance in the short term, but will also put a black mark on future BPR projects. Employees could resist change and potentially try to undermine the success of future reengineering projects.

IT Staff

The employees responsible for deploying and supporting software systems have an important role in reengineering efforts that rely on information technology. Often, their dedication to the project's success is critical for its introduction and use by the other employees. These are the team members that will need to work with the hardware and software as well as provide support for users as the system begins operation. Their ability to contribute or detract from the system's eventual success should not be overlooked.

Executive Suite

Every reengineering effort needs a champion of sufficient status such that employees will understand how committed the company is to making the necessary changes. Executive sponsors must often stake their reputation on the project's success and should be willing to address many of the issues that are brought up as objections by peers or subordinates that might have an interested in resisting the need to change. The higher the rank of this champion, the less likely these objections will derail the project.

Business Partners

Change implies disruption and business partners are often wary of any disruption in the activities that support a business relationship. Placating these concerns requires a willingness to share information about the pending changes as well as a commitment to address specific issues that arise as the changes take place. Partners will often have to enact their own changes to avoid any adverse effects caused by the necessary disruptions. On the other hand, changes in one partner's processes are often opportunities for the other partner to take advantage of new, more efficient activities.

Upstream Supply Chain

Suppliers are often beset with uncertainties about their customers' demand for their product. Acting with imperfect information, they tend to overproduce and overcharge in an effort to protect themselves from factors that may arise from circumstances of which they are not aware. If a reengineered process can provide better information to suppliers, they will be able to affect greater accuracy and efficiency in their operation and may be able to pass along those savings to their customers.

Downstream Supply Chain

Customers not only gain similar benefits of improved visibility and efficiencies that can lead to lower costs, but the most impressive improvements are typically those that arise from improved customer relationship management techniques. Reengineered processes that focus on this relationship are great for customer retention and profitability.

Auditors

Verifying that information is used appropriately and accurately can be complicated by unwieldy information systems. As processes are reengineered and systems are integrated, they can usually be configured to support auditing requirements with greater efficiency.

Regulators

As new systems are brought online to support reengineered processes, they can be configured to meet regulatory demands and provide the information necessary to meet the requirements arising out of compliance with those regulations.

Interested Parties

Interested parties include other divisions or departments that either input or consume elements of work being reengineered, industry associations that support given markets, local communities, political lobbyists or governing bodies, and shareholders and investors. All of these could positively or negatively impact the reengineering effort. To avoid any detrimental influence these parties may effect, reengineering plans should include analysis of the impact of the effort to these parties and plans to help mitigate any negative consequences quickly and effectively. If a company does not do this, they could lose valuable time, support and money fast ... and potentially - reputation - the hardest thing to win back.

Reengineering and the Competition

Companies should ask the following questions regarding their competitors: Will they follow? Can they follow? How fast will they follow? Will they be able to do it better? Ideally, companies want to choose a vector that distances them so much that competitors cannot or will not follow. If they achieve this, they will achieve competitive differentiation, which means higher potential profit margins. However, as Geoffrey Moore states in *Dealing with Darwin: How Great Companies Innovate at Every Phase of Their Evolution*, there will come a time when competitors do catch up. It is not a question of "if", but "when." Companies should factor this into their project and business plans

Summary

Implementing an ERP system gives companies the opportunity to look closely at existing business processes and decide whether to reengineer these processes to achieve maximum cost reductions, improve customer satisfaction, and increase profits. However, companies must understand the challenges that go along with such a dramatic change, and should alter their implementation method to best suit their needs. There are two methods for reengineering, clean slate and technology-enabled. Using an ERP system to reengineer is an example of the latter. Reengineering requires that companies adhere to certain principles, and there are certain processes that are good candidates for reengineering. Stakeholders in reengineering include employees, supply chain, executives and customers. These constituents are all affected by the initiative.

Keywords

Benchmarking

Business process improvement

Business process redesign

Business Process Reengineering (BPR)

Clean slate reengineering

Constrained reengineering

Core competencies

Key performance indicator (KPI)

Quality controls

Reengineering principles

Technology-enabled reengineering

Total Quality Management (TQM)

Quick Review

1. True/False: Business process reengineering can be defined as incremental improvement in business processes.

2. True/False: An advantage of technology-enabled reengineering is that it is more cost effective than clean slate reengineering.

3. True/False: A drawback to clean-slate reengineering is it can inhibit innovation and creativity.

4. _____ means using KPIs to compare the firm's processes and performance to industry best practices and standards.

5. The Three Cs include _____, _____, and _____.

Questions to Consider

1. What is the definition of business process reengineering?

2. How does reengineering relate to ERP?

3. What are the two types of reengineering? What are the disadvantages or advantages of each approach?

4. What are Hammer's seven reengineering principles?

5. What are some issues to consider when selecting a process to reengineer?

References

Bandara, W., Gable, G., & Rosemann, M. (2005). Factors and Measures of Business Process Modelling: Model Building through a Multiple Case Study. *European Journal of Information Systems, 14*(4), 347-360.

Bashein, B., Markus, M., & Riley, P. (1994). Preconditions for BPR Success. *Information Systems Management, 11*(2), 7-13.

Bradford, M., Gingras, B., & Hornby, J. (2008). Business Process Reengineering and ERP: Weapons for the Global Organization. In C. Ferran, & R. Salim (Eds.), *Forthcoming in Enterprise Resource*

Planning for Global Economies: Managerial Issues and Challenges (pp.108-125). Hershey, PA: IGI Global.

Bradford, M., & Florin, J. (2003). Examining the Role of Innovation Diffusion Factors on the Implementation Success of Enterprise Resource Planning Systems. *International Journal of Accounting Information Systems, 4*(3), 205-225.

Davenport, T., & Stoddard, D. (1994). Reengineering: Business Change of Mythic Proportions? *MIS Quarterly, 18*(2), 121-127.

Hammer, M. (1990). Reengineering Work: Don't Automate, Obliterate. *Harvard Business Review, 68*(4), 104-112.

Hammer, M., & Champy. J. (1993). *Reengineering the Corporation: A Manifesto for Business Revolution.* New York, NY: HarperCollins.

Hammer, M., & Stanton, S. (1995). *The Reengineering Revolution: The Handbook.* London: HarperCollins.

Harmon, R. (1996). *Reinventing the Business-Preparing Today's Enterprise for Tomorrow's Technology.* New York, NY: The Free Press.

Jarrar, Y. (1999). Business Process Re-engineering: Learning from Organizational Experience. *Total Quality Management, 10*(2), 173-186.

Klein, M. (1994). The Most Fatal Reengineering Mistakes. *Information Strategy: The Executive Journal, 10*(4), 21-28.

Moore, G. (2005). *Dealing with Darwin: How Great Companies Innovate at Every Phase of Their Evolution.* London, England: Penguin Books, Ltd.

O'Leary, D. (2000). *Enterprise Resource Planning Systems.* Cambridge, UK : Cambridge University Press.

Romney, M. (1994). Business Process Reengineering. *The CPA Journal, 64*(10), 30-33.

Sumner, M. (2005). *Enterprise Resource Planning.* Hoboken, NJ: Prentice Hall.

Tonnessen, T. (2000). Process Improvement and the Human Factor. *Total Quality Management, 11*(4-6), 773-778.

Chapter

4

Systems Diagramming and the Process Map

Objectives

- Understand the application of systems diagramming (SD) today.

- Be familiar with the types and methods of system diagramming.

- Understand how process maps are used.

- Recognize the benefits of process mapping.

- Know the steps involved in mapping a business process.

System Documentation and System Diagramming

As information systems become more process-oriented, the need to document these processes and the ability to communicate their proper execution also becomes more important. Information systems documentation includes narratives, checklists, and questionnaires as well as **system diagrams (SD)** that provide a graphical representation of the flow of the process, the interactions between employees and external entities, and the information generated by the work they accomplish. System diagrams help employees gain an understanding of information system(s), including ERP, and their role in the processes these systems support.

Given the more stringent regulation of business that arises from legislation such as the **Sarbanes-Oxley Act of 2002 (SOX)**, and accounting guidelines such as **Enterprise Risk Management (ERM)**, the ability to provide a concise, visually simple description of business processes also becomes more important. For instance, SOX Section 404 requires that management attest to **internal controls** over information processing, including the role business professionals play in information system access and change. This need to concisely articulate business processes and demonstrate an understanding of the flow of information in ERP systems make the diagramming of these systems extremely valuable. Consequently, business professionals should have knowledge of SD techniques and be able to read and prepare these diagrams as a matter of routine.

A 2006 survey of 403 Institute of Management Accountant members holding accounting and IT-related job titles indicated that the ability to:

- Read system diagrams was "very important" or "somewhat important" (77%)

- Prepare system diagrams was "very important" or "somewhat important" (60%)

Additionally, the study found that 82% of public companies have increased emphasis on reading or preparing information systems documentation post-SOX. Finally, results found that 72% of private companies and non-profits have also increased their desire to more fully document and diagram their processes, even though the regulations did not apply to them. These findings emphasize the importance of SD in many different types of organizations and underscore its importance in the marketplace. This increasing interest in SD also drives the growing importance of SD in business and technology education.

System Diagramming Techniques

Some SD techniques originated from industry or practice and seek to describe the specific processes in focus. Other techniques take a more academic approach, originating from Accounting Information Systems (AIS) theory or Management Information Systems (MIS) theory and describe process theories or models. Still others have no clear origin. Figure 4 - 1 presents a framework for classifying SD techniques. At the top, this framework proposes that educator focus, course curriculum, and organization characteristics will affect the SD technique taught.

At the bottom of Figure 4 – 1 are three basic purposes for teaching SD techniques. These include:

- Assessing the internal control environment.

- Describing business processes.

- Evaluating, designing, or changing information systems.

Whether the choice of a technique is determined by the preferred theoretical approach from the top or the functional approach from the bottom, a number of techniques are presented in the body of Figure 4 - 1 that will provide an optimum technique for the specific objective of a given SD.

The remainder of this chapter will focus on one of these techniques, the **process map**. This technique has emerged more recently and arises from common industry practices. It is widely used to flowchart business processes involved in initiatives such as ERP implementations, business process reengineering and business process improvement. The other techniques noted in Figure 4 – 1 are briefly described in the chapter appendix.

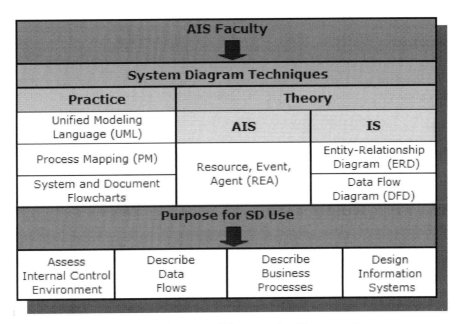

Figure 4 - 1 System Diagramming Framework

Source: Bradford and Taylor, 2007

The Process Map

The process map dates back to the 1980s when General Electric sought to improve their manufacturing processes and developed the process map as a highly effective graphical technique used to assist with their analyses. Since then, the process map, also known as a **cross-functional flowchart**, has expanded to all types of industries and processes, gaining widespread acceptance by leading global organizations seeking to document, analyze, streamline, and redesign business activities.

The process map clearly defines:

- A process input or a set of inputs.

- Process outputs.

- The participants that transform the defined inputs into a set of defined outputs.

Process maps help to answer the questions "who" and "what" and define functional units, or **roles**, denoting the participants in the process. They will also define the activities these roles perform as they complete a specific process. Process maps often represent a snapshot in time, allowing the reader to identify the current status of the process and outline the activities remaining ahead in the process life cycle. Analyzing process maps will:

- Show the specific combination of roles, steps, inputs and outputs that an organization employs to provide value to its customers.

- Facilitate the understanding of how processes interact in an organization's business system and evaluate which activities add value.

- Highlight workflow inefficiencies and redundancies such as delays, queuing times, excessive handoffs, and unproductive utilization of resources.

- Identify opportunities to streamline and improve work flows, pointing out processes that can be improved or that may benefit from reengineering.

Process maps prove the adage: "A picture is worth a thousand words" by giving management a picture of the organization they may never have been able to envision otherwise. They provide a broad, macro view, perspective of organizational processes or they can focus tightly on the smallest units of work providing a detailed, micro view, perspective. The visual nature of process maps makes them easy to understand; anyone involved should be able to recognize their role in the processes being mapped and understand the importance of their role in relation to the entire system.

Finally, process maps facilitate analysis of process design and process management, both key  components of successful information systems. As discussed in Chapter 1, a business process is a collection of activities that takes one or more kinds of input and creates an output that is of value to the customer. Organizations use process maps to document the **"as is"** state, describing how work is currently accomplished. This diagram can then be used as a basis for improvement or reengineering the process to arrive at a more efficient **"to be"** state. ERP systems and their best practices will typically define the "to be" state with maps provided by the vendors. The "as is" process map can be compared to processes supported by the ERP system under evaluation to identify the current business processes that must be changed to gain the advantages of the ERP system's best practices.

Benefits of Process Maps

Process mapping techniques are invaluable skills for anyone involved with analysis, design, or control of business processes. Well constructed process maps provide a number of benefits to an organization including:

- Tightly defining the "as is" business process and clarifying the changes necessary to transform the present process into the optimum, "to be," process.

- Determining whether "as is" measures of performance are appropriate and potentially developing new performance measures that may promote efficiency and focus on adding value.

- Identifying the value each role adds to the overall process as well as the value the process adds toward the goals of the company.

- Defining employee roles and setting employee expectations for the efficient support of those roles.

- Promoting awareness of employees' responsibilities such as during training or performance reviews, as well as the impact their performance has on upstream and downstream activities in the process life cycle.

- Finding ways of gaining efficiency and reducing complexity.

Drawing Process Maps

Compared with other types of system diagrams, process maps are fairly simple. Beginning with narrowly focused, micro view processes, preparers are typically able to overcome the initial difficulties associated with learning to use the small number of symbols involved. Subsequently, they are typically able to master more complicated processes approaching macro views.

Process mapping uses specific symbols to designate:

- Trigger event.

- Activities.

- Decision points.

- Information flows.

- Data stores and information systems that support the process.

- Termination of the process.

- On-page/off-page connectors.

While these symbols are simple enough to be sketched with pencil and paper, ordinary office suite software applications can be used to create high quality process maps. Other flowcharting applications, such as Microsoft Visio, provide specific functionality to support process mapping. These applications have varying learning curves but generally allow beginners to quickly learn how to generate visually striking and informative process maps.

Standard process mapping symbols are shown in Figure 4 - 2. Every process has a series of steps, or **activities**, that create value and transform inputs to outputs. Activities, also known as **events**, are depicted in process maps with rectangles. Along the way there may be **decision points**, depicted as diamonds, which fork the process one way or the other. Every decision must have a "yes" or "no"/positive or negative outcome that describes the remainder of the process that results from the decision and the flow lines out of the decision diamonds must be labeled with the outcomes of the decision. Decisions can be chained together to represent multiple decision points. Information flows/process handoffs are depicted with one-way arrows between activities. **Data stores**, or information systems that support the process such as ERP systems, are depicted with a flowcharting data store symbol. Flow lines to and from data stores are generally depicted with two-way arrows indicating that data records in information systems are created, read, updated and deleted in the associated databases, and the changes are viewed and confirmed by the user. Finally, the **termination** symbol is used to end the process.

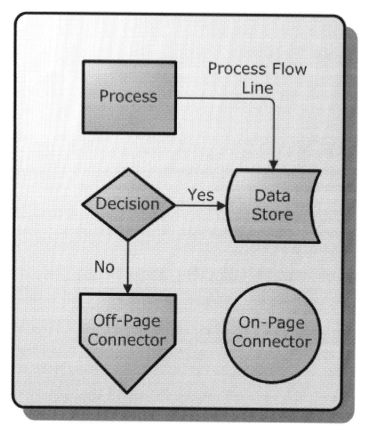

Figure 4 – 2: Process Mapping Symbols

One of the first steps in constructing a process map is to label the name of the business process being mapped at the top of the map. The roles in the process become horizontal or vertical **swim lanes** across or down the page. If swim lanes, or bands, are drawn across the page, it highlights the process; in a vertical layout, bands highlight the functional units, or roles, performing activities in the process. The information systems, if there are any, are generally the last swim lane in the process map. If several different computer systems support a process, which is the case in many organizations, the information systems band will include a simple label for the various systems such as "Database" or "ERP System" or "Information System." Each data store symbol would then contain the name of the specific system that supports parts of the process. If an ERP system is involved, multiple data store symbols can denote the names of modules accessed as part of the process.

Process maps generally portray events in chronological order; horizontal process maps present time from left to right, whereas vertical process maps present time from top to bottom. Processes, activities, decisions and systems are connected with arrows indicating flow. To provide simplicity, these flows can be broken into segments with **on-page connectors** represented as small circles. To maintain consistency, swim lanes retain the same role throughout the map even if the map carries over to other pages. An **off-page connector**, shaped like a 'home plate" pentagram, is used when connected processes span page breaks. For reference, the page numbers should be entered inside off-page connectors and letters of the alphabet entered into on-page connectors.

As hinted to earlier, process maps can quickly become complex as the number of events and roles increase. Creating these complex maps, however, involves a simple process using the following additional guidelines:

1. List the roles down the left column of the first page. Separate them with horizontal lines across the page to create swim lanes. Often, the participants in the target process can be interviewed to determine the process players, roles, people or departments.

2. Determine the **trigger event**, which is the point at which the customer, or consumer of process output, first interacts with the roles involved in the process being mapped. Something must occur to get the process started. This event can be as simple as a customer entering a store or a file getting dropped into an in-basket. Oftentimes, like an on-line purchase, the trigger event is information or data entered into a system that indicates the need to begin the process.

3. Starting at the left by the role designation created in Step 1, add the trigger event and subsequent events to the appropriate swim lanes moving to the right to indicate the passage of time.

4. Add the events in the process. The trigger and all events following are represented by rectangles. The descriptions inside the rectangles should begin with an active verb such as "Enter," "Inspect," or "Input." Passive activities such as "Receive" can generally be excluded because these activities are represented by the flow lines, (i.e. the flow of data into a rectangle means that that data has been received by the recipient).

Figure 4 - 3 presents guidelines for recognizing activities in a process. The information being exchanged is entered on the flow lines. Each decision is labeled with a question, and the flow lines coming out of the decision are labeled with possible outcomes of the decision.

Since the software applications that render process maps are widely available, practically anyone can create quality process maps, particularly for small, simple, new or short term ad hoc processes. Larger, more sophisticated operations often benefit from a more formal process that may include group meetings, collaboration efforts and the use of a skilled facilitator. Skilled facilitators, often from outside the company, promote and focus the discussions questioning conventional wisdom and noting the important aspects of subject processes. Their unbiased, objective point of view allows the groups of process participants to provide detailed process knowledge resulting in cross-functional, multi-department, or end-to-end process maps. On the other hand, the participants in the subject processes are usually able to provide substantial detail in these groups settings. Anecdotal accounts of failures, unnecessary delays and pain points often focus these efforts on particular processes that can benefit most from detailed analysis and a quality process map.

> Recognize the first event in a process occurs when a person or department within an organization becomes responsible for an activity
>
> Ignore activities that do not require participation by an internal agent.
>
> Recognize a new event when responsibility is transferred from one internal agent to another.
>
> Recognize a new event when a process has been interrupted and resumed later by the same internal agent. After the interruption, someone outside the organization or the process may restart the process. Alternatively, the process may continue at a scheduled time.
>
> Use an event name and description that reflects the broad nature of the event

Figure 4 – 3: Guidelines for Recognizing Events

Source: Jones and Rama 2004

Electric City – A Process Map Example

Figure 4 - 4 provides an example of a process map at a hypothetical company, Electric City. The process being mapped is described as follows:

1. After customers have browsed through the merchandise at Electric City, they fill out an order form for the item(s) they wish to purchase.

2. At the sales counter, the sales clerks enter the order into the accounting system software (a legacy system called MTS900.)

3. The sales clerk prints out a picking ticket and hands it to the warehouse stock person. The stock person locates the items in the warehouse and places them on a conveyor belt for the sales person to retrieve. If the item is not in-stock, the sales clerk communicates to the customer and the process starts over.

4. Once items are delivered to the counter, the customer inspects merchandise and confirms their satisfaction with the items.

5. If the customer decides to purchase, they pay using cash, credit card (including their very own Electric City credit card) or check. Sales clerks process the payment. Customers can always decide not to purchase at this point and this ends the process.

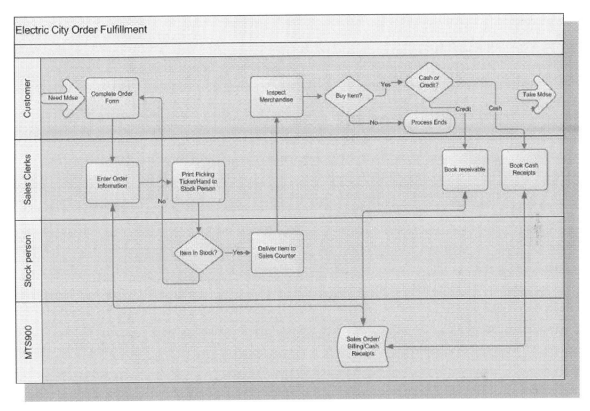

Figure 4 – 4: Electric City Order Fulfillment Cross-Functional Process Map

Since we are highlighting the process, we will create a horizontal cross-functional process map. The first step in constructing a process map for Electric City is to label it, in this case *Electric City Order Fulfillment*. Next, we identify the four roles involved in the process: the customer, the sales clerk, the warehouse stock person, and the information system, MTS900. The swim lanes, horizontally spanning the page, represent each role.

The team mapping the process must next identify the trigger event. The narrative states that potential customers browse the merchandise first. However, this is not a trigger event. The trigger is the point at which customers first become involved in the process, which is when they complete a sales order from. The next activity is when the sales clerk enters the order information into the MTS900. Notice there are two-way flow lines from the event to the data store symbol. This is because the sales order event is created in the system, and then the sales clerk reviews the results on the screen and saves the record. The screen may state "Enter" or "Ok," and this is a response that is viewed by the sales clerk; the two arrow heads indicate the two-way flow of data.

The process map identifies the three distinct decision events in Electric City's order fulfillment process. All the connectors, or flow lines, are labeled with suitable descriptions. Once processes lead to a decision point and the appropriate decisions are made, each potential outcome is labeled as the connectors lead to subsequent events. Like events, the decisions points appear in the swim lane of the role that is making the decision. Process termination symbols are also placed in the swim lane where the process ends.

Extensions to the Process Map

The Electric City example in Figure 4 – 4 includes the basic symbols we have discussed. However, the process map toolset can be broadened, depending on the environment being documented and the level of task detail. For instance, in a manufacturing environment the **flow time**, or distance a part travels, is of critical importance. Symbols can be used to denote delays, such as queue time or setup time, inspection of parts, rejection of parts and storage of parts. These symbols can be found in any flowcharting software palette. Using these symbols to document the flow of materials from raw material to shipping can pinpoint excessive delays and handoffs and inefficient movement of goods. Isolating these problems through the use of process mapping can lead to dramatic improvements in flow time.

The simple, yet effective presentation is one of the strengths of a process map since it can illustrate complicated organizational interdependencies. However, business processes can be mapped at a high level and then expanded to provide greater detail at successively lower levels often uncovering flaws, difficult or time consuming interactions, or inefficiencies. Once these issues are identified they can be mitigated by addressing them in performance monitoring, inter-department communications or employee training.

For instance, at a high level, most manufacturers engage in exactly the same process:

- Inbound logistics – Firms buy goods and services from their upstream supply chain.

- Internal operations – Firms process these things to add value to them.

- Outbound logistics – Firms sell these new things to their customers.

This high level process may not provide sufficient detail to identify where problems arise and where improvements can be made; each of these high level activities should be explored in greater detail to identify these issues. These more detailed process maps may examine:

- Vendor management, receiving and quality control processes that support the firm's inbound logistics.

- Inventory control, manufacturing controls or performance monitors that support the firm's internal operations.

- Customer relationship management, distribution or marketing programs that support the firm's outbound logistics.

Process maps can also be expanded by associating task instructions with specific process events. For example, the flow line labeled *Deliver Goods to Sales Counter* could be accompanied by task instructions that articulate the steps and specific instructions used by the warehouse staff to perform this activity (Figure 4 – 5). The methods used to associate events on process maps with task instructions could be as simple as noting the title of the task instruction or a task instruction number or other identifier.

On the other hand, these associations could be embedded in the software used to generate the process map so that users could access the process map online, identify the task, and navigate interactively to the task instructions.

Date:	25-May-07
Author:	J. Doe
Process Owner:	Warehouse
Customer:	Sales Clerk

Step	Instructions
1	Retrieve picking ticket from Sales Clerk
2	Using MTS900, enter Item Number into Item Number field ; Determine availability of item
3	If Item is not in stock, notify Sales Clerk. Otherwise, locate Item using Bin Location on Picking Ticket.
4	Tape Picking Ticket to Item and place on carousel A for heavy items, carousel B for lighter items.

Dependencies:	None
Inputs:	Picking Ticket
Outputs:	Delivery of Item to Sales Clerks

Figure 4 – 5: Detailed Documentation for Deliver Goods to Sales Counter

Additional Hints for Constructing Process Maps

The following are additional hints for developing process maps that are visually appealing and easy to understand:

- Make sure each area of the map contains roughly the same amount of effort.

- Make sure process maps are not too busy; use a detailed documentation worksheet to back up activities (Figure 4 – 5).

- Take notes while mapping and create a glossary for acronyms so that information generated in the process mapping session is not lost or later becomes ambiguous.

- Use on-page connectors when flow lines become too complicated.

- Use off-page connectors to provide process details or alternative flows that result in significant additional activity.

- Use humps when flow lines intersect on the process map but not in the subject process.

- Use slightly curved corners on flow-lines to indicate the direction flows take when they begin to flow together.

A review of Figure 4 - 4 shows that some of these helpful hints have been incorporated into the Electric City process map.

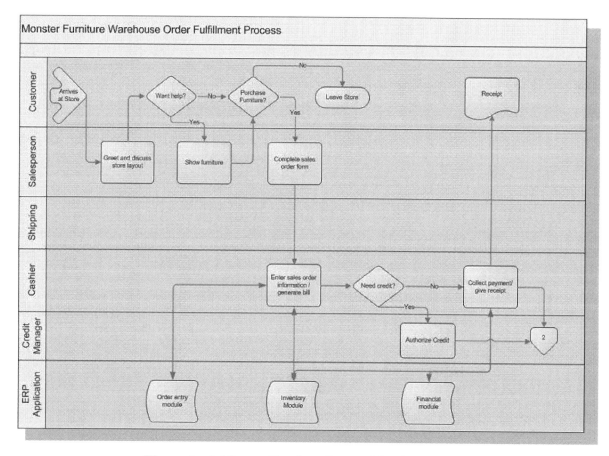

Figure 4 – 6: Monster Furniture Process Map (Page 1)

Monster Furniture Warehouse– An Advanced Process Map Example

A second, more advanced process map for Monster Furniture Warehouse (MFW) follows. The process map consists of two pages, Figure 4 – 6 and Figure 4 – 7. The narrative below describes MFW's Sales and Billing Process. A customer enters MFW and is greeted by a salesperson.

1. The salesperson will introduce himself/herself and explain the layout of the store and will either show the customer items in the store or let the customer wander around on his/her own.

2. If the customer decides to purchase furniture, the salesperson (that greeted this particular customer) will complete a paper sales order document and give it to the cashier.

3. The cashier will then enter the order information into the order entry module of the ERP system. This entry also reserves inventory in the inventory module.

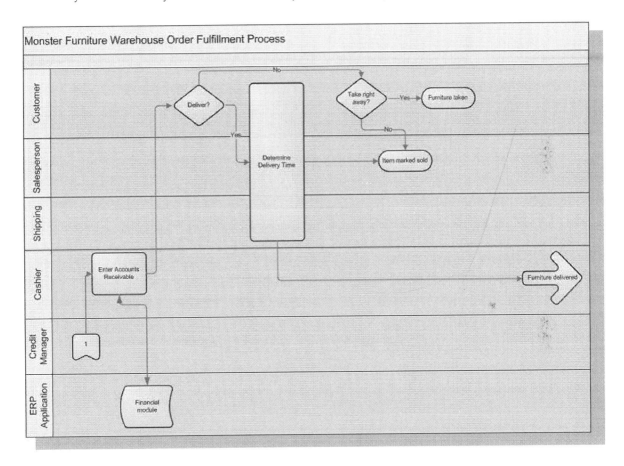

Figure 4 – 7: Monster Furniture Process Map (Page 2)

4. An invoice is then generated by the billing (financial) module. The invoice contains all items sold and amount due.

5. The cashier then collects a payment (credit card, check or cash) for the total amount and the receipt is handed to customer.

6. This closes out the sale (and also reduces inventory levels in inventory module).

7. If the customer needs to purchase on credit, Max, the Credit Manager, will authorize an accounts receivable, which is then entered in the billing system by the cashier.

8. After the sale is made, the question becomes "how to deliver?" If the customer wants MFW to deliver the furniture, the salesperson consults with shipping and the time of shipment is agreed upon with the customer.

9. If the customer is going to arrange his or her own delivery, then either he or she takes the item(s) then, or notifies salesperson return date and time.

10. A sold tag is put on the furniture; either way the items waiting for delivery are moved to the back holding room, where pick-ups or shipping occur. Logistics are handled totally manually.

Using Process Maps

The objective of mapping business processes is not simply to produce a perfect or professional graph of an organization's activities. Rather, the objective is to define the "as is" process, which describes how the company currently works or the "to be" process, which defines how the company ought to work.

"As Is" Process Maps

The "as is" map establishes a starting point from which implementation of the eventual design will be launched. The development of a draft "as is" cross-functional process map is best accomplished by conducting a series of interviews with design team members and others familiar with the process. When this approach is followed, design team members often get an idea how the entire process works from end to end for the very first time. Often, these exercises will generate questions such as:

- "Do we still do that?"

- "Why does this happen there?"

- "Why are we doing it that way?"

- "I did not realize...."

As the team reviews the map and starts asking "why," they will find many opportunities for improvement.

Each activity in the process should be examined for:

- **Handoffs** – Processes that involve departmental interaction or the transfer of responsibility from one role to another, provide opportunities for mistakes, miscommunication, or delay.

- **Bottlenecks** – When a number of flows lead to a single role, the process may be hindered by insufficient resources dedicated to the roles and events downstream. Bottlenecks can be a stage in a process that can delay or completely stop a process.

- **Rework** – Process maps that indicate roles are dedicated to fixing errors or remediating problems might lead to modifications of the subject process to eliminate or reduce the source of the errors.

- **Role ambiguity** – Process maps can firmly identify which participants are responsible for filling which roles, thereby eliminating confusion among the participants in the process.

- **Data duplication** – Flows that point to and from information systems can be analyzed, to identify the extent to which the necessary data and the activities that create or use that data can be shared among the organization's many processes.

- **Cycle time** – The time consumed during process flow can provide a suitable subject for performance measurement, providing focus on the length of time it takes from the start to the end of the process.

- **Flow time** – Time between process events can be measured to identify substantial contributors to delays and underutilization.

- **Value added** versus **non-value added** steps – Looking at processes from the customer's point of view provides focus on events, roles or activities that add little or no value.

- Unnecessary or **repetitive steps** – Flows that dead-end with suboptimal results or wind back around to the same event or role a number of times can indicate processes that would benefit from modifications to move that flows back toward the value added steps.

Each decision in the process should be examined to determine:

- Authority ambiguity – By clearly defining who owns the decision point, the process map eliminates a potential source of confusion.

- Decision necessity – When decision point output flows lead toward the same or similar events, the process may include unnecessary decisions that may generate unwarranted delays.

- Decisions too early - When decision point output flows continue for a long time before encountering subsequent events, the decision point may, in fact, be made too early leading to unnecessary downstream complications.

- Decisions too late - When flows lead to errors or rework, decision points can provide quality assurance or confirmation of customer satisfaction eliminating costly remediation.

"To Be" Maps

Firms adept at improving large, cross-functional processes realize the importance of having specific goals and objectives that clearly answer the question "what do we want to accomplish by when?" A customer-centric view in this activity is vital whereby the following key questions are asked and answered:

- Who is the customer?

- What is the customer willing to pay for?

- What does the customer receive?

- What level of performance does the customer expect?

- How well are we satisfying the customer?

- How can we increase customer satisfaction?

- What is our first interaction with the customer that starts our process?

- What are the most important value added steps?

- Where do our processes end and which endings are optimal?

- If we are going to adopt this "to be" process, what activities are in scope that we can change and what activities are out of scope that we cannot change?

Summary

One way an organization can gain a better understanding of their processes is through documentation. This chapter focuses on one type of system documentation, SD. There are several types of SD, while the most common is process mapping. A process map clearly defines process inputs, process outputs, and the participants involved in the process. This type of SD can be used to analyze an "as is" or "to be" state for an organization. There are many benefits to be gained from process mapping, such as the identification of bottlenecks and clearly defining employee roles. Process mapping is easily performed through several prescribed, key steps using standard symbols, which produce a visual system diagram, allowing management to understand and identify areas for improvement within their organizations processes.

Keywords

"As is"

Activity

Bottleneck

Cross-functional flowchart

Cycle time

Data duplication

Data store

Decision point

Enterprise Risk Management (ERM)

Events

Flow time

Information flows

Internal controls

Handoff

Non-value added

Off-page connector

On-page connector

Process map

Repetitive steps

Rework

Role

Role Ambiguity

Sarbanes-Oxley Act of 2002 (SOX)

Swim lane

System diagram (SD)

Termination

"To be"

Trigger

Value added

Quick Review

1. True/False: Systems documentation is the graphical representation of information systems, which falls under the general umbrella of systems diagramming.

2. True/False: Process mapping is used primarily to model databases.

3. True/False: Only experienced IT professionals and senior level executives should be able to decipher process maps.

4. The _____ shows how work is currently accomplished and the _____ shows an improved or reengineered process.

5. The _____ is the point in which the customer is first involved in the process.

Questions to Consider

1. What is the difference between systems documentation and systems diagramming?

2. How can organizations use process maps?

3. What are the benefits of process mapping?

4. What steps are involved in creating a process map?

5. What kind of problems can be identified by process maps?

References

Andrews, C. (2007). Drawing a Map of the Business. *Internal Auditor, 64*(1), 55-58.

Bradford, M., & Taylor, E. (2007). *AIS Educators' Choice of Systems Diagramming Techniques: A Framework and Analysis.* White Paper. Retrieved from http://www.fdewb.unimaas.nl/marc/ecais_v2/ pdf/2008/Paper%207.pdf

Bradford, M., Roberts, D., & Stroupe, G. (2001). Integrating Process Mapping into the AIS Students' Toolset. *Review of Business Information Systems, 5*(4), 61-67.

Bradford, M., Richtermeyer, S., & Roberts, D. (2007). System Diagramming Techniques: An Analysis of Methods Used in Accounting Education and Practice. *Journal of Information Systems, 12*(1), 173-212.

Bradford, M. (2004). Reengineering a Process: A Group Project Using Hammer's Reengineering Principles and Process Mapping Techniques. *Compendium of Classroom Cases and Tools for AIS Applications (C3), 2*(1),

Chen, P. (1976). The Entity-Relationship Model--Toward a Unified View of Data. *ACM Transactions on Database Systems, 1*(1), 9-36.

Damelio, R. (1996). *The Basics of Process Mapping.* New York, NY: Productivity Press.

Demarco, T. (1979). *Structured Analysis and System Specification.* New York, NY: Yourdon Press.

Gelinas, U., Sutton, S., & Hunton, J. (2005). *Accounting Information Systems.* Cincinnati, OH: Thomson South-Western College Publishing.

Hurt, R. (2006). *Accounting Information Systems: Basic Concepts and Current Issues.* New York, NY: McGraw-Hill Irwin.

Jacka, J., & Keller, P. (2002). *Business Process Mapping: Improving Customer Satisfaction.* New York, NY: John Wiley & Sons.

Jones, F., & Rama, D. (2006). *Accounting Information Systems: A Business Process Approach*. Cincinnati, OH: Thomson South-Western College Publishing.

McCarthy, W. (1982). The REA accounting model: a Generalized Framework for Accounting Systems in a Shared Data Environment. *The Accounting Review, 57*(3), 554-578.

Smith, M. (2007). *BOLO (Be On LookOut) List for Analyzing Process Mapping*. Retrieved November 15, 2007, from www.isixsigma.com/library/content/c040301a.asp

Wang, S. (1996). Two MIS analysis methods: An experimental comparison. *Journal of Education for Business, 61*(3), 136-141.

Chapter

5

ERP Life Cycle: Planning and Package Selection

Objectives

- Explain why organizations change their information systems.

- Describe activities that take place in the Planning and Package Selection stages of the ERP Life Cycle.

- Identify the four major rationales used by companies for investing in ERP.

- Recognize the cost components of an ERP system.

- Understand the steps to choosing an ERP system.

Introduction

An organization's relationship with its information systems is a long one, especially if they include an ERP system. At any point in time, a company will find itself in one stage or another in this relationship, whether it be planning for ERP or post-implementation support. The stages of a company's experience with ERP can be thought of as a life cycle, from the early stages of planning, to the latter stages of maintenance and consideration of future upgrades, at which time the life cycle may start all over again.

From planning for to its ultimate retirement from service, an ERP system will move through distinct life cycle stages. Though experts vary on their names and definitions, this life cycle can be divided into five distinct phases:

- Planning

- Package selection

- Development

- Implementation

- Maintenance

This chapter focuses on the first two stages, planning and package selection. These two stages involve activities needed before formal commitment to adopt a specific technology or engage a particular vendor or service provider. Each of these stages requires the dedication of specific resources. For example, the planning stage requires a high level understanding of a company's business processes while the development stage requires specific technical capabilities. Likewise, each stage produces specific deliverables. The planning stage, for example, will narrow the options from which a vendor will be selected, while the development stage will deliver a set of process configurations we can install and use. We can say, therefore, the stages of the ERP life cycle differ with regard to their inputs and their outputs.

A solid understanding of the ERP Life Cycle and the ability to differentiate between them is critical to a successful ERP implementation. Without such an understanding, project leaders are prone to dedicate insufficient resources and possibly at inappropriate times. Key executives, for example, may revisit complicated planning issues during the development stage negating substantial package selection and development efforts. Likewise, when expectations of each stage's outputs are unclear, the implementation team may be unable to proceed because of an inadequate definition of the outputs required of the development stage. It is often recommended that stakeholders of the project are part of an official sign off of each stage before moving to the next stage. This emphasizes the importance of alignment and commitment throughout the implementation.

Since the inputs and outputs of each stage are so important to the project's success, in Chapters 5 and 6 we discuss the stages of the ERP Life Cycle. First, however, we will discuss why organizations inevitably need to change their information systems.

Why Organizations Change Their Information Systems

In business and elsewhere, the only thing that never changes is that things are always changing. In the face of change, businesses will obviously contemplate changes to their information systems. The changes may be motivated by:

- Obsolescence – As systems age, they may be incapable of taking advantage of newer technologies. Their age alone is not necessarily a problem unless they cannot be upgraded to keep pace with advancing technology.

- Operational Costs – Older technologies are often more expensive to operate. They may require more hardware, have less efficient processes, and more manual intervention to maintain their operation.

- Support – Software vendors may go out of business or be acquired. Additionally, software vendors may retire their support for older software and cease to provide technical assistance, updates, security patches or additional development.

- Compliance – Government and institutional compliance requirements continue to grow. Publicly-traded companies and businesses in industries such as government contract work, banking, medical equipment, pharmaceuticals, food and beverage, and automotive are being forced to consider new systems to meet stricter corporate governance requirements.

- Business model change – A software system that was purchased years ago to meet specific requirements may no longer effectively support new corporate operations and strategic direction. A company may grow through acquisition, delve into a new line of business, need to meet a unique requirement for an important customer, add a direct sales force, initiate a field services operation, or begin doing business overseas. Any one of these examples can render an existing business system ineffective.

Since the mid-1990's, these motivations and others have led businesses to embrace more modern technology and implement ERP systems. During this time, ERP systems have been the predominant choice for organizational information management. This dominance seems likely to continue into the foreseeable future, partially because of the benefits they provide but also because companies have invested so greatly in them. Granted, ERP systems may one day fall out of favor, just as all innovations become yesterday's news. But, for now and for some time to come, they reign supreme as the cornerstone of organizational computing.

ERP Life Cycle: Planning

Investing in a new ERP system is one of the most strategic business decisions a company will make. Few other investments will present a greater opportunity for measurable business improvement. With that said, there is also significant risk of failure if a company approaches this project without the priority, commitment and attention to detail that is required to be successful. ERP is a significant financial investment; it is not uncommon for larger organizations to invest millions of dollars in the ERP software alone. Proper evaluation and implementation of ERP systems requires a significant internal resource investment; most companies dedicate their most valuable and knowledgeable employees (the ones they can least afford) to the project for a significant period of time (a typical implementation may take a year or more). When considering the opportunity, the investment, and the risk it becomes clear that effective planning is imperative to the financial success of this endeavor. Effective planning will lead to a sizeable ROI improvement over the system's life cycle. Poor planning often leads to missed opportunity, budget overruns, and a significantly shorter life cycle for the ERP system. Given the stakes, the potential for savings or the avoidance of expenses, a company's executive leadership needs to make sure they have clearly defined a solid business case for their ERP solution and clearly articulated the strategic objectives that the system is expected to support. The executive team should commit to be the champions of the initiative before they ask the Board of Directors to dedicate the necessary resources to the effort. An example of an ROI calculation is shown in Figure 5 – 1.

Purchasing	Current Hours	New ERP Hours
Sales Order Arrival and Data Entry:	0.50	0.25
Sales Order Review for Accuracy:	1.00	0.25
Phone and Check Prices with Suppliers:	0.25	0.25
Negotiate Prices & Delivery:	0.25	0.25
Create Purchase Order:	0.50	0.25
Issue Quote:	0.50	0.25
Conclude Transaction:	0.25	0.00
Confirm Delivery:	0.25	0.00
Total Time taken to conduct process:	**3.50**	**1.50**
Average Annual Salary of Purchasing Agents:	$40,000	
Multiplier to Convert Salary to Cost of Employment, Overheads etc (typically = 2.0):	2.00	
Total Annual Employee Cost:	$80,000	
Days of Operation per Year:	240	
Average Hourly Rate (8 Hours per Day):	$41.67	
Total Cost per Purchase Transaction:	**$145.83**	**$62.50**
Total Purchase Transactions per Day:	5	5
Transactions per Year:	1200	1200
Total Annual Cost of Transactions:	**$175,000**	**$75,000**
Annual ROI with New ERP System:		**$100,000**

Figure 5 – 1: Estimated ROI for a Purchasing Process

The Cost/Benefit Analysis

The ROI calculation is part of a larger cost/benefit analysis. Each alternative in an ERP system implementation involves certain costs. Some of these costs are common to most or all alternatives, while others are specific to a small number of alternative systems. Likewise, the benefits expected from the execution of various alternatives will differ to some degree. The analysis of the costs and benefits of an alternative and its comparison, with those of other alternatives enters into nearly every decision in a healthy planning effort. The following is an example:

Cost/Benefit Analysis: Procurement at Company X

Strategic Objective: Company X is a $100M company and has identified a strategic objective to lower the cost of purchased items and raw materials by 1.5%. Purchased parts and raw materials account for $20M of Company X's costs. If company X is able to meet their strategic objective with the current purchasing resources the result would be $300,000 to the bottom line.

Challenge: Currently Company X's purchasing resources are spending 100% of their time dealing with the administrative aspects of purchasing. To support expected sales growth in the coming year, Company X will likely need to add an additional full time purchasing agent if no improvements are made.

Solution: If Company X can successfully implement a planning system to electronically generate purchasing recommendations, implement a vendor managed inventory system with one of their key suppliers, and implement Radio Frequency Scanners at the receiving dock for real time visibility of inventory receipts, it is expected that the purchasing department will have the time to focus on vendor contract negotiation and avoid the cost of adding another purchasing agent.

Benefit: $300,000 material cost, $75,000 (loaded cost with benefits) avoidance for additional headcount.

Costs and the Total Cost of Ownership

A company's move from "As Is" to "To Be" can only be accomplished with the allocation of adequate resources to make the transition. The decision to make these allocations should focus, as accurately as possible, on the system's **total cost of ownership (TCO)**, the total amount that will likely be incurred throughout the system's life cycle. Generally, TCO can be influenced by:

> Tata Iron and Steel Company Limited adopted ERP technology to take a lead in the competitive steel industry and, through constant learning, innovation and refinement of its business operations, has transited seamlessly from a production-driven company to a customer driven one.
>
> *Source: Network Magazine India*

- Company size – Greater business volume requires a scalable system, capable of supporting the associated higher number of transactions.

- Number of ERP users – More users means more information management power and access to more input/output devices. Additionally, each vendor may charge a licensing fee per type of user. For example, "Power Users," those who use more of the systems functionality, may be charged a higher license fee than "Casual Users" who only view reports or a single module of the system.

- Functionality – The depth and breadth of functionality to be supported by the system is usually defined by the number of modules deployed.

Clearly, costs can be expected to rise with business volume, user counts and functionality. In addition, projects will include specific costs associated with implementation and ongoing operation. Implementation costs typically consist of:

- Software and database licenses

- Hardware

- Implementation services

- Internal costs

In addition, ongoing maintenance costs must be incurred to keep the soft-ware, hardware and database running smoothly. This includes annual licensing fees, updates and patches. One recent study found that software licenses, services and maintenance are the costs that are most often measured and considered when evaluating enterprise software or measuring ROI. Database license, internal costs, and hardware costs, on the other hand, are considered less important because these resources are shared with other business needs; they tend to be relatively equal between various ERP system alternatives and may even be outsourced. Consequently, they do not vary as much with the package selected.

Software License

ERP software purchases typically involve licensing expenses that govern the software's use. Generally, the price for this software depends on the number of end users and the number of modules implemented. For instance, if a company implements modules for financials, human resources, payroll, customer relationship management, and manufacturing or if it has a large number of employees, the software license costs will be higher than if it were smaller or chose to only implement fewer modules. Vendors tend to further complicate this calculation by providing volume discounts which reduce per module or per user prices.

Database License

ERP systems require the dedication of substantial data storage and processing power. While a company can avoid this expense by outsourcing the application, if the software will be loaded onto the company's servers, the database software required may also involve licensing costs. The database license cost is usually based on the number of users that will log into the system or the number/type of database servers required.

Hardware

ERP system operations rely on IT infrastructures supporting system servers, network components, wiring and power, and user workstations. Again, some of these costs may be avoided by outsourcing the application since the software will be running on the outsource provider's servers.

Implementation Services

Any or all stages of an implementation can involve the employment of external resources; in fact, service costs are the largest budget item in many ERP system implementations. External resources include consultants, implementation specialists, project managers, and training directors.

The expenses can be difficult to estimate. Whereas many project planners approximate these expenses using the ratio of software license costs to total implementation costs, it is important to recognize that implementation costs have more to do with the number and complexity of business processes being implemented than the number of licensed users. The number of users only impacts end user training service. A certain software product might have a 2:1 implementation ratio, meaning for every $1 spent on software, a customer can plan to spend $2 on implementation costs. Very often the ratio of services to software costs provides an indication of a system's ease of implementation or support for more advanced functionality. One study found that smaller companies, those with revenues less than $50 million, are more likely to implement ERP by engaging fewer outside resources, possibly because they have tighter budgets. The study also found that small companies are 58% more likely than their mid-size counterparts to achieve their first "go live" milestone in six months or less. Smaller companies often benefit from less corporate politics leading to faster decision making and faster implementations.

Internal Cost

The ultimate operation of an ERP system will involve specific costs arising from the additional activity it requires to adopt, use and support. Internal costs vary among companies and projects, so this component is difficult to estimate. The largest part of the internal cost factor is lost productivity for project team members who are pulled off their regular duties to work on the implementation. Most team members will spend 100% of their time on the project during peak times, which includes design, configuration, testing, training, and support. To estimate internal cost, project planners can calculate the number of **full time equivalents (FTE)** the project will require both during implementation and during the operational phase of the project's life cycle. FTEs are calculated by multiplying the percentage of the team members' time dedicated to the project, the length of their commitment to the project, and the team headcount. FTEs can be associated with an expected cost depending on skill level and market labor rates to arrive at a reasonably accurate internal cost calculation.

Maintenance

Finally, spending is not over after the system "goes live." Maintenance costs for items such as hardware upgrades, ongoing configuration issues and support must be taken into account. Like implementation costs, maintenance costs can also be calculated as a ratio of software license costs. Many vendors will charge periodic software maintenance costs to cover routine consulting, technical support, bug fixes, and minor upgrades. They may base these charges on the current list price of the software or consider the actual cost of the software, which may or may not include volume discounts.

Pervasive anecdotal evidence suggests that many companies have dramatically underestimated the TCO that arises from the areas we have discussed. The main culprit is usually underestimation of implementation services. In fact, experts cite that most companies underestimate the amount of external assistance they need. A lack of focus in the areas of system design and training can lead to poor user acceptance. Many lay the blame on employees, citing employees' resistance to change. There are also "hidden costs" associated with ERP implementations. One hidden cost is scope creep, where the scope of the project keeps on increasing. ERP systems are often integrated with legacy systems that are retained either due to budget constraints or the perceived lack of need to change them. Prior to converting data from a legacy system to the new system the data must be cleansed. Dirty data refers to data that is incorrect, out-of date, redundant, incomplete, or unformatted. This data must be "scrubbed" or "cleansed" by first detecting it and then removing or correcting the problem. The actual process of data cleansing may involve removing typographical errors or validating and correcting values against a known list of entities. The goal of data cleansing is not just to clean up the data in a database but also to bring consistency or symmetry to different sets of data that have been merged from separate databases. Another hidden cost is that of customization. Oftentimes companies do not adequately examine the application selected against their requirements and realize during the implementation that program code must be changed. Changing code is expensive because programming experts must be employed. Properly budgeting for an ERP system implementation requires the project team to perform significant due diligence during the planning phase of the ERP Life Cycle.

Identifying ERP Benefits

Against these costs, one must measure and weigh the benefits of undertaking an ERP implementation. Companies are drawn to ERP solutions for many reasons, and those reasons have changed in recent years with the creation of the Internet and other technologies that fuel technology as a competitive advantage. Often companies choose to limit the scope of their project and address a specific objective, such as improving cash flow or lowering inventory costs. Beyond that, objectives increase in scope, limited only by the size of the company undertaking the project. In between, companies find any number of rationales that motivate them toward ERP solutions. These rationales motivate companies to select alternatives that should be expected to produce quantifiable results when compared to the project's cost. Further, ERP projects tend to effect substantial fractions of company workforces and therefore can be expected to generate any number of beneficial process modifications. The methods employed to measure these benefits can be complex; the business cases supporting the benefit calculations should be defensible and clearly stated. They are not something that can be drawn up in an afternoon.

Finally, these motivations to invest in ERP systems have changed over the years. For example, in the late 1990's many businesses were concerned with Y2K issues. Many companies believed that their information systems would crash when the date rolled over to the year 2000. Faced with an alternative of funding large scale rewrites of nearly obsolete code bases, many businesses chose an ERP alternative. Over time, rationales supporting ERP systems have arisen from four major business areas:

- Technology – Like meeting the challenge of Y2K, technology rationales have included gaining better visibility and utility of data in areas such as inventory control and labor cost management and extending information to speed customer and supply chain communication. Other rationales include those supporting upgrades to network infrastructure in the interest of increasing throughput or capacity or systems frameworks enabling various software delivery methodologies to work more efficiently.

- Competition – Technical solutions are widely communicated among the business communities in which ERP solutions are found. News of the technologies deployed and the best practices that surround their deployment seldom stays secret when those technologies provide a clear and effective advantage. The possibility of a competitor gaining such an advantage in their information systems should concern business leaders and often they are forced to adopt ERP solutions to maintain competitive advantage.

- Strategy – ERP solutions can be focused by specific corporate strategies such as those to drive growth, support mergers and acquisitions, market diversification, or globalization. Often the nature of corporate strategy impacts the package selection stage, which we will discuss in the next section, and provides any number of opportunities to impact the measurement of the ultimate solution's benefit.

- Process – Often ERP solutions focus on specific business processes with the objective of attaining targeted, specific, and measurable performance improvements. The functional managers responsible for these processes and the IT managers responsible for delivering the solution can identify these "pain points" and can often provide methods to quantify any gains resulting from the deployment of the ERP system.

In earlier years, the motivation to change or invest was driven more by the first two, technology and competition. In more recent years we have seen strategy and process as the primary motivation for new and better systems. Benefits may arise from improvements in any or all of the noted sources. Management should study each carefully and may use all of these to justify their company's decision to implement an ERP system.

Benefit Measurement

A business process rationale normally includes both tangible benefits, which are quantitative in nature, as well as intangible benefits, which are qualitative in nature. Examples of tangible benefits include reduced headcount, improved cash flow, reduced time to market, reduced costs, and accelerated shipments. Examples of intangible benefits include improved customer satisfaction, improved customer service, and more timely access to financial information.

Despite the complexities that arise in these calculations, the basic methodology is simply comparing baselines, "As Is" measurements to projected "To Be" measurements and calculating the difference. Continuing after deployment, this process can include an ongoing comparison between the old, baseline measures and current measures. The need for these measurements should be addressed early in the deployment project, so companies can begin measuring processes prior to implementation. Compared with these valid baseline measures, measurements taken after "go live" will provide accurate, quantifiable results.

Business Process Reasons to Implement ERP

There is no better time for a company to consider making changes to the processes that drive their business than when implementing a new ERP system. While many ERP deployment efforts are motivated by concern about technology, competition, and strategy, ERP systems remain tightly associated with Business Process Reengineering (BPR). Consequently, performance gains attained through improved business processes often provide the greatest measurable benefit. According to CIO Magazine, companies embrace ERP solutions seeking performance improvements in five major business processes:

- Integrate financial information – ERP systems allow for only one version of the truth. Before ERP, finance may have its own revenue numbers, the sales department another version, and different business units yet another. ERP creates one version of the truth, which cannot be questioned because everyone uses the same system.

- Integrate customer order information - In ERP systems, a customer order travels from the salesperson through credit, picking, packing, shipping, invoicing and cash receipt. Before ERP, this order may get stuck in a department, in an in-box, or lost in the shuffle because of a lack of coordination among departments and excessive hand-offs and repeated data entry. By having this information in one system, companies can keep track of orders more easily and coordinate manufacturing, inventory and shipping across locations at the same time.

- Standardize and speed up manufacturing processes - Manufacturing companies often find that multiple business units make the same product using different methods. ERP systems come with standard methods for automating many of the manufacturing processes. Standardizing those processes and using a single, integrated system can save time, increase productivity and reduce personnel head count.

- Reduce inventory - ERP systems help the manufacturing process flow more smoothly, improving the visibility of the order fulfillment process. This can lead to reductions in raw materials and work-in-progress inventories. A smooth flowing manufacturing facility can also help with planning deliveries to customers, thereby reducing finished goods inventories at the warehouses and shipping docks. Supply chain functionality, which comes with many ERP systems, further helps in the management of inventory among suppliers of materials to the production process.

- Standardize human resource information - Especially in companies with multiple business units spread across multiple geographic areas, HR may not have a unified, simple method for recruiting, training, tracking employees' time and communicating about benefits and services. ERP can fix this by consolidating employee information in a single system.

According to Aberdeen Group, manufacturing companies use the following metrics for evaluating success of their implementation.

- Reduced levels of inventory.

- Inventory accuracy.

- Manufacturing schedule compliance.

- Percent on-time and complete shipments.

- Number of days needed to close out a production campaign.

Other benefits of ERP include reductions in:

- Order to cash process cycle time.

- Manufacturing flaws and rework.

- Number of late orders.

- Duplication of data entry.

- Lead time to close financials at the end a period.

Executive Leadership

Clearly, the ERP planning stage can be filled with research and number crunching. We should recall that the output of the planning stage is a set of solution alternatives with sound business cases for each. Regardless of the relative merits of the various alternatives, the likelihood of the project's success is largely dependent on the quality of the project's executive leadership. At the earliest point in the planning stage, the appropriate executive should take ownership of the entire project and be highly involved in its activities. Project team leadership should have ready access to this executive who should be responsible for both representing the project in the executive suite as well as exercising effective and timely decision-making authority over the project. This kind of leadership goes beyond "executive support," which merely denotes that they are "on board." Rather, they are personally responsible for its success; they are "driving" the project doing whatever is necessary to remove the normal organizational roadblocks that inevitably crop up. If the directors of the company have become educated on how the tool will impact business processes, reporting and other essentials for efficiency, they will then be prepared to "champion" those working with them. This helps the project gain the priority it needs and benefit from the attention executive sponsorship provides.

Only adequately ranking executives are able to effectively communicate the goals the project is trying to attain and the vision of the "to be" state. The ideal choice would be the CEO because the CEO is in the best position to share this vision. As an example, a CEO of one company flew all managers into headquarters in the 4th quarter of business (when most attention was focused on making end of year sales) to an ERP "kick-off" event. In addition, he moved the project leader into the office next door to him, so he could talk to him every day. This is an example of how a C-level executive can display leadership and make clear to employees that no one should stand in the way of the ERP implementation.

The Implementation Team

Finally, the ultimate success of any enterprise system deployment depends on the effectiveness of the implementation team. Given the typical scope of ERP systems and their ability to span across departmental and functional boundaries, team members ought to be sought from key personnel familiar with the processes involved. These key process owners, experts, and decision makers should be gathered from across the organization as part of the project team that will span multiple functions, business units and organizational levels of the company. With this optimum mix of personnel, all areas of the company will have a "voice" in the package selection process, allowing for a best-case decision and a sense of ownership in the rest of the implementation process.

The project leader must have authority granted by a high level executive, preferably, the CEO. The leader and the rest of the team should include the best and brightest. Commitment to team efforts will conflict with regular job functions particularly when employees are leaders or are otherwise considered indispensable in their regular job functions; their participation in the implementation project can adversely impact their department's performance. Also, employees that are not indispensable and can easily be freed from their regular job requirements for the duration of the project may not be best suited for these activities. Creating the optimum team often requires accommodation of needs arising out of the dedication of key personnel to the implementation project.

The team's size is also an important factor. Larger teams are more difficult to manage, often react more slowly and provide greater cover for participants that are not contributing sufficient effort toward team goals. Smaller teams could exclude functional areas and deny them sufficient, perhaps critical, input. In this light, the CEO or other executive sponsor should give wide discretion to the project leader and the project team to make all important decisions regarding the ERP implementation and to add experts to the team as the need for such expertise becomes apparent. The most important decision that the team will make is the selection of which specific ERP solution to implement.

ERP Life Cycle: Package Selection

This step of the ERP life cycle presumes that the Board of Directors or other high level organizational group has approved funding based on the alternatives identified in the planning effort and the various business cases motivating the company to adopt an ERP solution. The Package Selection phase involves choosing the ERP package (or modules of various packages) that best meets the company's needs. Not only must the software match the functionality required by the organization, but the ultimate selection may be influenced by other factors such as its affordability, user-friendliness, and ability to be customized or other set of features it is able to provide.

The steps in the package selection phase include:

- Outline Specification

- Market Survey

- Request for Proposal

- Narrowing down the Choices

- Site Survey

- Requirements Analysis Review

- Demo Days

- Implementation Methodology Discussion

- Proposal

- Reference Visits

- Decision

- Final Negotiations

Outline Specification

The package selection team must gain a broad consensus on the type of system that will support the best business case. A shared understanding of the project's objectives among team members is essential. When this aspect of the life cycle is mismanaged or faulty, teams will not be able to clearly define the objectives of the ERP solution and fail to understand exactly what the new system is designed to achieve.

> Cisco spent 10 days writing an RFP to ERP vendors. However, the project team was so familiar with Cisco's needs that the process of writing the proposal was unusually short. Oftentimes, the RFP takes much longer to prepare and just as long – if not longer – for the vendor to answer. In the case of Cisco, the project team gave each vendor two weeks to respond.
>
> *Source: Cisco Systems, Inc.: Implementing ERP Harvard Case Study*

By drafting an outline specification, the team clearly articulates the scope of the project. In addition, this specification provides a flexible baseline for revisions and other modifications to the project's scope as the various business cases are compared.

This outline specification should consider the processes that will be reevaluated and reengineered. These are situations where expertise in reengineering and process mapping will be most valuable. The ERP systems typically support "to be" models that accommodate industry best practices, which can be mapped into the processes the ERP system will impact. Comparing these process maps with the "as is" process maps will provide clear definition of the processes that will be modified as the system is implemented.

Using these models, experts will begin to truly understand how these processes work now and how they will be changed as a result of the ERP implementation. Certain functionality will never change – a company will always have to issue purchase orders, approve invoices for payment, receive a sales order, pay salaries and wages, and book general journal entries. However, packages can also provide additional functionality the company never contemplated such as e-commerce capabilities, advanced planning and scheduling, workflow, or SOX compliance and governance. During this stage, the project team should identify all the current functionality, the processes targeted for improvement, and how the ERP system will improve them. The detailed analysis companies go through to determine all the functionalities they need and desire is known as **requirements analysis**.

Figure 5 – 2 provides an example of an analysis supporting an ERP package selection effort at a hypothetical company. One can see that along with functionality, other qualitative criteria should be considered. On the left side of Figure 5 - 2 are functional requirements followed by qualitative criteria. In this case, the functionality requirements are a high level "roll up" of more detailed functions. Companies may use all of these specifications and more, in order to choose an ERP system. The remainder of Figure 5 - 2 will be discussed later.

Market Survey

Before choosing an ERP package, firms should perform their due diligence by completing a market survey to determine which vendors' software might be potential alternatives. Appropriate vendors can be identified from any number of sources including web sites, industry magazines and trade exhibits. Elsewhere, vendors may be identified in specific research, through suppliers or customers or user groups at regional or national levels such as America's SAP User Group (ASUG) or Microsoft's Dynamics User Group.

Narrowing Down the Choices

From the responses of the prospective vendors, the project team will narrow down the ERP vendor candidates based on solution fit, technology, vendor viability and estimated software investment. The list should generally include no more than two or three vendors due to the time it takes to evaluate each one. It is important when evaluating the vendors to focus on what the vendor can deliver now (not promises in future upgrades.) When narrowing down the choices, the project team should focus on "must haves," "nice to haves," and "bells and whistles." While the latter two are luring, the main focus should be on the "must haves."

A methodology used to quantify the comparison of system functionality to system requirements is the **Gap-Fit Analysis**. The ways systems fit business requirements can support comparisons between the systems. On the other hand, the implementation team should understand the gaps between the way a system works and the way the business needs it to work. These differences can pose troublesome problems, unexpected costs and delays. The project team should provide an unbiased analysis of the alignment of the software and the organization.

Commonly, when planning for substantial system upgrades, the existing supplier is advised the company is looking to replace software. The current supplier may propose alternatives such as:

- Re-implementation of the current software.

- Re-training on the current software.

- Upgrade.

	Importance (1-3)	Vendor A		Vendor B		Vendor C	
		Rating (1-10)	Weighted Rating	Rating (1-10)	Weighted Rating	Rating (1-10)	Weighted Rating
ManufacturingFunctionality	3	8	24	10	30	7	21
Planning Functionality	2	6	12	7	14	8	16
Distribution Functionality	2	6	12	5	10	4	8
Financials Functionality	3	4	12	7	21	6	18
Ease of use	3	6	18	9	27	3	9
Customizability	1	5	5	9	9	6	6
Compatibility with Existing Applications	2	6	12	7	14	8	16
Matched to Our Growth	3	4	12	6	18	5	15
Pricing Structure	2	6	12	5	10	4	8
Implementation Costs & Time	3	2	6	8	24	6	18
Single Source - Total Solution	2	6	12	7	14	8	16
Integration with Third Pary Applications	1	4	4	6	6	8	8
Commonly Used in Our Industry	2	8	16	5	10	3	6
Quality, Accessibility & Cost of Support	3	3	9	5	15	7	21
Partnership Potential	1	3	3	8	8	10	10
Understands Our Business	3	7	21	7	21	2	6
Understands Our Processes	3	5	15	9	27	4	12
Business Stability	2	5	10	8	16	9	18
R & D Resources	1	5	5	8	8	7	7
Implementation & Training Resources	3	4	12	8	24	10	30
Totals:			232		326		269

Figure 5 - 2: Example Package Selection Criteria

Given their proposals, the alternatives may or may not turn out to be a suitable option, leaving a change in vendor as the only course of action.

Site Survey

After narrowing down the choices, it is worthwhile to invite each of the prospective vendors (at their cost) to meet with the project team on-site so that they can better understand functional requirements and the peculiarities of the business. This investment of time might range from four hours to two days depending on business complexity. A site survey should begin with a brief operational tour and a meeting with the executive sponsor of the project to discuss the strategic objectives of the project. The vendor should then be given an opportunity to meet with the functional area managers to ask any questions or get clarification. This process may help the vendor uncover additional value their solution might provide that the company did not think to ask about in the RFI.

Requirements Analysis Review

The demo that the vendor is preparing for will involve many of the most important people at the potential customer's organization. Planning for effective demonstrations is important. Prior to demonstration the vendor should provide a document or have a discussion to validate what they are planning to show and confirm that it meets expectations. Taking the time to review the vendor's observations and interpretations from the site survey and preparation for their solution presentation is important. What must be avoided is an incomplete demonstration that requires a follow up. This is costly for the company as it takes up valuable employee time.

Demo Days

A demo day is when the vendor must "walk the walk" and "show a day in the life" – meaning, the demo must be detailed, showing the software workflows using the real company data. Generally speaking, a demo can take up a whole day. Time is money! So below are ten rules to make each demo run as smooth as possible.

- Use the same team to view all vendor demonstrations.

- Agree the agenda with vendor well in advance and stick to it.

- Confirm the "must haves" first and then the "nice to haves" and lastly the "bells and whistles."

- Compare fits and identify gaps.

- Focus on the system's operation avoiding the influence of freebies, a flashy appearance and slick suits.

- Notice their culture.

- Allow the vendors to share their new ideas.

- Leave enough time for a post-demo Q&A.

- Consider a weighted score sheet for scoring and ranking.

- Cover implementation and support/maintenance separately.

The weighted score sheet is especially important. Each vendor will structure their demo somewhat differently, so it is helpful to prepare a score sheet (see example at Figure 5 - 2) that can be used by the project team to help make a more objective decision. This serves as a check-list of what is important and focuses on comparing "apples with apples."

As the project team watches the demos, they should consider how well the vendor applies their solutions to real company processes. Given the potential size of the investment, it is not unrealistic to expect demonstrations to use real data, such as real transactions and products. In addition to the obvious selection criteria – functionality, flexibility, requirements fit, user reaction, comfort with the vendor, price – the need for and cost of customizations should also be considered. Specific resources should be identified to provide the customizations and responsibility for the cost of these resources should be clear. Of particular concern is how maintenance and future upgrades will impact customizations made. Generally, these customizations will be written over with new releases and must be done again, unless the vendor has established "user-exits" to jump out to custom code and then return back to the vendor's standard application. These user-exits will not be impacted by upgrades.

This is also the time to evaluate each vendor's technology strategy. Solutions typically rely on a small number of underlying technology frameworks and each will present advantages and disadvantages when interacting with existing or other future solutions the organization may employ. A vendor's suitability may depend on it technical or corporate direction and the steps they take to drive down TCO. A final, critical element of a vendor's suitability is its commitment to satisfactory implementation and support. Their ongoing commitment to their system's effectiveness is essential in the best of cases.

The outcome of all this intense scrutiny is the ability to choose a single, preferred ERP vendor. Others may be ranked with one perhaps designated as an alternate. Sometimes, this choice often comes down to "chemistry": how each group has gotten along so far. This seems like a frivolous factor, but since an implementation can take months up to years, it is important to have confidence that a working relationship can exist. One Aberdeen Group study of mid-sized companies selecting ERP software, found that three factors: functionality, ease of use, and total cost of ownership, are weighted the most heavily when selecting an ERP package.

Implementation Methodology Discussion

Before a proposal can be finalized, a clear understanding of the implementation needs to be agreed upon. The project team and the vendor's implementation services team should have a clear understanding of expectations for the project scope, roles and responsibilities, approach, and methodology with defined deliverables that will be used to guide the project. Once these are defined and agreed upon, a proposal for the software configuration and services estimate can be completed along with a statement of work that clearly defines the project and what the vendor and the company mutually agree to.

Proposal

After a review of the proposed implementation methodology, the parties should agree on the scope, approach, roles and responsibilities for the implementation and begin to develop a proposal. The proposal should include the recommended solutions for the defined scope. The company may consider purchasing more application modules as part of the initial purchase if they expect to implement additional functionality in a future. Typically, software providers are more generous with incentives or discounts included with the initial purchase in an effort to gain the customer. The proposal should include any annual fees for support and software assurance that provides rights to upgrade to future releases of the system at little or no cost. The company may wish to inquire about a reduced annual fee in exchange for agreeing to a multiple year contract. The proposal should include a high level project plan with the identified consulting services time and cost and should describe how these relate to the various phases of the plan. Often travel and similar expenses become significant so the company may want to establish limits on these types of expenses or provide for some way of controlling them. Lastly, the company will need to know if it needs to upgrade any of its hardware, network resources, or supporting software such as operating system specifications, database capacity or connectivity requirements. To help make this determination, the proposal should include well defined hardware, network and software requirements necessary to support the new ERP system.

Reference Visits

Before making a decision, the project team should visit vendor reference sites to observe how the ERP system works in real life from a user's perspective. Usually, vendors already have a list of references that they would prefer to give out (the ones that are very happy with their software or implementation expertise!); however, the more objective the references, the better. Therefore, the team should seek out reference installations in companies comparable in size, industry, and geographic location, using the same software version and similar hardware platform. These commonalities will boost the relevance of the reference site to the selection process. The team should be able to confirm if the ERP system is right sized, if it fits their industry, how good the local support is, and the how the current version runs. Special notice should be taken of different software versions, particularly when the versions are markedly different; comparisons with dissimilar versions may have minimal value.

Example issues to discuss with references include:

- Overall satisfaction with functionality and performance.

- Overall satisfaction with look and feel of system.

- Implementation time and cost - did they go over the original budget? If it took longer and cost more than was estimated, how accurate is the vendor's quote?

- Impression of the vendor, as an implementation partner.

- Local vendor support – it can get costly flying consultants in every week!

- Lessons learned from problems and issues that were not anticipated but arose after the implementation began.

Decision and Negotiations

After all the work, it is finally time to make a decision. The team should discuss information obtained from demos and reference visits and rate each vendor (see Figure 5 – 2 for example). At this point, it is time for the project's executive sponsor and the vendor's account executive to get to know each other and for serious negotiations to begin. The visits can be formal or informal, but the two can work to reassure management their decisions are supported with appropriate due diligence and that the parties have compatible corporate cultures.

The executive sponsor should see that the CIO compares the suitability of the technology and its cost. The CFO should evaluate the vendor's financial health and the contract as well as consider purchasing, leasing and outsourcing options. Purchase and lease terms may involve differences in relative bargaining power and each can have specific tax advantages or suit specific corporate financial goals. For example, many outsourcing vendors will allow a five year contract with an option to reevaluate after three years. This will provide flexibility for the company but also lower overall cost since the outsource vendor can depreciate any purchased hardware over a longer period of time.

Additionally, paying for one or more years of annual support fees in advance may induce a vendor to discount the maintenance fee. Usually the services component that call for dedicated personnel to provide full time support can be the most expensive and least negotiable cost component since experienced personnel are scarce and at a premium. The implementation schedule can also effect the negotiations and include built-in incentives and penalties based on timely performance. Final negotiations may include rapid interaction as terms, prices, contracts and the teams from both parties reach an agreement. Finally, the big day arrives. The contract is signed and the journey begins.

Summary

There are five main stages of the ERP life cycle. This chapter discussed the first two stages: planning and selection. For an organization to justify such a large commitment of resources, both financial and non-financial, four major business rationales are typically used: technology, competition, strategy, or process. Once an organization has decided to go ERP, there are several steps that should be followed in choosing the correct ERP package for their particular organization. Some key points to take away from this chapter should be correct identification of benefits to be achieved, clearly defined roles of key players in the implementation, reasonable estimates of cost, and vendor selection is a complex decision with multiple variables.

Keywords

Cost/benefit analysis

Full time equivalents (FTE)

Gap-fit analysis

Request for information

Requirements analysis

Return on investment (ROI)

Total cost of ownership (TCO)

Quick Review

1. True/False: Implementing an ERP system to drive firm growth is an example of a strategic rationale.

2. True/False: The total cost of ownership should be assessed in the Package Selection phase of the ERP Life Cycle.

3. True/False: The goal of a request for information is for vendors to submit information about themselves and the ability for the solution to support the functional requirements identified as critical to the business.

4. A _____ should include key process owners and decision makers from different business units and organizational levels of the company.

5. A methodology used to quantify the comparison of system functionality to system requirements is the _____analysis.

Questions to Consider

1. What are the stages in the ERP Life Cycle?

2. What are the four major rationales used by companies when deciding to invest in ERP?

3. What are the cost components of enterprise software?

4. What steps are involved in choosing an ERP package?

References

Arnesen, S., & Thompson, J. (2005). How To Budget For Enterprise Software. *Strategic Finance,* (January), 43-47.

Austin, R., Cotteleer, M., & Nolan, R. (2002). Cisco Systems, Inc.: Implementing ERP. *Harvard Business School,* (May), 9-699-022.

Koch, C., & Wailgum, T. (2007). *ABC: An Introduction to ERP.* Retrieved August 10, 2007, from http://www.cio.com/article/print/40323

Kordysh, D., & Welch, J. (2007). Seven Keys to ERP Success. *Strategic Finance*, (September), 41-61.

Mabert, V., Soni, A., & Venkataramanan, M. (2001). Enterprise Resource Planning: Common Myths Versus Evolving Reality. *Business Horizons, 44*(3), 69-76.

O'Leary, D. (2000). *Enterprise Resource Planning Systems*. Cambridge, UK : Cambridge University Press.

OSD Comptroller iCenter. (2008). *Change Management*. Retrieved January 30, 2008 from http://www.defenselink.mil/comptroller/icenter/learn/changeman.htm

Pearl, M. (2008). *How to Buy your Next ERP System*. Retrieved February 20, 2008, from http://www.techexchange.com/thelibrary/buyERP.html

Sood, B. (2002). *An ERP and a Steely Resolution*. Retrieved December 11, 2007 from http://www.networkmagazineindia.com/200210/case5.shtml

Taleo Research. (2008). *Configurability vs. Customization: Implications for Staffing Management Systems*. Retrieved from http://www.taleo.com/research/articles/vendor/configurability-customization-implications-for-staffing-management-47.html

Chapter

6

ERP Life Cycle: Development, Implementation, and Maintenance

Objectives

- Differentiate between Phased and Big Bang approaches to an ERP implementation.

- Understand the basics of change management.

- Identify what conference room pilot tests seek to deliver.

- Identify the risks and benefits associated with using consultants to assist in ERP implementations.

Introduction

In the previous chapter, we examined the activities involved in planning for and selecting an ERP system. Once these activities are complete, a company is prepared to commit resources to the tasks of bringing the selected ERP system into operation. This commitment will include designating the necessary personnel to the project and may include engaging any number of ERP vendors and consultants and may involve any number of hardware changes and software packages. This is an important point in the system's life cycle because, up to now, the company could walk away from its plan at little expense. From this point forward, the company will begin to commit to contracts, purchases and other expenses; from a financial point of view, given the magnitude of the financial commitments and the costs of changing directions, the ERP project has reached the "point of no return." This chapter discusses the remaining stages in the ERP Life Cycle: Development, Implementation and Maintenance.

ERP Life Cycle: Development

In our introduction to ERP systems, we discussed how ERP implementations are motivated by a company's desire to replace or integrate any number of legacy, "stove-pipe," solutions and support business process reengineering efforts.

Commercially available ERP systems cannot be expected to perfectly suit these objectives. In Chapter 1, we discussed that an ERP implementation is not a simple software installation; the technical complexities of integrating with legacy systems, on the one hand, and effectively fitting reengineered processes on the other, will generally require that the software be modified to gain its maximum return on investment. These modifications must be developed by suitable technical experts and deployed as defined in the project plan.

Also, in Chapter 1, we described these modifications as either configuration or customization. While we will explore these two activities in detail and provide examples later in the chapter, at this point one should understand that configuration involves setting options that are built into the software, while customization involves modifications to the software code to make it behave in a way the software manufacturer had not contemplated or was willing to include in the version. While many configuration and customization options can be identified and addressed during the planning and selection life cycle stages, many times these decisions are best addressed during the development stage. Of course, the easiest development method is to merely accept all the defaults with which the package is shipped. This is known as a **vanilla implementation,** which eliminates all customization and configuration requirements and relies explicitly on the software vendor's prescribed methodology and the best practices built into its software. So while these projects introduce very little "flavor" that addresses specific business requirements, usually these implementations run on time and under budget.

To summarize, the ERP implementation will involve new software, and unless a vanilla implementation is suitable, that software must be modified to meet the specific requirements and needs of the organization. A solid appreciation of the difference between configuration and customization will allow implementation team members to identify the advantages of one over the other in given situations. The proper choices of acceptable configuration and customization alternatives are essential to ERP system development and are further discussed next.

Configuration

The simplest steps away from a vanilla implementation include an ERP system's configuration options. While software manufacturers seek to provide business process solutions, they understand their product should be flexible enough to accommodate the basic differences between their customers. They provide this flexibility by building options into their software and allowing the company to choose among these options. Software administrators select alternatives in radio buttons, check boxes or drop down menus. These selections then behave like switches that make the software behave differently based on the values selected.

Configurations tailor the system to fit the business by allowing system administrators to choose from a limited number of alternatives. For example, configuration options may allow the company to specify:

- Whether inventory accounting should be based on LIFO or FIFO.

- Whether the company wants to recognize revenue by geographical unit, product line, or distribution channel.

- Which database technology the system will use.

- Whether system data is available to external business partners.

SAP's R/3 system, one of the most comprehensive and complex offerings on the market, has over 3,000 configuration tables. Navigating through them can be a formidable task. In fact, when Dell computers implemented R/3, the configurations alone took over a year to complete. As software vendors attempt to broaden their target customer base, they will continue to provide configuration options to address more and more system requirements, thereby gaining an advantage over alternative systems.

Customization

Customizing software means deploying new programming code. Often a company will choose to customize ERP software to support a business process that may be unique or provide a competitive advantage. On the other hand, the company may need custom functionality to meet unique requirements presented by a valuable market niche of a particularly important customer. As we discussed, while configuration entails selecting from alternatives the software supports, customization involves building functionality into the software that otherwise would not exist. The objective of customizing software is to perfectly match business processes; in theory, the purchaser gets exactly what they require. However, **customization** requires a sophisticated approach to software development and adds substantially to a project's complexity and risk. For example:

- Customization adds cost, both for the initial development as well as for long-term support. This new code may need to be rewritten each time the customer wants to upgrade to a new version of the vendor's software.

- Creating custom code can be a time consuming process and involves inherent risks that can only be eliminated with exhaustive testing. This burden can challenge the most careful project managers to avoid the possibility of the project dates slipping due to scope creep and other factors. Too often, quality assurance is undercut in order for the project to come in on time, giving rise to risks associated with software that may be full of bugs.

- Vendors that customize their solutions for individual customers may commit significant resources away from the rest of the project; the focus on heavy customization efforts may detract attention away from other aspects of the project.

- Customization may hamper the system's ability to support interaction between departments and between the company and its suppliers and customers.

Customization is generally done in order to fill "gaps" found in requirements analysis. Interfaces to legacy and third party applications are generally the "bread and butter" of customization efforts for larger implementations that can include dozens of ancillary systems with which core ERP software has to interact. Additionally, ERP packages differ in the ease with which they are customized; some ERP packages are very generic in their reports, functions and queries, such that customization is expected in every implementation. For these packages, it oftentimes makes sense to buy third party software, referred to as bolt-ons that can extend the system's functionality reducing the need for customization or to reinvent the wheel.

Configuration vs. Customization

At some point, planners will have to decide whether to implement a vanilla solution, where various options may be reconfigured from their from their defaults values, or to embrace complicated and extensive customizations. Vanilla implementations have the advantage of dealing with known issues and predictable cost and time requirements. On the other hand, their fit with the company's "to-be" processes may be poor and overcoming that poor fit may require complicated workarounds or extensive training. The project's leadership will have to decide between configuration options that may get close to the "to-be" model and customization efforts that will get closer. Consideration of these alternatives includes:

- Existing systems can be retained if programmatic interfaces are built to connect the ERP system and the legacy system. The advantage of this approach is having the ERP system's code is left intact. The interface may have to be rewritten when the ERP software is upgraded but those solutions should be less costly and less risky than rewriting the code of the ERP system itself.

- Several ERP vendors offer fixed "user exits" within their existing code that provide a sanctioned jumping off point for custom coding. The benefit of this approach is the vendors' guarantee these user exits will not be affected by future upgrades to their software.

- Rewriting ERP system code introduces a number of costs, risks and complications that range from the need for exhaustive testing, the inability to quickly install updates and upgrades, and the inability for the vendor to support code it did not provide.

- Customized systems may be difficult to integrate with other systems, particularly those used by external partners.

- Quality assurance is greatly affected by the need for customized solutions that may be less stable and less reliable.

Finally, when confronted by a need to develop custom solutions, the project team should consider approaching the software vendor for consultation and support. Often the vendor may assist by internalizing efforts to provide unique solutions that would otherwise require customization and making them configuration options. This approach may be advantageous to both parties because:

- These custom enhancements or additions of new functionality may have widespread appeal and applicability allowing the vendor to expand their target customer base.

- The vendor would gain the benefit of having all their customers running identical programs reducing their overall support burden and therefore allowing them to provide better support to all their customers.

- The vendor will gain valuable insight into the real world application of their software and learn to provide a more configurable, flexible system.

In general, as customization increases, risks, complexity, costs, and time increases. Among the risks are additional complications arising from the need to test, support, patch, update or upgrade the system, as well as the need for the system to interact with other systems inside and outside the host organization. Each time a customization effort is considered the impact of these issues on the system's ROI should be quantified and supported, with an accurate and detailed business case. Often the best approach is to maximize effective configuration and minimize necessary customization; and then, reengineering business processes to match the resulting system as efficiently as possible.

ERP Life Cycle: Implementation

The implementation stage of the ERP Life Cycle includes a number of distinct efforts: testing, change management, and training. Each of these elements calls for different skills and impacts different audiences. Depending on the scope of the project, these efforts may be focused on a single business entity such as a local office or department, or the project may impact all or nearly all offices or departments. The project team needs to decide between the two distinct implementation methodologies known as the "Big Bang" or "Phased" method. First, we will look at each of the elements of the implementation stage. Once we have gained an understanding of the skills and people involved, we will consider implementation methodologies.

Testing

Once the system has been selected, installed, configured and custom code has been developed and deployed, the system will need to be tested. While one of the major objectives of the testing effort is to confirm the software behaves as expected, more importantly, the testing effort should determine if the business, its people and its processes are prepared to make use of the software. If these components are prepared they are able to do so with limited business interruption or detrimental impact to customer satisfaction.

To accurately measure a system's performance, it needs to be installed and operational, and then support business operations by employees. These operations may take the form of:

- Real business transactions – Real business data is entered into the system and then system outputs are monitored carefully to avoid any negative impact. This is a risky alternative and may cause any number of unforeseen problems.

- Duplicate business transactions – As employees execute transactions in the legacy system, the same transactions are executed in the new system and the two outputs can be compared. This is best at assuring that the new system adequately addresses typical business events. However, these comparisons may be complicated if the new system requires more or different data entries or changes the way transactions are recorded to addresses more precise accounting or compliance details.

- Model business transactions – Prior to testing, key business experts create an exhaustive list of all possible business transactions and identify the expected or required result as these transactions are executed. This is the most time-consuming method, but is least risky and can provide assurance the new system can handle nearly every possible business scenario.

The cornerstone of testing is the **conference room pilot (CRP) session.** Very often, conference rooms are dedicated as temporary locations to support these efforts, where actual employees can execute these real, duplicate or model transactions in the new system. As these transactions are executed, expected results can be compared to actual results. Differences between the two will identify areas where the system or the expectations might need to be tweaked. A number of CRP's may be warranted to address different business units, different system modules or geographical locations. Typically, initial CRPs focus on specific functions such as converting purchase requisitions into purchase orders. As these processes are demonstrated and found to meet expectations, cross-functional processes can be demonstrated and tested such as converting that purchase order and several others into shipping orders and accounts receivables while simultaneously adjusting inventories and production schedules. As a real example, Cisco held three CRP sessions for their original Oracle implementation.

Effective conference room pilot sessions will:

- Allow key personnel to learn the software and become leaders in its adoption.

- Allow technical experts to fine tune the configuration of the software.

- Help the project team design the models for new business processes supported by the new systems.

- Allow the project team to identify gaps between the software and the specified "to be" process.

- Allow management to develop organizational remedies, policy requirements or workarounds to eliminate any detrimental effects arising from those gaps, to identify and test new procedures, and to confirm the desired business process improvements.

- Allow the project team to set real expectations of system performance and confirm the software can meet the previously specified requirements.

- Determine training requirements for end users. Often, errors arise from unfamiliarity with the system. Many times these issues can be avoided by intense training efforts.

- Include tests for change management procedures. The processes used to remediate errors as they are uncovered should be tested.

- Confirm data definitions. One question to ask is "will the system interpret the data codes devised and be able to use them?" This is particularly important in cases where the new system will run in parallel with existing systems and each will generate data that must eventually be integrated.

- Confirm data conversion rules. A question to ask is "Will the new system use the data converted from the previous system properly?" This is more important when old systems are being retired and the data in those systems must be migrated to the new system with an acceptable loss in fidelity.

- Confirm that unit tests are focused on smaller segments of system functionality, will perform acceptably in integration testing where they must interact with one another. For example, batch processes, job streams, and interfaces can be tested separately but also need to be tested when they interact in a repetitive production environment.

Change Management

One of the main advantages of installing an ERP system is the organization takes advantage of best practices supported by the software. However, changes in workflow and procedures can disrupt an organization. The implementation of an ERP system can require a paradigm shift in the way employees do their jobs. People are naturally hesitant to change. This hesitancy must be anticipated and managed, allowing employees to:

- Provide input into the implementation process and see their input considered.

- Become acclimated to the look and feel of the new system.

- Learn to appreciate the system's objectives and the business cases that support its selection.

- Take ownership of the mission to successfully implement the new system.

The body of knowledge that has evolved to address change within the context of an organization is called **change management**. For the meaning of change management, one could turn to any or all of these three definitions:

- "A systematic approach to dealing with change, both from the perspective of an organization and on the individual level."

- "Making change happen – to flexibly adapt the organization to ongoing external changes."

- "A structured approach to change in individuals, teams, organizations and societies that enables the transition from a current state to a desired future state."

Without change, performance would never improve. Successful companies have a culture that keeps moving and changing all the time. But changes need to be properly managed and orchestrated so that the results meet expectations. Thus, change management is the "what-to-dos" and "what-not-to-dos" in the midst of a transition. Organization of these "what to dos" promotes awareness and sets reasonable expectation that may be missing when adopting an ad hoc approach to change. Organizational changes should be managed with a formal process that:

- Defines the objectives of the change.

- States the business case supporting the change.

- Identifies the actors or agents responsible for the change.

- Defines the schedule of the events that will result in the change.

- Lists specific steps involved in implementing the change and defines the results confirming each step's success or failure.

- Identifies risks and potential points of failure in the change or the changed processes involved.

- Identifies roll back methods, allowing the business to revert back to unchanged processes, in the event of unacceptable complications.

There are many practices used to manage change; with these, executives can understand what to expect, how to manage their own personal change, and how to engage the entire organization in the process. In major transformations of large enterprises, executives usually focus their attention on devising the best strategic and tactical plans. But to succeed and encourage the desired results, they must have an understanding of the human side of change management - the alignment of the company's culture, values, people, and behaviors. Change management involves getting employees from point A, prior to change, to point B, where all employees are fully trained and new processes are in operation providing ROIs within the expectations established in the business case.

As with any major initiative, change management starts with leadership. High level executives need to set the tone at the top. If management has an optimistic attitude towards change, this will "trickle down" through every level of the company from executives to entry-level employees. Leaders should clearly define the new roles for employees as a result of the change, taking care to promote inclusion and ownership. As changes are undertaken, employees should be led to appreciate why the change is important. This appreciation will require education; not just "how" to execute the new processes, but also "why" the new processes are important to the company and the employee. This understanding of "why" promotes feelings of ownership and enthusiasm for the change.

Apart from simple change management, a company's culture should also be considered because it will define the challenges management will face when they choose an implementation strategy. Implementations tend to roll more smoothly when a company's culture is open to change and when employees are more experienced with juggling many different responsibilities. A culture not open to change or a workforce set in narrow, rigidly defined responsibilities will present greater challenges and may take longer, requiring more communication, training or call for a more patient strategy.

Guiding, nurturing, and shepherding human capital are the skills needed most to ensure organizational change is accepted enthusiastically, rather than with suspicion and fear. The degree to which leaders are able to manage change, develop consensus, and sustain commitment will determine the success, or failure, of any initiative.

Oftentimes a person is designated to lead change in the organization. This person can be a consultant, implementation partner, or someone from within the company. This person is known as the **change agent** and is someone with the clout, conviction, and charisma to make things happen and to keep employees engaged. In essence, they must bring order out of chaos. Change agents employ a number of skills. They must:

- Understand, but not participate in, an organization's politics.

- Be able to "deconstruct" an organization or process and put it back together in original, innovative ways.

- Be keen analyzers, who can clearly and persuasively defend their analyses to the organization.

- Speak many organizational languages such as sales, finance, IT, and manufacturing. Understand the financial impacts of change, whether brought on by reengineering or incremental continuous improvements.

Figure 6 - 1 lists ten best practices for change management. Many of these address the human side of the change; as the organization experiences change, this change impacts individuals working there.

Training

Employee training is often the most overlooked and under-budgeted ERP cost component. There are various ways to train employees. Training options can include on-site or off-site training classes, computer-based training, or train-the-trainer. A **train-the-trainer** technique is where someone in a functional area becomes a **super-user** by attending in-depth training conducted by the vendor, consultant, or implementation partner and then trains their coworkers using classroom, computer-based or on-the-job settings. Computer-based training is the least expensive mode of training, but is not as effective as face to face training. Train-the-trainer can combine the benefits of face-to-face training and computer-based training at little additional expense. This approach also positions super-users as a first line of support during the initial go-live period.

10 Principles of Change Management	
1	**Address the "human side" systematically**: People are innately resistant to change. Reengineering will change job positions and job descriptions for many employees and management needs to be prepared to alleviate potential struggles.
2	**Start at the top**: Employees will look to higher level management to set the attitude towards these dramatic changes. Executives should speak as one voice of the company with certainty and encouragement.
3	**Involve every layer**: A leader should be designated from every layer of the company to participate in training but also to provide input as a representative of their layer. This leader is responsible for bringing back all the training they received and the overall message of change to their individual layer.
4	**Make the formal case**: Management should present a formal case as to why change is absolutely necessary in anticipation of resistance and questioning. Include in this case, the process in which change will occur to help employees see the big picture.
5	**Create ownership**: Management needs to take ownership of this change; they cannot be indifferent because it will reflect on their employees. They need to project enthusiasm and take responsibility for the changes.
6	**Communicate the message**: Employees need to be reminded of the purpose of the change process throughout. They can lose focus as to why they are changing, so from time to time a little clarity and inspiration may be necessary.
7	**Assess the cultural landscape**: Some company cultures are more willing to change. The cultural landscape of a company needs to be evaluated to foresee problems and predict the motivation needed at each layer of the company.
8	**Address culture explicitly**: Once the culture is mapped, management should come up with the culture that is best suited to accept the change process and the end product. Management should then direct changes in the current culture to create a culture that can use the end product the best.
9	**Prepare for the unexpected**: Companies need to realize that every phase of change is not going to be perfect. A strong change leader should be ready to deflate these situations and provide encouragement that everything will still turn out in the end.
10	**Speak to the individual**: Each employee needs to know what is expected out of them individually. Time should be spent with individuals, providing clarity and also definite rewards with achieving attainable changes.

Figure 6 – 1: Ten Principles of Change Management

Source: Aguirre, Calderone, & Jones

The type and length of implementation depends on the company and specific factors. A few main considerations include:

- What is the scope of the implementation?

- How many modules are going to be implemented?

- How complex is the business in terms of products, geographical locations, and different currencies being used?

- How much reengineering is going to take place?

- How much customization is going to be required?

- How many resources (e.g., people, consultants) are going to be devoted to implementation?

- What is the size of the company?

- Will we use an **Application Service Provider** (hosted solution) or will we install the software on our own servers?

There are two major ways to implement an ERP system: Phased and Big Bang. The **Phased approach** (or **incremental approach**) is a slower approach to deployment in which the ERP system is rolled out by function (module by module) or geographical area. The **Big Bang approach** (or **direct cutover approach**) is the more aggressive approach to implementation, in which the entire scope of the project is addressed at once across the organization.

Phased Implementation Approach

The appeal of the Phased approach to deployment is the project team can focus on certain functional areas of the company, while the remaining functional areas continue with their normal operations. The Phased approach is also less risky than the Big Bang approach, as phases of the project are completed one at a time leading to successive "wins," which can be used to encourage the project team and company employees as a whole for the remainder of the project.

The luxury of time can also be a downside to the Phased approach, as the lack of urgency can lead to "change fatigue," causing employees to become burned out by lingering and constant change. Instead of getting the project over in a shorter time period, these projects involve change over longer periods, which can be draining to employees. This can ultimately lead to resentment, complacency and doubt that the project will ever end.

Finally, another problem with the phased approach is each module relies on information from other modules during the phasing in of the new system; therefore, many technology "bridges" must be laid in the form of code capable of talking to the old system and new ERP module. These bridges were discussed in Chapter 2 as middleware, or more specifically Enterprise Application Integration. If more than one business unit is involved, one option would be to first implement the system in a relatively easy but not atypical business unit and then begin rolling out the system to other units.

Big Bang Implementation Approach

The Big Bang implementation approach is the preferred method for organizations that feel a sense of urgency and are compelled to deliver the majority of the solution as soon as possible. This approach focuses the organization for an intense but shorter period of time compared to a phased approach; and as a result, requires the dedication of substantially more resources and planning earlier in the project.

Companies that use the Big Bang approach to implementation are generally smaller and less complex than those using Phased, making it easier to "go live" with the ERP system all at once. With the Big Bang approach, benefits are recognized sooner as the implementation is over within a shorter time period. However, the downside is the implementation is often rushed and important details can be overlooked due to the hectic nature of this approach. More often than not, projects using the aggressive Big Bang method are more risky and can result in less satisfaction with the system's abilities to meet important business requirements.

Which Approach is Better?

Both implementation approaches have their pros and cons and work best in certain types of companies. Large, complex enterprises with differing business models may find Big Bang too difficult to pull off. Organizing a global company with multiple languages, currencies, rules and regulations to go live all at once, with all the modules (or at least the ones in scope) is a major feat. Not many large organizations can do this; in fact, it has caused some to go bankrupt such as the well-known FoxMeyer SAP implementation in the 1990's.

In some situations, one method will obviously be preferable to the other. In cases where the choice is not so obvious, other issues need to be considered such as:

- Is there strong leadership in the company that could drive a dramatic and quick overhaul of systems and processes?

- Is managing change difficult for the company?

- Is the company very decentralized, making it difficult to mobilize?

- Does the IT group within a company have the capability and resources needed to develop any required customization and bridges between the ERP system and retained legacy systems?

The implementation project team should focus on these and other issues as they work to choose an implementation method. Typically, the best solutions are those that strike a balance between the two approaches. Implementation schedules should be aggressive, but not so much so they cause the team to overlook important details or make sub-par decisions. Breaking the implementation into multiple but aggressive phases can help focus the organization and create a valuable sense of urgency. These details should be carefully ironed out as part of the planning stage.

Risks to a Successful Implementation

The main reason that ERP projects fail is because of people, the "soft stuff." The main groups of people involved in ERP implementations are top management, employees, the ERP vendor, integration partners (which could be the same company as the vendor), and outside consultants. Top management may fail because they have not successfully shared the vision and rallied the troops – thus, there is no impetus to drive transformation, and the project lurches to a halt, or even worse, a slow and steady demise. Implementation partners can also fail if part of their job is to enable change management and they don't deliver. The vendor could fail if they don't deliver on customization promises. Consultants could fail if part of their job is project management and they don't deliver. All of these issues can cause employees to fail in properly accepting the new system and the accompanying new processes.

Elements of a Successful Implementation

Figure 6 – 2 presents key factors leading to a successful implementation or upgrade. Some additional elements are:

- Reengineering instead of customization where possible.

- Spending a lot of time planning upfront to define implementation details.

- Don't hand over the project to integration partners. Manage the project internally with help from consultants.

ERP Consultants

Throughout the ERP life cycle, consultants can augment the project team involved with implementation activities. While they may add to the project's cost, they are often highly beneficial and can bring critically important skills to the project that may not be available otherwise. Consultants should be objective, knowledgeable, experienced professionals who can provide top level management with analyses that support important decisions with clear articulation of the associated issues, relevant evidence and a candid discussion of alternatives. As an outsider, their unbiased recommendations can be invaluable in an ERP implementation. Yet, while their expertise may be substantial, teams should refrain from allowing consultants too much decision making authority; ultimate responsibility and authority belongs to the company and is exercised by the implementation team leadership and its executive sponsor. Under no circumstances should a company "hand over" decision-making to consultants. Rather, decisions should be made by the team with advice from the consultants. Good consultants empower their host teams to make the best decisions by effectively transferring knowledge throughout the project lifecycle to the implementation staff.

Factors That Lead to a Successful ERP Implementation
Team Composition
An appropriate team composition should include the project sponsors, end users, and a steering committee.
Organization Fortitude
Strong, executive level support. Employees at all levels can envision success and commit to the project from start to finish.
Communication
Communication should be honest, direct, and timely. It is important to bring any problems out in the open so team members can respond appropriately. Project team leaders should be accessible, providing feedback and responding quickly.
Documentation
Document project-specific configurations. Keep user and training manuals updated. Have a central repository of business rules and requirements.
Project Management
From the onset of the project, have a designated team, budget, plan, and deadline. Ensure there are sufficient resources committed to the project. Have a methodology to identify and correct problems. Sign off on project milestones.
Testing, Training and Quality
Ensure proposed features are thoroughly investigated in deciding whether or not to include them. Bring in consultants early to provide technical expertise.

Figure 6 – 2: Factors that Lead to a Successful ERP Implementation

Before choosing a consultant, or integration partner, the project team should consider these questions:

- Do they have experience in the company's particular industry? This can be described as vertical expertise, since it implies greater knowledge in a narrowly focused industry segment.

- How many successful implementations have they completed?

- What are the sizes of those companies?

- Are those companies in the same industry?

- Do they provide ongoing service and support?

- Do we need consultants to train us to continue rolling out the software without their help after the first implementation, or do we just need a single implementation configured for our use?

Using Consultants	
Benefits	**Risks**
Unbiased and Objective - Fixed contracts tend to reduce bias.	Consultants' experience, association with particular software vendors and participation in technical communities may result in bias toward favorite packages.
Knowledge of Vendors - Consultants can offer valuable knowledge regarding suitable software providers and their relative strengths and weaknesses.	Initial lack of knowledge of the host company's business, processes, and culture mean consultants must get up to speed and learn on company time.
Knowledge of Best Practices - Consultants can provide expertise designing processes to address best practices and to include them in implementation plans.	Advocacy of best practices may threaten company differentiators and competitive advantages.
Implementation Experience - Familiarty with technical details eliminate many potential points of failure.	Expensive - Consultants with proven successful track records command market power.
Big Picture Focus	Unaware of Process Details
Able to envision valuable opportunities to integrate company processes with software functionlity.	Knowledge may not be transferred to company employees, thus inadvertently "handing over" project ownership to consultants.
Senior Management Endorsement	May hesitate to offer legitimate criticism of management actions and decisions.

Figure 6 – 3: Benefits and Risks of Using Consultants

Source: strategy+business.com

Consultants are commonly used to provide assistance for many steps in the ERP life cycle including:

- Building the business cases.

- Documenting "as is" and developing "to be" business processes.

- Gathering requirements.

- Supporting the vendor selection process.

- Training, both on site and in classroom facilities.

- Project management and change management.

- Performing infrastructure readiness and security assessments.

- On-going support and maintenance.

Figure 6 – 3 summarizes benefits and risks of using consultants in an ERP system implementation.

Approach	Time	Internal Cost	External Cost	Change	ROI	Risks
Recommended	Medium	Medium	Medium	High	High	• Internal resource capacity
Turnkey	Low	Low	High	Med	Med	• User Acceptance • Change Management
Customer Driven	High	High	Low	Low	Med	• Missed opportunities • Maintaining momentum over time • Internal resource capacity
A la carte	High	High	Low	Low	Med	• Implementation success • Lack of control & guidance • Missed opportunities • Maintaining momentum over time • Internal resource capacity

Figure 6 – 4: Implementation Approach Comparison

Source: mcaConnect

Implementation Approach Options

Figure 6 – 4 presents various implementation approaches and an assessment of the implementation time, internal and external costs incurred, amount of change required and ROI. The different types of approaches include:

- Recommended – a cooperative approach between the company and vendor providing a shared effort for all implementation aspects.

- Turnkey – an accelerated, delivered solution, reducing internal investment by minimizing customer contribution.

- Customer driven – maximizes customer involvement, with minimal involvement from consultants

- A la carte – Customer owns the process, with consultant involved as requested.

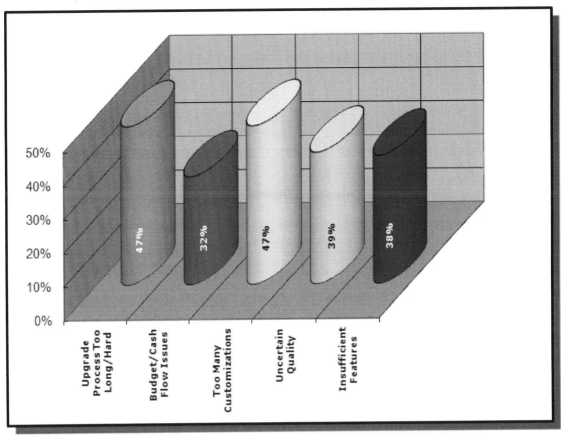

Figure 6 – 5: Reported Percentages for Company Decisions Not to Upgrade Systems

Source: Aberdeen Group

ERP Life Cycle – Maintenance

Post go-live, companies enter the Maintenance stage, which starts with a period of stabilization. According to Deloitte Consulting, the time period for stabilization is normally between three and nine months and in this time many companies will experience a dip in performance due to continued training needs and fine-tuning of "to be" processes. Also during this time while the implementation is still recent, a project review and analysis session should be conducted to ascertain what went right, what went wrong, and lessons learned. After stabilization, companies will enter the synthesize and synergize stages, in which they will put more effort into people and process improvements. Complementary applications such as CRM and Business Intelligence may be added. These stages are ongoing as companies are continually upgrading and building on their ERP platform.

Companies must allocate for annual maintenance activities as well. Annual maintenance expenses for ERP systems can cost approximately 25% of initial ERP implementation costs and upgrade costs as much as 25-33% of the initial ERP implementation. Maintenance can take the form of patches, fixes, additional customization, supplementary training, and help desk. The help desk is a support department/call center that is supported by the ERP vendor or managed in-house and staffed with super users. The integration partner will often stay on after go live to assist with the operational learning-curve and provide support for initial, critical deliverables such as month-end closing.

One truism of an ERP implementation is that the project team can never stop. Companies cannot afford to send their project members back into the business because there is still so much to do after ERP is installed. Writing and customizing reports to pull information out of the ERP system is one task that will certainly be going on past go live. Another important activity is the infamous ROI calculation, which should be conducted as soon as the company stabilizes and continue every month, quarter, and year. Most ERP systems do not reveal their value until after organizations have had them running for some time and can concentrate on making improvements in the business processes affected by the system. Team members should return to their business case rationales and expected benefits and measure progress against baseline performance metrics to show the value of the ERP implementation.

After some period of time companies will elect to upgrade their ERP system. Some companies rush to be the first movers in a version upgrade in order to take advantage of the most advanced technology and functionality. Others try to delay upgrades as long as possible. Figure 6 – 5 presents reasons why companies delay upgrades and the percentage of survey respondents that cited a specific reason.

Summary

The ERP Life Cycle consists of five main stages. This chapter discussed the last three stages: development, implementation and maintenance. During the development phase, a company will have to decide among a vanilla approach, customization and/or configuration. Customization will increase the costs of an implementation due to programming of code; however, the resulting solution will be unique and provide a competitive advantage. Conference room pilots can ensure that models chosen will work for the company and output of the system is accurate. Two main implementation approaches are Big Bang and Phased. Company-specific characteristics usually dictate what the best choice will be for a particular implementation. All through the Life Cycle, organizations will want to commit resources to change management as well as for knowledgeable external consultants. Both factors can ensure a successful implementation. Finally, the maintenance phase of the Life Cycle is replete with activities as well that demand thorough analyses of cost and benefit options. One of these activities is the consideration of future upgrades.

Keywords

Application Service Provider

Big Bang implementation approach

Change agent

Change management

Conference room pilot (CRP) session

Configuration

Customization

Direct cutover implementation approach

Incremental implementation approach

Phased implementation approach

Super-user

Train-the-trainer

Vanilla implementation

Quick Review

1. True/False: Configurations tailor the system to fit the business by allowing system administrators to choose from a limited number of alternatives.

2. True/False: The appeal of the Big Bang approach to deployment is the project team can focus on certain functional areas of the company, while the remaining functional areas continue with their normal operations.

3. A _____ implementation eliminates all customization and configuration requirements and relies explicitly on the software vendor's prescribed methodology.

4. Return on investment calculations and upgrades are accomplished during the _____ phase of the ERP Life Cycle.

5. Large, complex companies usually use a _____ (or incremental) implementation approach.

Questions to Consider

1. Discuss why conference room pilots are used in the development phase of an ERP implementation.

2. What is the difference between the Phased and Big Bang approaches to ERP implementation?

3. List the 10 principles of change management.

4. List benefits and risks associated with using consultants.

5. What factors can help ensure a successful ERP implementation?

References

Aguirre, D., Calderone, M., & Jones, J. (2004). *10 Principles of Change Management*. Retrieved from http://www.strategy-business.com/resilience/rr00006

Austin, R., Cotteleer, M., & Nolan, R. (2002). Cisco Systems, Inc.: Implementing ERP. *Harvard Business School, (* May), 9-699-022.

Collett, Stacy. (2007). *Big Payback From Big-Bang Projects*. Retrieved March 21, 2008, from http://www.computerworld.com/action/article.do?command=viewArticleBasic&articleId=275150

Kimberling, E. (2007). *ERP's Big Bang Theory*. Retrieved March 21, 2008, from http://blogs.ittoolbox.com/erp/roi/archives/erps-big-bang-theory-11954

Koch, C., & Wailgum, T. (2007). *ABC: An Introduction to ERP*. Retrieved August 10, 2007, from http://www.cio.com/article/40295/ABC An_ Introduction_to_CRM

Kordysh, D., & Welch, J. (2007). Seven Keys to ERP Success. *Strategic Finance*, (September), 41-61.

Mabert, V., Soni, S., & Venkataramanan, M. (2001). Enterprise Resource Planning: Common Myths Versus Evolving Reality. *Business Horizons*, *44*(3), 69-76.

O'Donnell, S. *5 Steps To Successful ERP Implementation*. Retrieved from http://www.datacorinc.com/articles/news/erp.pdf

O'Leary, D. (2000). *Enterprise Resource Planning Systems*. Cambridge, UK : Cambridge University Press.

OSD Comptroller iCenter. (2008). *Change Management*. Retrieved January 5, 2008, from http://www.defenselink.mil/comptroller/icenter/learn/changeman.htm

SM Thacker & Associates. (2000). *Testing you ERP Computer Software Using a Conference Room Pilot*. Retrieved January 5, 2008, from http://www.smthacker.co.uk/conference_room_pilot.htm

Sood, B. (2002). *An ERP and a Steely Resolution*. Retrieved January 5, 2008, from http://www.networkmagazineindia.com/200210/case5.shtml

Chapter

7

ERP and Customer Relationship Management

Objectives

- Explain the reasons for the growing importance of CRM solutions.

- Recognize the differences between Sales Force Automation and CRM.

- Understand the "Customer's Point of View."

Introduction

Generating revenue is critically important to every organization. Whether the revenue is generated from selling products, providing services or accepting donations, an organization cannot survive without revenue to cover expenses. ERP systems are adept at processing customer orders and integrating customer and sales order information with other relevant information such as inventory, manufacturing and logistics. Traditionally, core ERP systems have supported these processes with functionality that focuses on the flow of revenue from the ordering through manufacturing and ultimately to delivery. However, as one of the primary objectives of reengineering is to view processes from the customer's viewpoint, many companies have discovered that software that focuses on customers and potential customers can drive revenue growth and reduce sales-related expenses. The modules that have evolved to provide this focus are known as **Customer Relationship Management (CRM)** solutions. CRM solutions have demonstrated phenomenal growth over the last few years as businesses have embraced the opportunity to actively manage customer relationships to generate substantial market advantages.

While CRM applications were originally considered bolt-on modules that could be added to core ERP, they are now considered by many ERP system designers to be an extension of core ERP processes. This chapter will explore how ERP systems provide support for sales and marketing activities and how CRM functionality can be used to gain greater focus on customers, their behavior and the value of the relationships. A CRM solution empowers the organization to drive performance by fostering and maintaining strong customer relationships thereby providing support for operational and strategic goals. In the sections that follow, we will look at sales activities in ERP systems, distinguish between ERP and CRM, and define clearly front-office processes that CRM systems seek to automate and support.

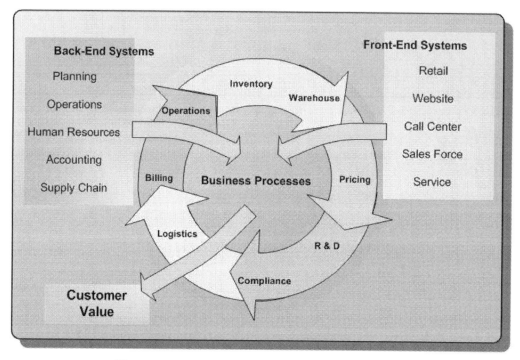

Figure 7 – 1: Back-Office and Front-Office Systems

Sales Activities in ERP

Traditional ERP systems were considered **back-office systems**, implying that they supported transactional processing and operational support for activities that are not visible to the customer. These back-office functions include accounting, human resources, and operations. In addition, ERP systems are particularly effective at reengineering back-office order fulfillment activities that include picking, packing, and shipping. The goal of ERP has always been to integrate these back-office systems. However, as we can see in Figure 7 – 1, many of these back-office systems can either use information from, or provide information to, systems that employees use as they interact with customers. These **front-office systems**, such as CRM, support activities that directly involve the organization's customer interface. They seek to capture all customer related information and use that information to improve the organization's interactions with its customers. In addition, an effective CRM system will integrate seamlessly with back-office systems, transferring sales order information to modules that support order fulfillment, billing and revenue recognition. Integrating CRM functionality with traditional ERP functionality such as sales, marketing and service data, allows data, once captured in the system, to be used throughout the ERP system without re-entering the data into separate systems.

Figure 7 – 2: NetSuite Functionality Wheel

Source: NetSuite

One way to understand the relationship of CRM to core ERP is to take a look at a real business system, NetSuite, a widely used, mid-sized ERP application. Figure 7 - 2 presents NetSuite's "Functionality Wheel" used to describe the system. NetSuite's primary functions include three major modules: ERP, CRM and Ecommerce. We highlight a few of the components of NetSuite CRM below:

- **Order Management** – Functionality to capture and track customer orders through fulfillments, billing and payment.

- **Sales Force Automation (SFA)** – Discussed later in this chapter, SFA provides functionality that reduces the burden typically associated with sales efforts.

- **Partner Portal** - An interface that manages all correspondence related to implementation partners, customer support and marketing campaigns.

CRM in Action

To begin to appreciate the value of CRM solutions, one could consider a typical commercial call center where customers call to place orders. In this example, the telephone system and computer workstations are connected so that, as customers call in, they are routed to a Customer Service Representative (CSR) and information about that customer would be provided in a "screen popup" on the CSR's monitor. This popup application would include important information including the customer's purchasing history and buying habits. With this information, the CSR may be able to lead the customer to complementary items that would go well with what they have already purchased. In addition, using information from other ERP modules, the CSR is able to quote any unpaid invoices on the customer's account or may be able to suggest financial arrangements suited to the customer. By having this information available at the point of contact, the CSR is able to enrich the interaction, increase customer satisfaction and possibly up-sell and cross-sell the customer adding to sales revenue.

> CRM is a business approach that integrates people, processes and technology to maximize the relations of an organization with all types of customers. The true value of CRM is to transform strategy, operational processes and business functions in order to retain customers and increase customer loyalty and profitability.
>
> *Source: Aris Pantazopoulos – Founder, CRM Today*

CRM: The Front-Office Interface to the Customer

These days, customers have high expectations:

- "Know me and know my business."

- "Help me solve my business problems."

- "Make it easy for me to do business with you."

These are the customer perspectives where CRM systems add value. CRM systems support these perspectives by:

- Providing current, complete and accurate customer data throughout the company.

- Reducing administrative overhead costs associated with gathering and managing customer data.

- Increasing profitability by organizing detailed information about customers and facilitating more efficient and personalized service.

- Solidifying customer loyalty by promoting stronger relationships with customers.

- Serving as a front-office interface between the customer and the sales, marketing and customer service departments.

Another indication that CRM is becoming more closely associated with core ERP functionality is the confusion in the marketplace about what exactly CRM entails. Pepper & Rogers Group, a marketing consulting firm, conducted a survey of business leaders from companies that are at the forefront of CRM. When they asked leaders how they define CRM, they found that:

- Sixty-five percent said CRM is moving a company from product-centric to customer-centric focus.

- Fifty-one percent felt CRM is using IT tools to achieve incremental business improvements.

- Forty-one percent viewed CRM as making customer information available to all customer contact personnel.

These varying answers raise a good point: CRM is not all things to all people. Further, while these perceptions reflect different perspectives, each describes a different way of arriving at the same goal: reaching the customer, fostering a relationship with that customer, and managing that relationship in order to boost long term profits that relationship generates.

CRM is a strategic process that helps better understand customers' needs and how to meet those needs to enhance the bottom line. The foundation of a successful CRM solution consists of three elements:

- People – Company staff, from the CEO to the front-office customer service representatives, need to buy into and support CRM.

- Processes - A company's business processes must be reengineered to reinforce its CRM initiative, often from the viewpoint of "How can this process best serve the customer?"

- Technology - Firms must select the right technology to drive the processes, provide high quality data to employees and be user friendly.

If any of these three elements is unsound, the CRM system will never reach its greatest potential return on investment. Worst case, the entire CRM structure will crumble. Organizations that understand the strategic value of CRM technology to achieve dramatic increases in revenue, productivity, and customer satisfaction will have a significant advantage over their competitors who lag in the adoption of this technology. As we have seen in our discussions of other ERP solutions, a key component of a CRM initiative is its business case. A solid business case should be justified by its ability to provide measurable business performance improvements. Generally, performance should be measured before the system is implemented to establish **baseline performance measures.** These baseline measures can

> "SaaS is increasingly popular for its ability to simplify deployment and reduce customer acquisition costs; it also allows developers to support many customers with a single version of a product."
>
> *Source: Microsoft*

subsequently be compared with post-implementation metrics to gauge the effectiveness of the solutions implemented and the extent to which the business process objectives are being achieved. Figure 7 – 3 provides examples of key sales, marketing, and service performance indicators that could be used to justify the adoption of a CRM system.

Marketing Metrics	Sales Metrics	Service Metrics
Number of new campaigns	Number of new customers	Cases closed same day
Number of responses per campaign	Amount of new revenue	Number of cases handled per agent
Number of customer referrals	Number of sales calls made	Complaint time-to-resolution
Revenue generated per campaign	Sales cycle duration	Customer satisfaction level

Figure 7 - 3: Example CRM Metrics

CRM versus ERP

CRM and ERP both offer ways to automate processes and run the organization more efficiently, but the systems were originally designed to streamline different functions. CRM solutions focus on front-office operations and are used to manage customer interactions including sales, marketing and service. ERP systems, on the other hand, focus on back-office operations and are used to manage inventory, purchasing, human resources, accounting and other back-office processes. So while CRM requires customer service acumen, ERP requires knowledge of financial and manufacturing processes.

However, as enterprise solutions continue to evolve, the lines between CRM and ERP are beginning to blur. ERP vendors are incorporating CRM functions into their software, and CRM vendors add ERP capabilities to their offerings. Both industries are working to develop all-encompassing applications to streamline internal operations and customer activities. NetSuite is an example of this "blurring of the lines" as they have included both CRM and ERP into their business suite in order to provide seamless business workflows from front-office, customer facing activities through to back-office fulfillment and accounting activities.

CRM: On Premise versus On Demand

The traditional method of implementing software, including CRM, is to install it **on premise**, which means on the company's own servers. Of course, this involves purchasing the hardware and database license along with the software license. Other companies are finding that the fastest and least expensive way to get up and running with enterprise software is the **on demand** model in which the software is hosted by a third party, such as NetSuite. This model, also referred to as **Software as a**

Service (SaaS) in which an application is delivered over the Internet on a "pay as you go" basis, is a form of IT outsourcing called **application outsourcing**. In application outsourcing, the host maintains the software on their servers and licenses it over the Internet to many different companies on a subscription basis. Of course, certain security measures must be put in place such as encryption and firewalls and a **service level agreement (SLA)** must be drawn up and agreed upon by the parties involved. The SLA should define responsibilities of both parties such as payment responsibilities of the client and minimum level of availability by the provider. This method of paying for software is also known as **off-Balance Sheet financing** in that no amounts are capitalized on the Balance Sheet as assets; license fees are paid on a subscription basis and run through the Income Statement. Figure 7 – 4 outlines some of the comparisons between the two approaches.

Advantages of Hosted Solutions	Advantages of Premise-based Solutions
Faster deployment.	Easier to customize.
Lower up-front costs.	Easier to integrate with other applications and data.
Reduced upgrade/maintenance requirements.	Generally less-expensive long-term - generally treated (capitalized) as an investment rather than an ongoing expense.
Simpler remote/field support.	Easier to use with more complete functionality in disconnected/remote environments.

Figure 7 – 4: Comparison of Hosted vs. On-Premise Systems

Source: Reservoir Partners, L.P.

The Evolution of CRM

The term "CRM" first emerged in the mid-1990's, created with the intent of describing how Sales, Marketing and Customer Service needed to work not just within their respective departments, but also together. CRM evolved from SFA software. The main purpose of SFA software is to sell more with less and is oftentimes called "technology for the traveling salesman" because its aim is to make field staff more productive. Primarily used by sales personnel as opposed to marketing personnel, these applications automated the sales cycle from lead generation, contact management, order processing and tracking all the way to billing, receivables and sales analysis. SFA is often used interchangeably with CRM, but CRM is generally considered to include more than functionality that automates the processes that make for an effective sales force. In addition to typical SFA, CRM systems might include:

Figure 7 – 5 lists the top hosted CRM software vendors for 2007.

Top 10 Hosted CRM Software Vendors	
1	**Aplicor** "Hosted Solutions for Higher Impact"
2	**Entellium** "Powerfully Simple CRM"
3	**NetSuite** "One System, No Limits"
4	**Oracle** "Unlock the Value of the Industry's Leading CRM Solution"
5	**Right Now Technologies** "Experiences that Make People Happy"
6	**Sage Software** "CRM Software Designed with Your Business in Mind"
7	**SalesForce.Com** "Success on Demand"
8	**SAP** "The Key to a Customer Centric Enterprise"
9	**Soffront** "Mid-Market CRM Leader"
10	**SugarCRM** "Commercial Open Source Leader"

Figure 7 - 5: Top Ten CRM Vendors

Source: www.business-software.com

- Directed Marketing that targets specific customers with specific marketing efforts.

- Market Intelligence that uses existing information to guide directed marketing efforts.

- Customer Appreciation and Rewards programs that promote customer loyalty.

- Data Analysis intended to support marketing and sales decisions.

- Customer Support and other after-sales management.

Sales Activities in CRM

The main objective of sales and marketing efforts is to capture and process the customer order. However, many important events take place before and after the customer order. These activities are collectively referred to as the **contact to contract to cash** process or sales cycle. The process can also be broken into separate parts known variously as:

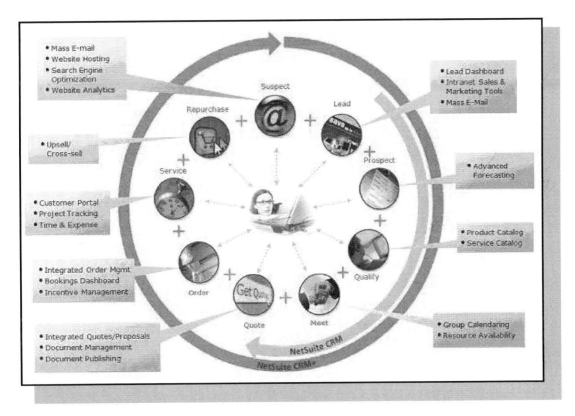

Figure 7 – 6: CRM Functionality Wheel

Source: NetSuite

- Contact to Contract - Activities that include identifying sales leads and working to secure their business.

- Quote to Cash - Activities that begin when a price is quoted and continue until the account is paid.

- Order to Cash – Activities that begin with the sales order and continue until the account is paid.

Regardless of which reference we choose to describe these processes, they are made of several distinct activities that require different information, different skills and they often depend on specific functionality in the CRM system for support. These activities make up the **sales cycle**. In Figure 7 -

6, NetSuite describes the cyclical nature of this process in their "Functionality Wheel" as they have incorporated specific functionality in their product to support these distinct processes.

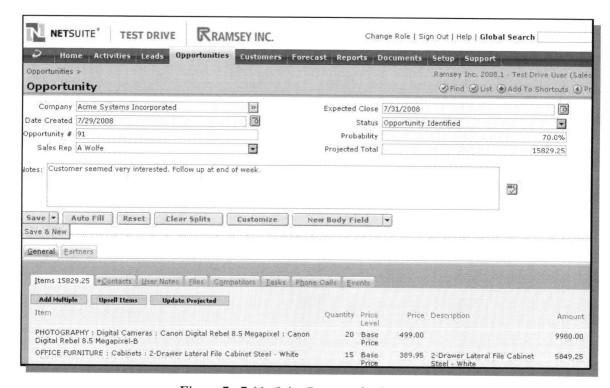

Figure 7 - 7: NetSuite Opportunity Screen

Source: NetSuite

While NetSuite's description is designed to match their software, in general, the sales cycle includes:

- **Sales Lead Generation** – Any number of tools can be used to identify potential customers. Often, marketing efforts will be specifically tailored to generate leads. Other lead generation techniques include trade shows, direct marketing, advertising, internet marketing. Any number of activities can generate interest in a company's products or services including cold calling where sales people engage potential customers from a random source like off the street or out of a phone book.

- **Contact** – The objective of this activity is to engage the customer and gather information in an effort to match their needs with the company's capabilities. During this process, the sale representative will be able to measure the likelihood that the lead may become a customer.

- **Qualification** – After engaging the prospect, the sales representative will need to determine if the prospect meets three important criteria:

    1. Applicability – Does the prospect have an immediate or nearly immediate need to purchase the company's products or services? This is an issue that requires the sales representative to know both the company's offerings and the prospect's needs.

2. Affordability – Does the prospect have the money needed to make the purchase? The sales representative will have to gain some assurance that the prospect can afford to make the purchase. Often a credit review or other payment support systems can help with this activity.

3. Authority – Does the prospect have the authority to commit to the purchase? The sales representative will need to gain some assurance that the prospect is the ultimate decision maker in the purchasing process.

- **Opportunity** - Only after we have identified a qualified prospect do we have a real opportunity to gain a sale. By tracking opportunities from start to close, companies can analyze potential sales by salesperson, territory, type, date, and many other criteria. This provides critical sales metrics that can be used to optimize sales efforts. It also is the start of the sales pipeline of all open opportunities, tracking the value, percentage chance to close and expected close date of each opportunity. Salespeople can use this to stay focused on their most promising opportunities.

- **Quote** – Given a valid sales opportunity, the company will present a quote for the products or services the prospect needs. Often, this quote will be stated as an estimate of costs and usually includes an expiration date. If the quote is accepted, it turns into a **customer order**, which becomes a **sales order** in the system.

Figure 7 - 7 shows the opportunity screen for NetSuite. In this scenario, Ramsey, Inc. has identified an opportunity to sell Acme Systems Inc. digital cameras and office furniture. The projected total is close to $16,000 and the **close probability** assigned to this opportunity is an optimistic 70%. This opportunity is now in A. Wolfe's sales pipeline, and he must work hard to close the sale. Figure 7 – 8 shows that A. Wolfe's hard work has paid off, and the opportunity has now become a sales order.

The remaining steps in the sales cycle (until we arrive at post-sales support and service) fall outside of CRM and rely more on ERP functionality. These are the steps triggered by the creation of the sales order and include the processes that deliver products to the customer (pick, pack and ship) and manage Accounts Receivable and postings to the General Ledger. While these processes are not under the purview of CRM, the information they generate can be valuable if it is added back into the CRM system. Information regarding cycle times, delivery performance, and service requests will add to knowledge that the sales representative can access as he subsequently reaches out to the customer in the interest of generating repeat sales.

Transactions and Events in CRM and ERP

While the link between ERP and CRM can be difficult to understand, we have seen how CRM systems sustain front-office operations by supporting the sales force and automating various activities in the Contact to Contract process. We have also seen how CRM efforts can take advantage of integration with ERP systems as orders flow into these back-office systems and the data generated in the order fulfillment processes populate the CRM system with valuable, customer-specific information. Finally, we discussed how CRM has moved closer to the core ERP functions essentially integrating these front-office activities with the entire enterprise.

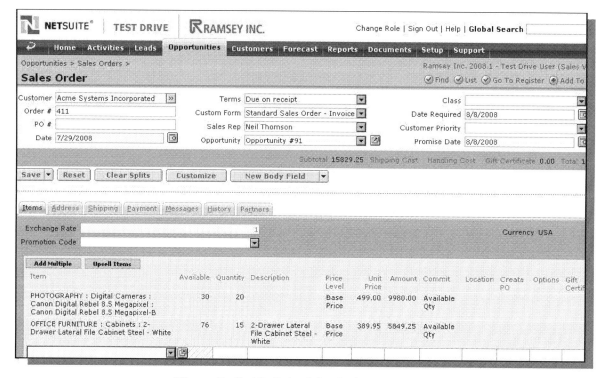

Figure 7 - 8: NetSuite Sales Order Screen

Source: NetSuite

Figure 7 - 9 can be used to explain the difference between transactions and events. **Transactions** have financial implications and are thus recorded in the books of accounts (e.g., Accounts Receivable Subsidiary Ledger). An **event,** or activity, is any step in the business process and may or may not have financial implications. Thus, transactions are a subset of events. In Figure 7 - 8, a sales order is generated in the CRM system where functionality supports the lead generation and qualifying activities. As the relationship matures eventually leading to a quote and an order, the workflow passes the customer and sales information first to fulfillment and ultimately on to the accounting module of ERP, which creates the invoice.

The transaction in the scenario thus far is the debit to accounts receivable and the credit to sales. Additionally, a simultaneous transaction would occur which decreases inventory and increases cost of goods sold. The rest of the steps are events because they do not "hit the books." Any adjustments to accounts receivable and ultimate collection of the cash would also take place within the accounting module and would also represent transactions. Figure 7 - 9 describes the many unstructured activities that can take place as part of this Contact to Contract to Cash process. If the prospect is to make an order, their needs and desires must be reconciled with the company's capabilities. This process can be supported by:

- The CSR, who can work with the customer to define the exact products or services the prospect wants to purchase.

- A product catalog, which can provide exhaustive lists and descriptions of products of various shapes, sizes, colors, or configurations. The customer can gather the associated catalog numbers and pass them along to the CSR who can prepare the quote.

- An automated software application or webpage that acts as a **product configurator**. This program will step the prospect through the various configuration options of the product and generate the specifications necessary to produce an accurate quote. The product configurator will check to make sure that different components of a product will work together and may suggest additional products or services in which the customer may find value.

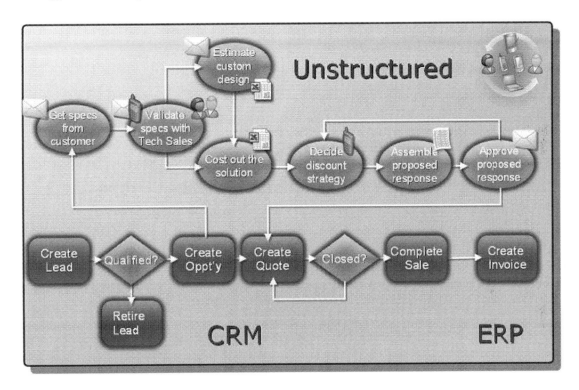

Figure 7 - 9: Where CRM and ERP Meet
Source: Microsoft Executive, Lisa Dion. North Carolina State University Presentation

While these order-shaping activities are important and may be structured or unstructured, other activities in the sales cycle may also be unstructured. These activities include:

- Pricing - CRM systems may help determine an initial price and may suggest a discount strategy based on information of which it is aware. However, other pricing factors may impact the company's ultimate quote. These factors include production and sourcing issues, logistic concerns and customer attractiveness. These quotes may be escalated to a sales manager who will assemble the response and approve it.

- Validation - Certain transactions may require some measure of technical expertise to assure that the appropriate items have been purchased. This is particularly relevant in build-to-order, where products are custom designed. Sometimes, as in the case of large equipment, when order fulfillment will require the dedication of substantial resources prior to delivery, the parties to the transaction may engage in some measure of due diligence to satisfy themselves that the other party will be able to deliver as contracted.

- Financing – Credit facilities reduce transactional friction and allow products and services to be bought and sold without the need to micro-manage invoices and payments associated with sale. On the other hand, the financing company carries some risk that must be considered as part of the transaction. In addition, often credit facilities may be a third party to a transaction and may require certain information transfers from the purchaser or the seller in any given transaction. CRM and ERP systems may support this type of data exchange to varying degrees.

Benefits of CRM

Customer relationship management systems have many benefits focused on both generating revenue and decreasing selling-related expenses. CRM systems can generate more revenue by acquiring new customers and retaining customers. By knowing existing customers better and focusing attention on profitable customers, customer satisfaction increases which should lead to higher retention. CRM systems can decrease selling expenses by making fewer and more productive sales calls, speeding data analysis, lowering communication and transaction costs, eliminating data redundancy, and reducing personnel headcount.

These goals are attained using a set of capabilities unique to CRM solutions. These capabilities include:

- Effectively identifying **cross-selling** and **up-selling** opportunities with customers based on prior information about that customer or market segment.

- Providing timely and precise information about where an opportunity is in the sales pipeline.

- Targeting and launching marketing campaigns with specific and measurable objective and subsequently analyzing their effectiveness.

- Integrating a multitude of channels, including phone centers, email, website and electronic data interchange resources into the sales process

- Providing accurate order fulfillment information such as delivery dates and inventory status by integrating CRM with ERP.

- Tracking and following through on customer service and support issues and inquiries.

- Managing the customer information through lead generation all the way through post-sales support.

- Empowering telemarketing capabilities with the updated and complete customer history information.

Tracking and analyzing sales performance by region, marketing campaign, customer, product, or sales unit including margins, commissions, or specific sales representative. CRM systems also offer more advanced analytics such as:

- **Event monitoring** - When specific, defined events happen, CRM users are notified. For instance, when a customer's purchases reach a certain amount, gift cards are mailed to the customer as a reward.

- **Personalization** - The ability to sell to the **market of one** (versus customer segments) based on data collected such as buying history and market or personal demographics. For example, once a customer logs into Amazon.com, a personalized webpage appears advertising merchandise specifically targeted toward that customer.

- **Segmentation** - Grouping customers according to attributes such as region, age, gender, or purchasing power allows for more efficient targeted marketing. An analysis of segmentation could compare sales in various segments of a population or territory and support the analysis of sales against budget, marketing campaign, sales unit, or product.

- **Pricing** - Supporting pricing decisions with various models based on logistics, expected consumer disposable income, or short-term fluctuations in production volumes, labor costs, or raw material costs.

- **Trending** - Taking measurements of interest over time. Providing data to operations managers to highlight potential shortfalls or excesses in stock levels earlier allowing for accommodations to mitigate the effects of otherwise unforeseeable market activity.

- **Advertising** - Identifying channels that will be most effective, cross-selling and up-selling opportunities, and making decisions on promoting or avoiding certain products or market segments.

- **Forecasting** - Estimating unknown situations in the future. Firms can use customers' purchase histories to forecast customers' future needs.

CRM helps businesses use technology to increase their bottom line by capturing pertinent data about customers and responding efficiently and effectively to their needs as well as forecasting future needs. ERP systems enable the smooth flow of information to speed the order fulfillment, billing, and cash collection processes. While CRM may be seen as a bolt-on to ERP now, it is becoming more important to companies that use ERP systems, and therefore the market for these systems is likely to experience continued growth.

Summary

Sales and marketing are key tasks in an enterprise and are supported by front-office CRM systems with ERP handling the back-office tasks of managing accounts receivables and collecting cash, which represent transactions in the order to cash process. CRM systems are considered bolt-ons to ERP and evolved out of early sales force automation tools. The distinguishing characteristic between SFA and CRM is that CRM involves analytics, whereas SFA merely enables the sales and contact management activities. Companies can use CRM systems to better understand the customer through integrated sales histories, service records and preferences. Many organizations have taken advantage of the on demand model for CRM that can allow for a faster and less expensive implementation.

Keywords

Application outsourcing

Back-office system

Baseline performance measure

Close probability

Contact to contract to cash

Cross-sell

Customer order

Customer Relationship Management (CRM)

Event

Event Monitoring

Forecasting

Front-office system

Market of one

Off-Balance Sheet financing

On demand

On premise

Opportunity

Order Management

Partner Portal

Personalization

Product Configurator

Qualification

Quote

Sales cycle

Sales Force Automation (SFA)

Sales order

Segmentation

Service level agreement (SLA)

Software as a Service

Transaction

Trending

Up-sell

Quick Review

1. True/False: CRM software focuses on customers and allows companies to drive revenue growth and reduce sales-related expenses.

2. True/False: Segmentation refers to the ability to sell to the market-of-one.

3. _____ provides functionality that reduces the burden typically associated with sales efforts.

4. A quote that is accepted turns into a _____, which becomes a sales order in the system.

5. Activities that begin when a price is quoted and continue until the account is paid are called - _____ to _____.

Questions to Consider

1. What is CRM?

2. List CRM functionalities.

3. How did CRM evolve?

4. How does CRM integrate with ERP?

5. What activities are involved in order fulfillment?

References

AllBusiness.com. (2007). *Qualifying Sales Prospects*. Retrieved April 10, 2008, from http://www.allbusiness.com/sales/selling-techniques/1360-1.html

AllBusiness.com. (2007). *Sales Force Automation: Managing CRM and ERP Solutions*. Retrieved April 10, 2008, from http://www.allbusiness.com/sales/sales-tracking-reporting-software/375-1.html

Business-Software.com. (2007). *Top 10 Enterprise CRM Vendors Revealed*. Retrieved April 10, 2008, from http://www.business-software.com/pdf/top_10_ enterprise_CRM.pdf

DestinationCRM.com. (2002). *What is CRM?* Retrieved April 30, 2008, from http://www.destinationcrm.com/articles/default.asp?ArticleID=1747

Koch, C., & Wailgum, T. (2007). *ABC: An Introduction to CRM*. Retrieved April 20, 2008, from http://www.cio.com/article/40295/ABC An_ Introduction_to_CRM

SAP Global. (2007). *SAP Customer Relationship Management Solution Overview Brochure.* Retrieved January 4, 2008, from http://www.sap.com/solutions/business-suite/crm/brochures/index.epx

SearchCRM.com. (2007). *CRM Analytics.* Retrieved April 20, 2008, from http://searchcrm.techtarget.com/sDefinition/0,,sid11_gci745647,00.html#

Selland, C. (2005). *Customer Relationship Management: 10 Steps to Success.* White Paper. Retrieved from http://www.bitpipe.com/detail/RES/1126199232_867.html

Chapter

8

Accounting, Finance and Asset Management

Objectives

- Differentiate between financial and managerial accounting.

- Understand the different methods of cost accounting and the advantages and disadvantages of each method.

- Understand the cash cycle.

- Understand the Asset Management Life Cycle.

Introduction

In today's increasingly complex and global economy, financial professionals are challenged to manage an increasingly wider range of business processes and information. The financial modules of ERP systems include a suite of integrated applications that encompass all financial activity including accounting, finance, and asset management. ERP Financials are the essential building blocks of enterprise software because it includes the General Ledger, which produces the financial statements. Additionally, Financials supports the preparation of internal reports used by decision makers in the organization to measure performance and plan future financial activities. This chapter discusses the ERP financial tools that provide these critical functions. Figure 8 - 1 presents the benefits of implementing ERP Financials.

Financial versus Management Accounting

The primary difference between financial accounting and management accounting is one of target audience; the two activities produce output that is geared towards different groups of people. Management accounting meets the needs of internal users - those information consumers that act inside the company to further the organization's objectives. On the other hand, financial accounting is targeted to external users, such as shareholders, governmental agencies, financial analysts, creditors, and the general investing public. Both types of accounting are critical to ERP Financials.

Improve corporate performance	The ability to quickly read, evaluate, and respond to changing business conditions strategically – such as defining financial targets, developing a suitable business plan, and monitoring costs and revenue during execution.
Faster time to close the books	Streamline consolidation, process scheduling, workflow, and collaboration.
Improve corporate governance and transparency	Provides broader support of accounting standards, federal regulations, and improved administration of internal controls.
Shorten days sales outstanding	Automate dispute, credit, and collections management – including electronic invoicing and payment capabilities that supplement traditional accounts receivable and accounts payable functions.
Optimize global cash management	Report, analyze, and allocate cash in real time, and establish in-house banks or payment centers.
Improve financial and managerial reporting	Report performance by business unit, organization, or cost center.
Improve process integration between finance and treasury	Integrate risk and treasury transactions with core accounting and financial reporting processes.
Make finance costs more competitive	Innovate processes, collaborate with supply chain partners, and establish global shared-service operations.

Figure 8 - 1: Benefits of ERP Financials

Source: SAP

Financial Accounting

The primary objective of **financial accounting** is to produce financial statements, which include the Income Statement, Statement of Retained Earnings, Balance Sheet, and Statement of Cash Flows. Financial statements must conform to **Generally Accepted Accounting Principles (GAAP)**, which are the standards and conventions US-based companies follow in recording and summarizing transactions and preparing financial statements. Discussed below are the main components of financial accounting in ERP systems. Figure 8 – 2 shows that Finance is at the core of Oracle's ERP system and drills down into Oracle Finance components.

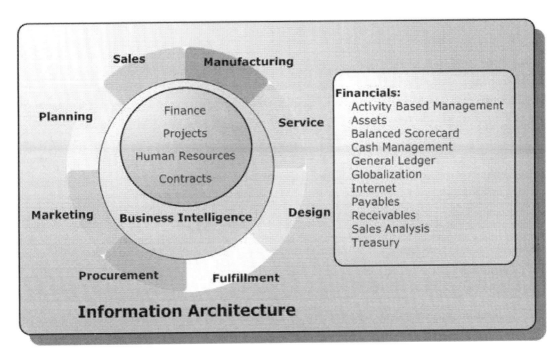

Figure 8 – 2: Oracle Financials Offerings

Source: Oracle

General Ledger

The backbone of financial accounting is the **General Ledger (GL)**, which includes the balance of every account within the **Chart of Accounts**, the listing of all accounts and their numbers tracked by the accounting system. All financial statements are generated from the General Ledger, so having accurate, real-time information is of critical importance. Before globalization of business, accounting professionals only had to maintain a single general ledger in one currency and generate financial statements monthly and yearly. Now, many organizations need to maintain sets of accounting books in multiple currencies and multiple languages as well as country-specific regulations for taxes, reporting, and payment transactions. **Parallel accounting** enables a company to keep several GLs simultaneously according to different accounting principles to ensure that local and international reporting requirements are met.

Accounts Payable

The **Accounts Payable (AP)** subsystem, also known as the **AP Subsidiary Ledger**, identifies the balances owed to every supplier calculated from purchases, returns to the supplier, allowances from the supplier and purchase discounts. The total amount of every creditor's balance at any point in time must equal the AP account total in the GL. The AP subsystem serves as an important information source for the purchasing department regarding delivery status and quality of merchandise and for the AP department regarding supplier invoicing and payment due dates. Organizations often try to pay invoices early to take advantage of discounts using either standard written forms or electronic means such as Electronic Data Interchange, which we will discuss later in the text.

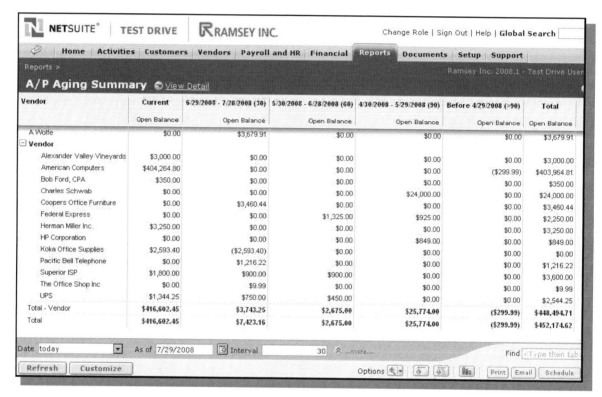

Figure 8 – 3: NetSuite A/P Aging Summary Report

Source: NetSuite

Accounts payable functions in ERP systems should support international methods of payment, track open items, provide account analyses, due date forecasts and risk assessments for issues such as foreign currencies translation. Documents generated from the AP subsidiary ledger include checks to suppliers and debit memos for returns to suppliers. Checks should be authorized through a **voucher system**, which matches the purchase order, receiving report and supplier invoice prior to payment. For cash management purposes, the **AP Aging Report** is used to group vouchers by due date in 30 day increments, providing focus on those payable items that may be past due. The finance department will use reports such as this for cash budgeting. Figure 8 - 3 shows a NetSuite screen shot of an AP Aging Summary Report for Ramsey Distribution, our hypothetical company.

Accounts Receivable

The **Accounts Receivable (AR)** subsystem, also known as the **AR Subsidiary Ledger**, identifies the balances customers owe to the firm and is calculated from sales less sales returns and allowances and sales discounts. Similar to the AP subsidiary ledger, the AR subsidiary ledger must balance to the

AR account in the GL. Financial amounts for AR come from orders through CRM or Sales and Distribution and cash receipt and other transactions through AR.

Customer:Job	Current	6/29/2008 - 7/28/2008 (30)	5/30/2008 - 6/28/2008 (60)	4/30/2008 - 5/29/2008 (90)	Before 4/29/2008 (>90)	Total
	Open Balance	Open Balance	Open Balance	Open Balance	Open Balance	Open Balance
Academy Avenue Liquor Store	$151.90	$3,424.75	$0.00	$0.00	$0.00	$3,576.65
Academy Sports & Outdoors	$0.00	$363,555.00	$27,500.99	$0.00	$0.00	$391,055.99
Acme Systems Incorporated	$0.00	$25,747.97	$0.00	$0.00	$0.00	$25,747.97
AcuVision Eye Centre	$0.00	$0.00	$10,340.00	$0.00	$0.00	$10,340.00
Adley Electric Systems	$23,499.00	$2,808.00	$0.00	$0.00	$0.00	$26,307.00
Advanced Machining Techniques Inc.	$541,250.00	$0.00	$0.00	$423.93	$0.00	$541,673.93
Alesna Leasing Sales	$150,005.00	$0.00	$0.00	$0.00	$0.00	$150,005.00
All Outdoors	$25,050.00	$0.00	$0.00	$0.00	$20,209.80	$45,259.80
Amsterdam Drug Store	$651.08	$0.00	$0.00	$0.00	$0.00	$651.08
Anderson Boughton Inc.	$750,005.00	$0.00	$0.00	$0.00	$0.00	$750,005.00
Apfel Electric Co.	$10,005.00	$12,505.00	$0.00	$0.00	$0.00	$22,510.00
Art Institute of California	$0.00	$5,302.00	$0.00	$0.00	$0.00	$5,302.00
Atherton Grocery	$1,645.64	$0.00	$0.00	$0.00	$0.00	$1,645.64
Avani Walters	$989.95	$0.00	$0.00	$0.00	$0.00	$989.95
B-Sharp Music	$0.00	$166,010.00	$464,788.40	$0.00	$0.00	$630,798.40
Bakkala Catering Distributors	$0.00	($218.00)	$0.00	$0.00	$0.00	($218.00)
BaySide Office Space	$0.00	$0.00	$0.00	$19,009.90	$0.00	$19,009.90
Benge Liquors Incorporated	$1,897.76	$0.00	$0.00	$0.00	$0.00	$1,897.76

Figure 8 – 4: NetSuite A/R Aging Summary Report

Source: NetSuite

ERP functionality for AR includes account analyses, alarm reports for various issues including over credit limit and non-payment, due date reports, invoices, account statements and dunning statements, all of which make it easier to keep track of open items. **Credit management** in ERP financials supports the automatic update of AR balances, which is important for credit analysts so that they have up-to-date information on customer balances and credit limits.

Accounting and finance personnel would be interested in viewing the **AR Aging Report**, which groups receivables into 30 day increments, supporting cash flow projections and providing focus on those balances that are oldest. This report is also used for the estimation of bad debts. Figure 8 - 4 shows a NetSuite screen shot of an AR Aging Summary Report for Ramsey Distribution.

Both the AP and AR subsidiary ledgers interface with the cash management tools used in the finance department to prepare the cash budget. Calculations based on cash on hand, accounts payables and accounts receivables allow Finance to project future cash flows and prepare a cash budget accordingly. The **cash journal,** which interfaces with AP and AR, can be kept in separate currencies and separate company codes.

Management Accounting

Unlike financial accounting, which is geared toward external consumers of information, **management accounting** supports the information needs of internal decision makers. Management accounting need not conform to GAAP because its primary use is for internal managers, and what to compute is instead decided pragmatically. Information produced by management accounting is generally confidential and forward-looking rather than historical. According to the American Institute of Certified Public Accountants, management accounting practice extends to strategic management, risk management and performance management. Information is used for a wide range of planning and decision-making activities. These activities include:

- Designing, evaluating and optimizing business processes.

- Budgeting and forecasting.

- Implementing and monitoring internal controls.

- Analyzing, synthesizing, and aggregating information.

Different components of ERP Financials support various accounting activities. One such activity is **cost accounting,** which is that part of management accounting that establishes budget and actual cost of operations, processes, departments or product and analyzes variances and profitability. ERP systems typically support functionality that includes:

- Overhead costing

- Product costing

- Activity based costing

- Profitability analyses

- Cost/Profit Center Accounting

The integration of ERP software allows these components to provide accurate cost accounting estimates. The type and value of expense information captured through financial accounting is shared with management so that they can make informed decisions. Using ERP systems, managers have access to the necessary source information, allowing them to choose the most appropriate costing method to support a given decision. Next, we will take a look at this functionality in detail.

Overhead Costing

Overhead costing helps with planning, allocating and controlling overhead in a company – doing so will allow for the development of standards for direct labor, direct materials and overhead to help control costs and establish a value for internal activities. Indirect costs that cannot be assigned to a specific product are known as **overhead costs**. Examples of overhead costs include factory rent, insurance, and property taxes, indirect materials (e.g., glue, staples) and indirect labor (e.g., factory supervisor.) These costs must be allocated to products so that management can make accurate product costing decisions. Other costs that have a true origin can be treated as direct costs and assigned appropriately. At the end of the accounting period, budgeted costs are compared to actual costs, and variances can be analyzed for their root cause so that future projections are more accurate.

Product Costing

Determining the cost of products manufactured or services provided is the goal of **product costing**. This capability within ERP systems can help answer such questions as: How high are the actual costs by period in my area? How much should the actual production cost? Do some products perform significantly better than others, and can I identify the cause of these variances?

Product costing functionality in ERP uses information from overhead costing to calculate labor, machine, and factory overhead costs for products. It supplies information for profitability analysis to calculate contribution margins. Product costing can perform high-level analyses of costs by plant, area of responsibility, product group and so on. These areas can be designated as profit centers, cost centers or investment centers for reporting purposes, and ERP systems can treat these centers as independent account assignment objects.

Companies use product costing to:

- Predict the costs incurred when manufacturing a product or providing a service.

- Set prices for the valuation of finished goods or work in progress in materials management and sales.

- Calculate the cost of goods manufactured or the cost of goods sold for profitability analyses.

Activity Based Costing

Traditionally, companies applied overhead based on machine hours and/or direct labor hours. This proved to be less than accurate as these activities are not the only "drivers" of manufacturing overhead. **Activity Based Costing (ABC)**

functionality in ERP systems delivers business intelligence that supports strategic and operational decision-making by tracing overhead based on the cause and effect of relevant cost drivers to more objectively assign costs. Examples of cost drivers might be number of machine set-ups, number of purchase orders executed, or inspection time. Once costs of the activities are identified, the cost of each activity is attributed to each product to the extent that the product uses the activity. In this way, ABC often identifies areas of high overhead costs per unit and so directs attention to finding ways to reduce the costs or to charge more for costly products. When effectively executed, ABC efforts will process and present activity-based costing data so that it is relevant, compelling, understandable, and actionable to those who will be using it. No matter what the particular approach, companies begin ABC with a primary goal in mind: to provide more relevant information to the managers of specific activities.

ABC is used to evaluate activities in the organization to answer questions such as:

- Are activities being conducted efficiently?

- Are activities even necessary or do their costs outweigh the benefits?

- Are certain groups within the organization performing activities better than others?

- Do specific materials or tools help the company complete certain activities more efficiently?

Profitability Analysis

The **profitability analysis** functionality of management accounting considers certain profitability segments of the organization and determines the profit they generate. A **profitability segment** can be any number of entities such as products, customers, activities, or organizational units or the intersection of a few. This method may focus on such segments to determine:

- Profit generated by certain product line

- Sales made to certain industries

- Margins supported by specific distribution channels

- Performance of specific regions, decentralized sales offices or other semi-autonomous business unit

Since profitability is often a result of the peculiar characteristics of specific segments, some ERP systems provide for standard or default profitability characteristics and allow users to add and quantify their own without any time-consuming data entry. Accurate and effective profitability analyses allow management to embrace a philosophy that transfers more responsibly to the individual employee; the employee can see the impact of his or her efforts on unit profitability. Parallel accounting, mentioned earlier, assists in the analysis by generating a set of balanced and reconcilable financial statements by any dimension of the business – whether by region, industry, business unit, profit center, or geographical location.

Cost/Profit Center Accounting

Companies may choose to set up certain business units as cost centers or profit centers. **Cost centers** are part of an organization that does not produce direct profit (although may add to revenue indirectly) but add to the cost of running the business. Examples are research and development departments, marketing departments, and help desks. On the other hand, the fundamental characteristic of a **profit center** is that the manager is responsible for both revenues and costs of the center. This distinguishes it from a cost center, which merely reflects where capacity costs originate. The primary goal of **cost center accounting** is to determine the cost of the center, while **profit center accounting** determines the operating profit of a center.

Where traditional accounting systems have required the reconciliation of multiple applications for various views of the GL, ERP systems today can provide a more unified view by providing individual ledgers, such as the cost-of sales ledger and profit center accounting. This speeds the reconciliation process between the GL and various GL views and ensures transparency and auditability, while enabling companies to meet both internal and external reporting requirements.

Profit and cost data can be used in conjunction with asset management and cash flow analysis, for the following key metrics:

- Return on investment

- Contribution margin

- Working capital

- Cash flow

Executives can use this data to compare the relative profitability of comparable business units and to plan strategic initiatives.

Treasury

Functionality related to investments, cash and cash flow, the cash cycle and the accounting requirements these cycles generate is known as **treasury operations**. These operations include:

- Cash management – Using cash to generate greater returns. For example, if a payment can be delayed for 30 days, the cash used to make that payment can be left in interest bearing accounts until the payment becomes due.

- Cash flow analysis in any currency and in multiple time periods – There is often a great cost associated with *not* taking advantage of early payment discounts. Firms should consider paying within the discount period if it can be confident that future income is sufficient to meet other short-term cash requirements.

- Capital budgeting – Given the potential for future returns, plant expansion may be advantageous if the cost of capital is less than the minimum rate of return on the capital investment project.

A **liquidity forecast** integrates anticipated cash inflows and outflows from financial accounting, purchasing and sales in order to show mid- to long-term liquidity trends. Also included in the treasury modules are the electronic bank statement and reconciliation features. Figure 8 - 5 shows the NetSuite Cash Flow Statement.

Asset Management

Financials may include a module for tracking and controlling property, plant and equipment (PP&E) for capital intensive companies. **Asset management** is known by different names depending on the ERP vendor, but its basic function is to track financial and non-financial information about PP&E such as:

- The current fair market value of the asset given its age and life expectancy.

- Where the asset is located and who has control of the asset.

- Amount asset is insured for, deductibles, and premiums.

- Depreciation of the asset.

- Maintenance needs of the asset.

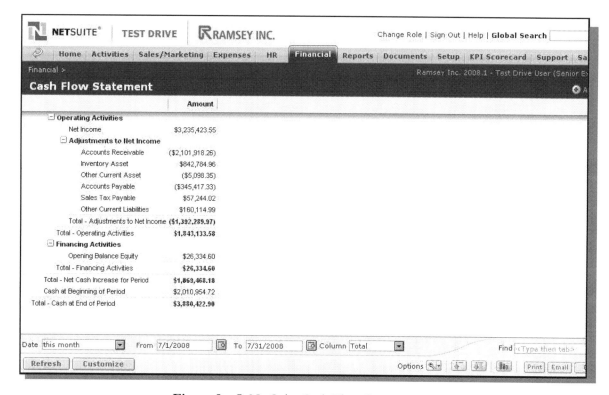

Figure 8 – 5: NetSuite Cash Flow Statement

Source: NetSuite

Figure 8 - 6 shows the **Asset Management Life Cycle**. In the example shown, the idea for investment is a machine overhaul. The ERP system will accept the input of the various actions the overhaul effort involves. In addition, the managers' decision-making power will be optimized by the reports the system can generate regarding the project's costs and benefits. ERP tracks the data and supports internal decision-making of PP&E throughout the following stages:

- Planning – Dedicating resources to the project and establishing expectations about the execution of steps necessary to overhaul the machine. Complete and accurate investment cost information, derived though integration with materials costs, contractor labor services and HR for labor costs, forms the basis for a capital asset budget request.

- Approval – Sanctioning the project. Once management decides which asset projects make the most sense to implement, they release appropriation requests. An **appropriation request** is a formal request for budget assignment and approval. Based on the business case, the initial planning, and capital budgeting models such as net present value and payback period, management can make objective decisions about which projects will be the most beneficial to undertake.

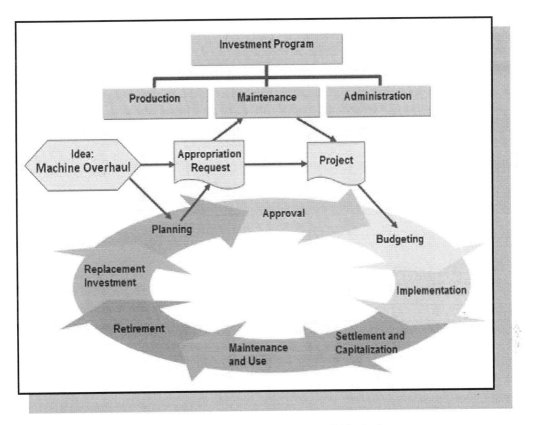

Figure 8 – 6: Asset Management Life Cycle

- Budgeting – Ensuring sufficient cash will be available to meet expenses as they arise. Each project must be assigned a budget based on the amounts that were requested in the appropriation requests. Project budgets are monitored from project implementation through execution.

- Implementation – Executing and validating steps of the plan. Many factors constantly affect the path of a project. The project manager must recognize internal and external factors that could seriously affect the proposed time-line and budget.

- Settlement and Capitalization – Since the overhaul may have affected the value of the machine, this new value will impact the PP&E account and related future depreciation. The execution of the project requires periodic settlement of vendor invoices, comparison of budget versus actual planned costs, and percentage of completion measured by actual costs incurred to validate and assess activities. Finally, an accurate cost basis must be capitalized and used for depreciation purposes.

- Maintenance and Use – The overhauled machine may present new maintenance requirements such as reduce the major maintenance in the near future. Once the asset is placed into service, maintenance costs associated with that asset are continually monitored. A separate module for plant maintenance is often used to track detailed maintenance activities.

- Retirement – The expected retirement date and the overhead associated with retiring the machine may have changed and may impact financial records. Asset management will provide information for an asset retirement such as its accumulated depreciation, salvage value, and whether the asset can be overhauled and put back in service elsewhere in the organization.

- Replacement Investment – The case to replace an asset is based on maintenance and operation costs. Once the decision has been made to replace an asset, the Asset Life Cycle starts all over again with the planning of replacement assets.

Investment Management

ERP systems support capital asset decisions by providing information concerning what new investments need to be made in PP&E, what PP&E needs to be replaced and when, which PP&E might be in need of expansion, what costs were incurred for PP&E in the previous years and what must be budgeted for maintenance measures in the near future. Decisions like the ones shown in Figure 8 – 7 can be answered through the use of an **investment management** module in an ERP system. This module of an ERP system provides the tools for pre-investment analysis to answer questions such as:

- What cost savings or revenue increases will the investment achieve?

- How can the investment improve the image of the enterprise?

- What will be the future payoff from the investment be using Internal Rate of return, Pay-Back Period, and Net Present Value?

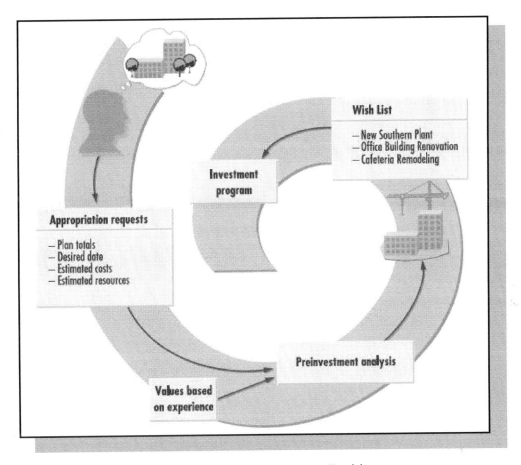

Figure 8 – 7: PP&E Investment Decisions

Corporate Governance

One of the more recent functionalities that ERP vendors provide is **corporate governance**, which is the structure and relationships that dictate how a corporation is directed, administered and controlled. **Governance** manages the strategic directives a company wants to follow; **risk management** assesses the areas of exposure and potential impacts; and **compliance** is the tactical action to mitigate risk. SAP has a module called **Governance, Risk, and Compliance (GRC)**, which supports controls for enterprise applications. These controls include enforcing proper segregation of duties in enterprise applications, reducing fraud with continuous monitoring of business transactions, and providing defensible evidence of a proper control environment.

Summary

ERP Financials is the backbone of a company's information system as it includes functionality to produce the financial statements, keep track of AR and AP, and support internal decision makers. Financial accounting handles the former, whereas management accounting focuses on the latter.

Financials also includes a module to track and control capital assets that support operations in the business. A recently developed bolt-on to Financials is Corporate Governance that enables segregation of duties, manages corporate risk, and provides continuous audit functions to support SOX Section 404 requirements and the financial statement audit.

Keywords

Activity Based Costing (ABC)

AP Aging Report

AP Subsidiary Ledger

Appropriation request

AR Aging Report

AR Subsidiary Ledger

Asset management

Asset Management Life Cycle

Cash journal

Chart of Accounts

Compliance

Corporate Governance

Cost accounting,

Cost center accounting

Cost centers

Credit management

Financial accounting

General Ledger (GL)

Generally Accepted Accounting Principles (GAAP)

Governance

Governance, Risk, and Compliance (GRC)

Investment management

Liquidity forecast

Management accounting

Overhead costing

Overhead costs

Parallel accounting

Product costing

Profit center

Profit center accounting

Profitability analysis

Profitability segment

Risk management

Treasury operations

Voucher system

Quick Review

1. True/False: The asset planning phase would include an assessment of a company's business needs and a justification for asset replacement.

2. True/False: The Chart of Accounts includes the balance owed to every vendor calculated from purchases, returns to the vendor, allowances from the vendor and purchase discounts.

3. True/False: Overhead costs are direct costs that are assigned to a specific cost object.

4. All financial statements are generated from the _____.

5. The _____ component of management accounting takes certain segments of the organization and determines the profit from those segments.

Questions to Consider

1. What are key ERP financial accounting components and what functionality do they provide?

2. What are key ERP management accounting components and what functionality do they provide?

3. List the steps in the Asset Management Life Cycle.

4. Explain why GRC would be a desirable module to adopt for publicly-traded companies.

References

BizBeginners.biz. (2007). *ERP and CRM*. Retrieved March 13, 2008, from http://www.bizbeginners.biz/erp_software.html

SAP Global. (2000). *SAP Functionality*. Retrieved March 13, 2008, from http://www.bfsgroup.us/FB/ENGLISH.HTM

Guan, L., Hansen D., & Mowen M. (2007). *Cost Management: Accounting and Control, 6th edition*. Mason, OH: South-Western Cengage Learning.

Lombana, R. (2007). *An Asset's Life: Its Harrowing Journey Through the IM/PM/PS Business Cycle*. Presented at the ASUG Conference, North Carolina State University. (September, 2007).

Oracle. (2008). *Oracle and LogicalApps*. Retrieved May 8, 2008, from
http://www.oracle.com/logicalapps/index.html

Oracle. (2004). *JD Edwards EnterpriseOne Fixed Asset Accounting*. Retrieved March 8, 2008, from
http://www.oracle.com/media/peoplesoft/en/pdf/datasheets/e1_fm_ds_fixedassetacct_5
1005.pdf

SAP. (2007). *mySAP ERP Financials*. Retrieved March 8, 2007, from
http://www.sap.com/usa/solutions/business-suite/erp/financials/brochures/index.epx

SAP. (2008). *ERP Financials: Business Benefits*. Retrieved May 8, 2008, from
http://www.sap.com/solutions/business-suite/erp/financials/businessbenefits/index.epx

Chapter

9

Human Capital Management and Employee Self-Service

Objectives

- Identify the traditional, core Human Resources functions.

- Understand the additional Human Resources modules provided in modern ERP systems.

- Understand the benefits of Employee Self-Service.

Introduction

Just as we have seen with other aspects of automating and integrating business processes with ERP systems, the processes that support the management of the organization's human resources can be automated and integrated into the enterprise systems. In terms of enterprise resources, the employees, executives, contractors and the other people that participate in and contribute to the organization's objectives can be viewed as **human capital**. In a typical organization, these people are its most valuable asset and the methods and strategies embraced to optimize the value of this asset are collectively known as **Human Capital Management (HCM).**

In ERP, the HCM modules allow the organization to take a coherent and strategic approach to the way it manages and supports the people who individually and collectively both empower the organization with their abilities and burden the organization with their personal agendas, their desires and their necessities. Put another way, HCM comprises the strategy and business processes that transform every employee into a competitive asset that supports operating and financial results.

In ERP terminology, HCM, also called **Workforce Management** or **Human Resources Management**, is also the name of the software solutions used by the **Human Resource (HR)** department. These solutions automate tasks and provide electronic alternatives to the typical paper-based business processes. With few exceptions, organizations will find that the application of ERP solutions to HCM can be extremely rewarding. These rewards arise because:

- People matter – HR has a tremendous impact on the organization's performance with both up-side potential and down-side risk.

- HR processes are data intensive - Each person requires access to a great deal of information, such as operation manuals and benefits information. Additionally, employees generate a great deal of information about themselves, such as their personnel file and training records.

- HR activities generate a high volume of records – Starting with help wanted advertisements and employee applications and throughout the employee life cycle to exit or retirement, nearly every action generates one or more records. These records have traditionally been paper and present various requirements with regard to care, custody and control.

- HR data is extremely sensitive – The information contained in HR files must be treated with the highest levels of security and confidence. The risks associated with mismanagement are enormous.

- HR data is extremely valuable to the rest of the organization – Whether measuring performance, forecasting revenue, or projecting stockholder returns, the information generated in HRM modules can be used in many ways.

In the past, HCM systems were typical stovepipe applications that specialized in only one area of HR such as applicant tracking, compensation, benefits, or time-keeping. These disparate systems contained redundant data, such as employee name and social security number and were not linked to each other or to any of the other business systems that could use this information. In addition, given its traditional use of mainframe computer technology, operations such as payroll would require IT staff to process source data in large computer runs or batch jobs. As we have seen in other cases, the ability to apply ERP style data integration leads to a number of operational benefits as the stovepipe is deconstructed, the data is shared among applications and business processes are reengineered to take advantage of this enterprise resource.

Modern HCM solutions are typically a suite of HR-related modules that automate the entire **recruit to retire process**, or **pre-hire to retire employee life cycle**. Since HCM is part of ERP, the data is integrated with all areas of the business as shown in these examples:

- CRM – An employee can be associated with a customer as the "primary contact" with the company. The CRM system would then use this information to provide contact information, service requests, or performance metrics.

- Financials – A salesperson can be associated with a sales order, and the data from that order could roll into the payroll system to calculate commissions.

- Cost Accounting – Employee payroll costs can be captured and transferred to the cost accounting module for financial analysis.

- Project Systems – Employee time information can be gathered and reflected in the project systems module to determine profitability of projects.

- Operations – Employee availability can be considered as production managers generate production forecasts.

- Performance Metrics – time tracked by employees supporting specific functions can be compared allowing managers to optimize the dedication of employees to specific products or customers.

As it evolved from more traditional paper-based operations, the earliest automated HCM solutions supported four primary functions:

- Personnel management

- Payroll

- Benefits administration

- Time and labor management.

As HCM systems grew more sophisticated and embraced the integration and process reengineering opportunities associated with ERP systems, they began to include a number of additional processes such as:

- Recruitment management.

- Organizational structure.

- Job descriptions and salary profiles.

- Career development.

- Training and performance management.

- Budgeting and cost control.

- Regulatory compliance.

- Travel and expense management.

- Health and safety

- Disciplinary actions and grievances tracking.

Human Capital Management Modules

> "With people-related costs averaging over 60% of total corporate expenditures, leading firms are paying attention to the contribution made by their workers and are developing a new model for HR. This model includes programs to improve the efficiency, effectiveness and productivity of the workforce and the ability to manage locally or globally. These programs require new processes supported by leading technologies.
>
> *Source: Oracle*

HCM functionality can range from very basic to more comprehensive support and can also be organized into various modules by different vendors. Vendors can be expected to provide solutions for the core functions we noted earlier - personnel management, payroll, benefits and timekeeping. In addition, while they will all provide one or more modules supporting the more advanced features we have listed above, they may extend these solutions further providing components such as employee self-service, talent management, mobility solutions, or other features that continue to evolve into more sophisticated solutions with time.

The **Personnel Management** module often covers all HR aspects from recruiting to retirement. The information captured in this module will include:

- Basic employee data – Name, address, social security number, and emergency contacts.

- Resumes, *Curriculum Vitae*, skills inventories – These records provide visibility for an individual employee's capabilities.

- Training, development, and skills management – These records track the progress of the individual and his or her accomplishments.

- Compensation – Accurate and secure salary information and payroll records are critically important. In addition, this information can be rolled into project and production forecasts in an effort to measure the costs those efforts may entail.

- Job descriptions, advertising and applicant tracking – The opportunity to hire qualified personnel can be optimized with effective management of these functions. In addition, these records present their own requirements regarding their Equal Employment Opportunity (EEO) compliance as well as the care, custody, and control of personal information.

Again, we see that the automation of these processes and the integration of this information into ERP systems provide a number of benefits throughout the enterprise. Likewise, as this information gains the benefits of the advanced data management solutions associated with ERP systems, it can be used in any number of reporting contexts such as EEO reporting, as we just mentioned, or others including the compliance and control documentation issues associated with the Sarbanes-Oxley Act (SOX).

The **Benefit Administration** module permits HR professionals to administer and track employee participation in benefits programs ranging from:

- Health and medical insurance plans.

- Life and supplemental life insurance plans.

- Accidental death and dismemberment (AD&D) and disability insurance plans.

- Flexible spending plans that provide income tax advantages available to employees in the United States.

- 401(k) plans, profit sharing plans, stock plans, retirement plans.

- Leave plans including vacation and sick leave accruals. In some ERP systems, this functionality is considered part of the Time Management module.

Using the advantages of ERP system data integration, these modules provide a number of valuable HR tools. One example of such an approach is a Total Compensation Report that displays the monetary value of each benefit that each employee is receiving, allowing the employee to fully understand the value of their compensation. Another example would be aggregated work-force metrics that can be used to promote the organization's work place environment among potential recruits.

The **Time and Labor Management** module allows workers to submit timecard data online and supervisors to review and approve time. This module supports cost accounting objectives by tracking time to specific efforts, activities or projects. At the same time, it helps the company control costs and time worked, consolidate timecard information, prepare information relevant for the payroll process, and support forecasting of labor requirements and utilization based on forecast demands.

The **Payroll** module automates accounting and preparation of payroll checks for employee salaries, wages and bonuses, calculation of various taxes and benefit deductions, and the generation of periodic payroll checks as well as the various local, state and federal tax information and forms. Data is generally fed from the Personnel Management and Time and Labor Management modules to calculate payroll. The payroll results can then be passed on to the accounting modules that record the liability for net wages and employee deductions. These amounts are transferred from Payroll to the General Ledger in Financials where entries are made for payroll accrual and employer payroll taxes. Also, labor is distributed to various cost centers and profit centers. This system may also manage payroll direct deposits that eliminate the security risks and fraud potential associated with issuing live checks. Because of the intricacies of keeping up with various local, city and country taxes for employees often spread out all over the world, many organizations choose to outsource payroll (and for that matter other HR functions as well.) Service organizations such as ADP will take on the responsibility for time and attendance, payroll, garnishments, payroll tax deposits, GL interface and 401K administration. Figure 9 – 1 presents 10 reasons to outsource payroll.

Ten Reasons to Outsource Payroll
Cost
Productivity
Accuracy
Reliability
Speed
Insight
Accountability
Flexibility
Security
Worry

Figure 9 – 1: Ten Reasons to Outsource Payroll

Source: HR World

The objectives of the next two modules, Recruitment Management and Talent Management, are to attract qualified candidates and retain them. Results of a recent survey found that these two factors are key to achieving strong financial performance (Figure 9 - 2), although a disparity exists between perceived importance of activity and how well organizations address each activity.

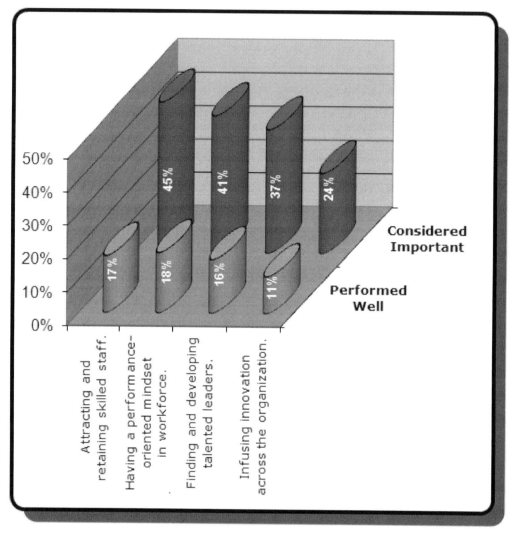

Figure 9 – 2: Key Factors in Achieving Strong Financial Performance

Source: Accenture's High Performance Workforce Study 2006

Recruitment Management typically supports the opening components of the employee life cycle including:

- Attracting potential applicants and managing resumes – Recently this has become a heavily web-based activity using job sites such as Monster.com or Dice.com. Also, HR systems can use data from professional networking sites where professional and personal acquaintances can support the recruitment process.

- Evaluating their suitability as an employee – HCM modules can track a set of personal and technical interviews providing the participants with a set of criteria with which to judge the recruit's responses.

- Analyzing the skills necessary to support various functions in the organization – This process should point to a level of skill and competency required to adequately perform the function.

- Articulating job descriptions for those functions – A catalog of all the organization's job descriptions will be a valuable resource for many HCM objectives.

- Matching potential new-hires with job descriptions – Experience, education and expertise can be confirmed in the screening processes and compared to the requirements noted in the job description.

Typical HCM modules contain many features that provide recruiters with industry knowledge, technical proficiency, and the job context so they can gain the insight needed to optimize the hiring process. An efficient and effective hiring process will lead to an increase in the productivity and value of the overall recruitment process. Among the most relevant benefits of Recruitment Management are:

- Communicating career opportunities to broad, qualified applicant pools.

- Streamlining application methods for job seekers, perhaps supporting the ability to accept data from third-party providers and on-line job services like the ones mentioned earlier.

- Reduce and simplify the paperwork associated with the on-boarding processes.

Talent Management works with Recruitment Management to analyze personnel usage within an organization and help retain good employees. By identifying the talents each employee possesses, managers are able to align people to objectives, and subsequently, objectives to business strategy. By assuring that each employee is placed in the most effective position, talent management can result in better control and transparency, lowering turnover rates by creating a challenging and rewarding work environment. Benefits of Talent Management to an organization include:

- Aligning each employee's contribution with organizational needs to establish appropriate rewards, performance plans, and career plans.

- Build a talent database to more easily identify high-potential employees for growth or development opportunities.

- Retain ideal employees to fit into the workforce plan.

- Optimize employee contribution by delivering the right employee learning in the most effective format at the lowest cost.

- Close skills gaps by assessing an individual's training needs and turning that assessment into a development plan.

Learning Management or **Enterprise Learning** as it is often referred to, is integral to Talent Management and includes employee training profiles, courses, sessions, instructors, and course evaluations. Learning management typically can support training programs presented in a variety of formats including:

- Instructor led, face to face – Courses are the traditional instructor/classroom environment.

- Instructor led, virtual – These courses can include students on site as well as those attending virtually, accessing audio over the telephone or computer audio and including shared computer workspaces and documents.

- Computer interactive – Courses run on a computer that involves one-on-one interaction with the student.

- Web based – Courses are accessed via web browsers and typically provide "anytime, anyplace, any pace" access. This type of training has gained tremendous momentum over the past few years and generally has an off-line capability, which is especially useful for the mobile workforce.

- On-line forums – Users can seek and find groups of employees with similar knowledge needs and can contribute to the organization's body of knowledge on specific subjects. These online forums are an extension of the traditional open seminar and more modern approaches include wikis and blogs where content is contributed, regulated and moderated by the user community.

In addition to providing access to specific courses, the Learning Management module can provide a number of additional solutions to enhance the learning environment such as:

- Online scheduling – Supporting both students in their need to schedule courses and also instructors as they prepare for their classes.

- On-line course material – Manuals, slide decks and course quizzes can be stored and accessed online. In addition, after classes, recorded audio and video can be made available as well as message boards where participants can exchange ideas and knowledge.

- Tracking – Class participation and completion information allow employees access to their transcripts. In addition learning management systems are favored by regulated industries such as medical professions, insurance, financial services and biopharmaceuticals, where compliance with continuing education requirements is essential. The purpose of learning management is to improve employee operational efficiency and report on learning effectiveness.

- Communication – Special events, new requirements and outstanding performances can be quickly communicated throughout the organization using the ERP system interface.

Many organizations have adopted a "University" metaphor shrouding their training efforts with the look and feel of a traditional institution of higher learning. Often these efforts are heavily based on learning management software solutions that allows the development of a true but virtual learning brand within the organization. One such example of this approach is implemented at Quintiles where its Quintiles University supports the ongoing training requirements outlined in its industry presentations.

Environment, Health, and Safety provides the tools to administer compliance with the health and safety regulations that arise from local, state, and federal agencies. The largest of these is the federal **Occupational Safety and Health Administration (OSHA)**. It and others, such as state industrial commissions and insurance regulators will impose any number of requirements that are mostly met with certifications of compliance signed off by corporate executives supported by data generated by the organization's ERP systems. Injuries and environmental threats impose significant down-side risks and ERP systems can provide the information that will empower decision-makers in their efforts to mitigate those risks. We will address risk specifically in a later chapter but, in terms of HCM modules, the organization's ERP system can be expected to:

- Provide reports regarding employee injuries and absences due to sicknesses that are work-related or otherwise.

- Provide information supporting an organization's effort to defend itself against charges of allowing dangerous or unhealthy conditions to persist.

- Support the efforts of industrial hygienists as they inspect the organization's operation looking for health threats.

- Provide decision-makers with data regarding compliance with safety guidelines, accident and injury reporting and expenses arising from those incidents.

Workforce Analytics allows the organization to measure the effectiveness of their HR strategies and programs and measure their workforce's contributions to the bottom line. Example key performance indicators and other analytics for HCM include:

- Recruiting success.

- Workforce trends by job, geography, minority groups, and business areas.

- Applicant statistics and dropout reasons.

- Absenteeism by reason over time.

- Training attendance, resource use, costs, and success rates.

- Value of benefits plans.

Employee Performance Management streamlines employee appraisal from goal planning and coaching to performance assessments and rewards. Managers, employees and HR administrators can collaborate on performance evaluations and goals, review performance history, and monitor and manage the overall performance process. Knowing where there is need for improvement in the HR processes is the first step to actually increasing performance. Figure 9 – 3 presents 10 things you cannot do without an EPM system.

Employee Self-Service

Activity and processes within Human Resource departments are peculiar in two ways. First, nearly every organization is faced with a similar set of HR requirements. This fact means that HR best practices in one organization are likely to also be effective in other organizations; HR best practices are readily transferable between organizations. As a result, the vertical set of HR solutions is well suited for integration into ERP systems and is also well developed among software vendors. Second, HR activities, administration and skills are usually not the primary focus of the HR department's host organization; organizational objectives include making products and/or providing services, not administering HR systems. Being outside the organization's core competencies also makes HR systems a prime target for reengineering and automation. Among the most advanced approaches to automating HR systems is **Employee Self-Service**.

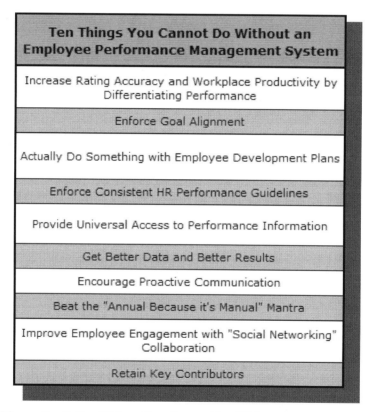

Ten Things You Cannot Do Without an Employee Performance Management System

Increase Rating Accuracy and Workplace Productivity by Differentiating Performance

Enforce Goal Alignment

Actually Do Something with Employee Development Plans

Enforce Consistent HR Performance Guidelines

Provide Universal Access to Performance Information

Get Better Data and Better Results

Encourage Proactive Communication

Beat the "Annual Because it's Manual" Mantra

Improve Employee Engagement with "Social Networking" Collaboration

Retain Key Contributors

Figure 9 – 3: Ten Things You Cannot Do Without an EPM System

Source: SumTotal Systems

We have also discussed previously how, even as paper records have evolved into electronic records, HR is still a highly document-centric activity, whether those documents are paper or electronic. HR systems attempt to track innumerable data points on each employee, including personal histories, skills, and capabilities and many of the other electronic documents we have described in the previous section. These records tend to churn a great deal. Employees come and go. They change their positions within a company and their supervisors and subordinates. Their skill, accomplishments, lifestyles and benefit choices change often. Recording and filing all of the information that arises as a result of this churn creates a substantial administrative burden. Figure 9 – 4 shows the NetSuite Expense Report where the employee, A Wolfe, is entering his expenses for meals and entertainment.

To the extent that these administrative activities are necessary to keep these records current, complete and accurate, often due to legal requirements, they command the time and attention of the HR staff and therefore distract the staff from more strategic issues that may indeed provide greater value to the organization. For example, instead of distributing, tracking and working on piles of employee benefit plan documents, the HR staff might provide greater value to the organization if it spent its time analyzing its current Benefit providers and plans to determine if changes would better serve the employees. Employee Self-Service addresses this need by allowing employees and managers to tend to the administrative burdens that arise from their activities that are relevant to their HR records.

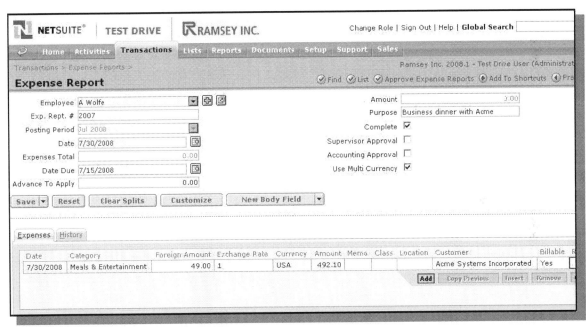

Figure 9 – 4: NetSuite Expense Report

Source: NetSuite

Employee Self-Service allows employees to enter and update worker-specific information by providing access to system interfaces that are tailored to the employee's role, experience, work content, language, and information needs. Employees can access and update their personal information and benefit allocations in the self-service system to manage the churn generated by their life events and benefit selections. As a result, countless paper records and HR administrative activities are eliminated, thereby allowing HR departments to reduce headcount as it must support a lighter administrative burden. On the other hand, with less demanding administrative overhead, HR staff can shift their focus away from administrative processes and provide greater support for objectives to optimize the value the HR department provides to the organization

Manager Self-Service provides managers an insight into their staff and their budget, two areas most pressing for managers. Managers can review and initiate recruitment for vacancies, perform annual reviews for employees, perform personnel change requests (position changes, hire, terminations and other actions) for employees via the use of workflow and even approve leave requests, to name only a small sampling of the functionality. By decentralizing these everyday tasks, organizations can respond flexibly and instantaneously to these changes with the use of tools such as Manager Self-Service.

Self-service applications for employee and their managers can provide the following benefits:

- Increases accuracy by embedding online advice to reduce errors by employees and by putting the data directly in the hands of the people who know it best.

- Increases timeliness by providing both managers and employees with a single point of entry to all their HR information and processes.

- Manages everything in employees' own languages, from profiles (including skills, resumes, contact details, and bank data) to self-appraisals, learning, benefits, payroll, expenses, and more.

- Gives managers the tools to perform activities such as transfers, employee training enrollment, terminations, compensation and performance reviews, and skills searches.

Human Capital Management Spending

In a 2006-2007 AMR Research study, companies were asked to estimate spending on HCM functionality. Figure 9 - 5 shows that talent acquisition, employee portals/employee self-service and employee performance management were spending priorities for 2006-2007. The Human Resource Management and Workforce Management modules show average spending for 2006-2007, although this may be because this functionality is the core part of a HCM strategy, and thus many companies may have already implemented them. Workforce Development can encompass both Talent Management and Learning Management. Rounding out the spending for 2006-2007 is Workforce Analytics and Professional Services Automation. The latter system is considered an ERP system for the professional services industry, such as for consultants and IT services organizations. This software is used to manage the delivery of client projects and the resources which are required for those projects, such as skilled personnel and equipment. Typically, functions include project management and documentation, time recording, billing, and reporting.

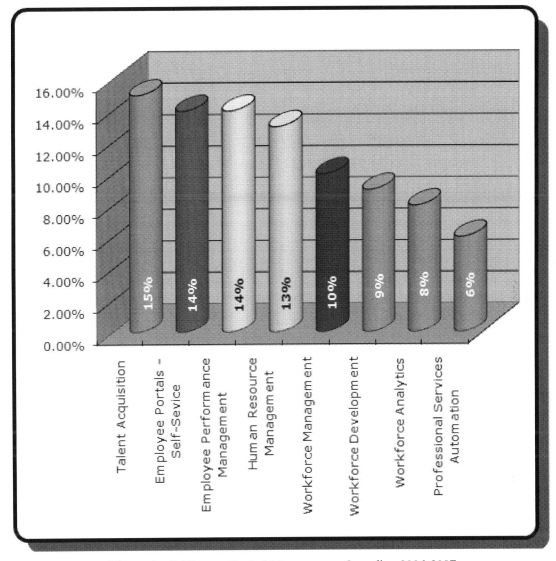

Figure 9 - 5: Human Capital Management Spending 2006-2007
Source: The Human Capital Management Spending Report, 2006–2007

Summary

An organization's workforce has become increasingly important to a company's success such that senior executives view people and workforce-related issues as a key differentiator in our competitive environment. The Human Resources modules of an ERP system manage the recruit to retire business process. Organizations can benefit from an ERP system to plan workforce needs, track applicants, onboard new employees, manage benefits, train and compensate. Using integrated components for these functions means that one record exists for each employee that is linked to all activities for that employee from payroll to professional development. Human Resources is also made easier for those operating in a global environment because ERP systems can keep track of legal issues regarding compensation and employment as well as constantly changing employee and employer tax rates for multiple taxing entities.

Keywords

Benefit Administration

Employee Performance Management

Employee Self-Service

Enterprise Learning

Environment, Health, and Safety

Human capital

Human Capital Management (HCM)

Human Resource (HR)

Human Resources Management

Learning Management

Manager Self-Service

Occupation Safety and Health Administration (OSHA)

Payroll

Personnel Management

Pre-hire to retire employee life cycle

Recruit to retire process

Recruitment Management

Talent Management

Time and Labor Management

Workforce Analytics

Workforce Management

Quick Review

1. True/False: The Personnel Management module covers all HR aspects from recruiting to retirement.

2. True/False: The Workforce Analytics module typically encompasses analyzing personnel usage within an organization, identifying potential applicants, and recruiting through a variety of means including the Web.

3. _____ allows employees to enter and update worker-specific information using systems tailored to the employee's role, experience, work content, language, and information needs.

4. _____ comprises the strategy and business processes that transform every employee into a competitive asset that supports operating and financial results.

5. Functionality in HCM that represents a top spending priority for companies is: _____.

Questions to Consider

1. List reasons why it benefits organizations to implement HCM modules.

2. What information is shared between HCM and other modules in an ERP system?

3. What are the main sub-modules of HCM and what functionality do they provide?

References

ADP. http://www.adp.com. Accessed January 5, 2008.

Balaguer, E., Cheese, P., & Marchetti, C. (2006). *The High-Performance Workforce Study 2006*. Accenture White Paper

Burger, A. (2008). *Enterprise Recruiting, Part 1: Powering Up the Process*. Retrieved March 11, 2008, from http://www.crmbuyer.com/story/61348.html

Edwards, J. (2007). *10 Reasons to Outsource Payroll*. Retrieved April 22, 2008, from http://www.hrworld.com/features/10-   reasons-outsource-payroll-092407/

Hall, J. (2003). *Accessing Learning Management Systems*. Retrieved April 22, 2008, from http://www.clomedia.com/content/templates/clo_feature.asp?articleid=91

Manning, C., Sweeney, J., & Sirkisoon, F. (2007). *The Human Capital Management Spending Report, 2006–2007*. White Paper. Retrieved from http://www.amrresearch.com/Content/View.asp?pmillid=20152

Oracle. *Oracle Human Resource Management System*. Retrieved April 22, 2008, from http://www.oracle.com/applications/human_resources/intro.html

SumTotal. (2008). 10 *Things You Cannot Do Without an Employee Performance Management System*. White Paper. Retrieved from http://www.sumtotalsystems.com/success/whitepapers/whitepapers.html#epm

Chapter

10

Manufacturing Systems and Supply Chain

Objectives

- Explain how ERP systems evolved from the manufacturing industry.

- Describe common ERP manufacturing modules.

- Understand the technologies used to support the supply chain.

Introduction

The objectives of manufacturing operations are to create a production plan, acquire raw materials, schedule equipment, design products, and produce appropriate quantities at expected quality levels. These efforts depend on two key systems for support: systems that support production planning and those that support inventory management. Together these two systems work to ensure that materials are available for production as needed. Prior to the advent of computerized systems, organizations relied on large amounts of inventory in the form of raw material and work in process in order to ensure smooth operations. Early computerized systems were used to optimize and lower inventory requirements. Optimizing this effort requires minimizing the amount of money needed to maintain materials before they enter the production cycle and the money needed to maintain completed product inventory after it is produced before it is sold. In addition, these systems can be integrated with other company systems such as human resources, cost accounting and asset management. ERP systems provide the integration that traditional manufacturing systems lacked. This chapter discusses the manufacturing and inventory modules of a typical ERP system. In addition, we will discuss, **Supply Chain Management (SCM)** functionality, considered a bolt-on to core ERP, as well as the technologies that support an efficient and smooth flow of materials to and from the enterprise.

Evolution of Manufacturing Systems

Before ERP systems, production systems lacked integration across organizational functions. Early systems focused on the management of inventory and production operations. Customer requirements and marketing forecast information was typically maintained in separate systems with unique databases. This means that material requirements, production plans and sales forecast information were not linked together. Information flow between operational systems and other important systems within an organization was accomplished with file exchanges resulting in slow response times and inaccurate information.

An efficient and smooth flowing manufacturing operation requires that a company maintain proper inventory levels to support an accurate production forecast. A shortage of inventory can stop the production process, idle production facilities, and delay shipments, events that increase costs, lead to customer dissatisfaction and lost sales opportunities. Producing too little or too much finished goods also carries a cost as excess inventories, both of raw materials and of finished products will impact cash flow and corporate profitability. ERP systems, particularly those that incorporate SCM functionality, empower a number of key production analyses that help reduce these negative impacts on profitability that arise from the need to finance the materials and inventory necessary to maintain efficient production levels.

Economic Order Quantity

Over the years, systems that support manufacturing activities have experienced a great amount of change, from stovepipe systems that supported a single purpose, to integrated systems that plan, manage and control complex manufacturing operations. Decades ago, businesses that carried raw materials relied on traditional inventory management techniques to ensure that those raw materials were available as needed to support efficient operations. The most popular of these methods is the **Economic Order Quantity (EOQ)** method, in which each raw material stock item is analyzed for its ordering lead time and carrying costs. The EOQ formula calculates the optimal ordering quantity to minimize both of these variable costs. Although the EOQ formula does a sound job at minimizing the cost of carrying raw materials, it does not permit effective rescheduling in response to dynamic changes in demand or production activities. It is a reactive, backward looking method rather than a proactive or forward-looking method as orders are placed to support projected needs based on prior experience.

Materials Requirements Planning

In the 1960's **Material Requirements Planning (MRP)** emerged as a more efficient material replenishment method. MRP is a software-based production planning and inventory control system used to manage manufacturing processes. It is a time-phased approach because it not only projects what and how much needs to be made and purchased, but also determines when those materials should be purchased. Its proactive manner of inventory management takes into account inventory already on hand, order processing and delivery time. Using sales forecasts to identify finished goods needed, this method uses a **Bill of Materials (BOM)** and explodes it based on the **Master Production Schedule (MPS)** to determine raw materials requirements with knowledge of the **Inventory Status File** for inventory already on hand. These three files which are integral to the MRP system of an ERP application are discussed next.

- Bill of Material - Each product consumes some amount of raw materials in its production. The Bill of Materials (BOM) is the full list of necessary raw materials to produce a single item. In anticipation of a desired quantity of finished products the necessary raw materials can be calculated to determine the amount of raw materials that must be on hand as production begins. Cooking is a form of production and the BOM is essentially the ingredients listed at the start of the recipe. This list is known as the **Engineering BOM**. In cooking, the recipe continues to specify what to do with the materials, what equipment to use, and how to go about cooking a specific dish and typically specifies a stated output, such as "serves six." To serve some multiple of six, such as in planning for a party, the recipe book quantities can be multiplied by an appropriate value to get an appropriate starting quantity of materials. This total quantity is the **Manufacturing BOM**.

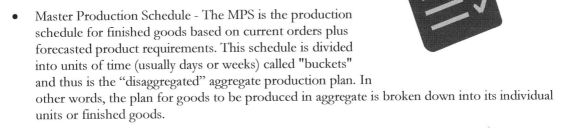

- Master Production Schedule - The MPS is the production schedule for finished goods based on current orders plus forecasted product requirements. This schedule is divided into units of time (usually days or weeks) called "buckets" and thus is the "disaggregated" aggregate production plan. In other words, the plan for goods to be produced in aggregate is broken down into its individual units or finished goods.

- Inventory Status File – This file contains a count of the on-hand balance of every part held in inventory. In addition, the inventory status file contains all pertinent information regarding open orders and the **lead time** (the time that elapses between placing an order and actually receiving it) for each item

With the MPS, the BOM and the Inventory Status Report, MRP systems:

- Identify raw materials needed.

- Calculate lead time for stock.

- Establish safety stock levels.

- Determine the most cost-effective order quantities.

- Produce a detailed schedule of accurate purchase orders.

- Reduce inventory levels and production and delivery lead times by improving coordination and avoiding delays.

- Make commitments more realistic.

- Increase efficiency in the raw material procurement process and ensuing production process.

Capacity Planning

MRP proved to be a very good technique for managing inventory, but it did not take into account other resources of the organization. In the 1970's, a modified MRP logic known as **Closed Loop MRP** emerged. In this technique, MRP was expanded to address other production capacities of the  organization such as the availability of production personnel, machines, space and warehouse capacity. These additional elements are taken into account by incorporating **Capacity Requirements Planning (CRP)** techniques. CRP uses the planned manufacturing schedule to analyze the requirements that will be placed upon manufacturing work centers. It compares these planned requirements with the capacity available to determine if a production plan is feasible. If a work center is over capacity, it will identify the production that is causing the problem allowing it to be rescheduled or allowing more resources to be allocated to the work center. Hence, a **feedback loop** is provided from the CRP module to MPS if there is not enough capacity available to produce the desired quantity. Product design and development is integrated with cost information which allows the comparison of alternatives to decrease expenses. Information needed for capacity planning includes HR data, the BOM, Work in Progress (WIP), Finished Goods, lot sizes, and orders in the plant.

Manufacturing Resource Planning (MRPII)

In the 1980s, MRPII emerged as an improvement over MRP. This method effectively plans all resources of a manufacturing operation addressing:

- Operational planning in units.

- Financial planning in dollars.

- A simulation capability to conduct sensitivity analysis ("what-if" questions).

MRP II is composed of several linked functions, such as business planning, sales and operations planning, CRP, and all related support systems. The output from these MRP II functions can be integrated into financial reports such as the business plan, purchase commitment report, shipping, budget, and inventory projections. It has the capability of specifically addressing operational planning

ERP Systems for Manufacturing

The shortcomings of MRPII and the need to integrate all activities of a business led to the development of a totally integrated solution, ERP. MRPII systems were built for manufacturing organizations; however, ERP has developed well beyond this industry, as we know. ERP allows for the merging of multiple databases by eliminating paperwork and bottlenecks, decreasing design costs, and increasing productivity. Tasks that need to interface with one another in a manufacturing company include:

- Engineering design (the best way to make manufactured goods.)

- Order tracking from acceptance through fulfillment, accepting customer orders, placing those orders into production, and delivering to customers.

- Purchasing raw materials and services, acquiring correct quantities of raw materials and supplies.

- Inventory receipts including quality control, inspection of delivered products and processing receipts by matching receipt with purchase order.

- Managing interdependencies of complex BOMs.

- Cost accounting including tracking the revenue, cost and profit at a detailed level.

ERP Manufacturing Modules

Modern ERP systems for manufacturing companies include major (core) modules that would encompass the production planning and inventory management functions as well as operation-oriented "bolt-ons" that can be purchased outside the core ERP. Let's take a look at the key manufacturing modules as well as several of these bolt-ons that facilitate operations activities.

Production Planning

Production Planning enables the production planner to create realistic production plans across the different manufacturing locations, including subcontractors, to fulfill demand in a timely manner and according to standards expected by the customer. For the medium and long-term time horizons, planning is based on time buckets and determines requirements of resources (machines, humans, production resource tools) and materials. Real-time, integrated data, KPI alerts and supply chain visibility support the planner's decision-making process.

Inventory Management

The **Inventory Management** module of an ERP system supports activities such as the tracking and control of raw material, stocked items, WIP and finished product in a single integrated inventory control environment. It specifies the activities needed to maintain adequate inventory levels such as ordering raw materials or transferring finished product from the warehouse to the loading dock. It can also address atypical inventory issues such as late specification changes, defects, or returns. As inventory moves from one production station to another, the necessary receipts and other documents can be produced to act as the foundation for on-hand balance calculations for use in both planning and financial valuation. The functions of Inventory Management include: MRP, material procurement (sourcing), invoice verification, material valuation, and external services management. Figure 10 – 1 shows the NetSuite Inventory Profitability Report including quantity sold, total cost and gross profit percentages.

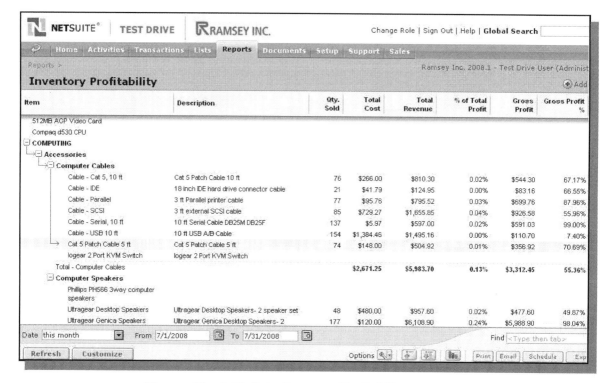

Figures 10 – 1: NetSuite Inventory Profitability Report

Source: NetSuite

Quality Management

Maintaining quality spans every activity in the manufacturing process, from purchasing through delivery to the customer. The **Quality Management** module of an ERP system helps an organization by building quality tasks into the production processes in all phases of a product - from the planning phase through the implementation and use phases. Management can set specific parameters (rules) into the application that can define what to inspect, when to inspect, and tolerance limits for acceptance. The system can then alert those responsible when quality deviations occur.

Improving quality improves the bottom line and increases customer satisfaction, and the earlier defects can be detected, the better. If a faulty product is detected early in manufacturing, it may cost a few dollars, but if found after the product is in the hands of the consumer, it could cost hundreds or thousands at that point.

Some of the key benefits of Quality Management include:

- Capture data regarding material quality of products.

- Record quality tests in a consistent and controlled way.

- Build quality management into processes.

- Minimize time spent inspecting material, collecting data, testing and retesting.

- Reduce scrap, rework and returns.

- Identify faulty products and inferior components.

Plant Maintenance

If an expensive piece of equipment stands idle waiting for a part, this can cost a company thousands of dollars in lost productivity. Additionally, if management cannot target problem equipment before a replace or repair decision needs to be made, this can also be costly for a company. The **Plant Maintenance** module of an ERP system helps an organization increase the availability of machinery and other fixed assets, reduce the number of breakdowns through preventive maintenance, coordinate and employ human resources to fulfill specific maintenance orders, and reduce costs of inspections and preventive and planned maintenance. Plant Maintenance integrates with Asset Management for the asset record and to track and report the cost and revenue data for plant equipment.

Benefits of implementing the Plant Maintenance ERP module include:

- Extend the useful life of equipment.

- Minimize downtime and maximize uptime of equipment.

- Support Lean manufacturing processes and other quality methods.

- Increase collaboration between production and maintenance staffs.

- Monitor equipment performance.

Service Management

Most companies are aware that retaining a current customer is cheaper than attracting a new customer; therefore, the ability of an organization to oversee their customer service is directly linked to their continued success. **Service Management** is the link between the order and the customer and manages the lifecycle changes to existing services or installed products after the initial order is fulfilled. The goal of Service Management is to optimize service-intensive supply chains, which are usually more complex than the typical finished-goods supply chain. Service Management can provide an organization with the necessary tools for quality customer service include integration with order management for the customer record, warranty and claims management, service contract management, service notifications, service order management, spare part deliveries, billing/settlement of services, and evaluations of services.

Benefits of employing the Service Management module of an ERP system include:

- Lower service costs by integrating the service and products supply chain.

- Lower service parts inventory levels.

- Optimized customer service or parts/service quality.

- Increase service revenue.

- Improve customer satisfaction levels.

- Minimize technician visits.

Warehouse Management

Some ERP systems contain a **Warehouse Management System (WMS)** as either part of the ERP system itself, or as an add-on module. Basically, a WMS controls the activities of movements into, out of and through a warehouse by using real-time information about the status of inventory supply

and demand. WMS include such basic functions as receiving, order picking, shipping, put-away, and inventory control, but what separates a modern WMS from the functions that are included in the core of an ERP system is the ability of a WMS to optimize activities. This difference is best explained with the following simple example.

Picture, if you will, a warehouse worker putting away items from a receiving area. The worker would pick an item(s) and travel through the warehouse putting the item(s) into designated spaces. Using a WMS, the worker is directed by the WMS through use of real-time information from a hand-held computer terminal device, to not only pick and place items from receiving, but to conduct any number of other activities. For example, the worker may be directed to put away an item at a location in the warehouse. While at that location, the worker also may be directed to cycle count an

item at a nearby location and while at that location, pick an item for delivery to the shipping area. The worker is in a continuous loop of activity directed by the WMS

In addition, the WMS will optimize the storage of items in the warehouse. For example, the WMS monitors movement of items, and will direct the placement of faster moving items towards the front of the warehouse and slower moving items in the back, thus minimizing put-away and retrieval times. It is this direction of activities by a WMS that optimize the entire operation and results in a more efficient operation, increasing accuracy, reducing labor costs with improved ability to service the customer.

Lean Manufacturing

Early manufacturing techniques focused on mass production techniques and large batches, which were then put on the shelf until used or sent to the customer. The problem with mass production is that the processes require large amounts of inventory, plant, equipment, and capital investment. **Lean Manufacturing** is a production approach that focuses on producing only what is required by the customer, at high qualities with no waste. The term "waste" in Lean Manufacturing refers to costs that add no value to a product and include:

1. Overproduction – not producing to customer demand. Every item should be produced only when it is need, or just-in-time.

2. Wait time – most of the time that material, parts, and finished goods spend in a typical manufacturing environment is in a **wait state,** usually caused by bottlenecks, long production runs, and poor synchronization of operations. Lean attempts to eliminate this waiting.

3. Transportation – moving items between production processes also contributes to waste.

4. Inventory – having too much inventory in the form of raw material, work-in-process, and finished goods is one of the largest forms of waste in a manufacturing operation.

5. Excess motion – differing from transportation, **motion** refers to the ergonomic issues of the producing process and includes repetitive lifting, bending, and reaching in a work place. Not only will eliminating motion reduce waste, but it will also improve the safety of the work environment.

6. Inappropriate processing – excess processing include sorting, unnecessary inspections, over designed products misallocation of resources, use of expensive, high precision equipment when smaller, flexible, low-cost automation can be used.

> Fabrikam, Inc., a leading bicycle manufacturer, produces high-end bicycles and custom bicycles for customers around the globe. The company purchases all of its parts from vendors, with the exception of the bicycle frames, which they manufacture from raw steel pipe. Fabrikam and each of its suppliers use RFID to share information about various parts, sub-assemblies, and inventory location. The following fictional scenario demonstrates how Fabrikam and its vendors have implemented RFID technology to create greater overall efficiencies in the supply chain, improve the response time for product recalls, and closely monitor delivery schedules.
>
> *Source: Microsoft*

7. Defects – processes that result in production of scrap and products that require rework.

By eliminating waste in production process, the pace of all of the processes in the plant can be set to the level of customer demand. Production smoothing techniques are used to smooth out fluctuating demand of the marketplace.

While the traditional approach to Lean Manufacturing includes a number of manual techniques, additional modules have been developed for ERP software to facilitate and enhance the achievement of Lean systems. For example, SAP has a module called Lean Planning and Operations based on the principles of Lean. This module helps companies respond to changes in customer demand effectively on the plant floor based on real-time information and decision support from their manufacturing execution systems. It can generate a leveled production schedule using sophisticated algorithms that take into consideration inventory targets, available capacity and customer demand.

Cost Accounting for Manufacturing

Cost accounting in manufacturing systems track the cost of manufacturing and relate those costs to established cost standards Cost accounting for manufacturing must track the dollars of inventory moving from raw material through the manufacturing process. A **move order** transfers the standard cost of raw materials to the plant and updates WIP. Cost accounting will compute raw material, direct labor and factory overhead variances and once the product is manufactured, will close the cost record and transfer Cost of Goods to Finished Goods.

Supply Chain Management and ERP

Systems that improve the way a company gathers the raw materials it needs and subsequently deliver products and services to its customer is known as a Supply Chain Management system. Initial ERP Systems focused on the manufacturing process within a plant. SCM systems extend benefits of the ERP to the entire supply chain, both up-stream and down-stream from the manufacturer. As organizations have outsourced components of their manufacturing processes, SCM systems have become a critical component of ERP systems.

SCM technology seeks to eliminate much of the guesswork between suppliers, manufacturers, retailers and consumers by enabling more visibility up and down the supply chain. Being a successful supply chain partner demands up-to-the-minute the kind of information visibility best provided by modern ERP platforms.

According to *The 2007-2008 Supply Chain Management Spending Report,* twice as many companies surveyed indicate that they will increase spending on supply chain software as compared to 2006 data. Additionally, the average spending on SCM technology will increase by nearly 12 percent for 2008. The report also states that both ERP vendors and best-of-breed vendors will benefit from this "investment resurgence" in SCM systems.

Benefits of implementing SCM include:

- Improved forecasting - Timely and accurate supply information upstream and demand information downstream allows the producer to make or ship only as much of a product as needed.

- Increased productivity - Greater awareness of customer trends allows more flexibility and responsiveness to valuable customer segments.

- Improved customer service and lower costs – The company is able to optimize production to meet but not exceed customer demand.

As mentioned earlier, Lean Manufacturing attempts to reduce inventory in the manufacturing process through a just-in-time approach. SCM extends these **just-in-time manufacturing** techniques to the supply chain. This approach, allows companies to minimize inventory without failing to have product on hand for sales opportunities. This can reduce costs substantially, since companies no longer need to pay to produce and store excess goods.

As with any enterprise system, companies must overcome obstacles in order to fully realize the value from a SCM system. A few of these obstacles include:

- Gaining trust from suppliers and partners - Supply chain partners must agree to collaborate, compromise and help each other achieve their goals.

- Internal resistance to change - Traditionally, operations personnel were accustomed to managing the supply chain with phone calls, faxes and guesses scrawled on pieces of paper. They will most likely want to keep it that way. The company has to convince them that it is worth their time to use the SCM system.

- Making mistakes at first - New supply chain systems process data as they are programmed but often lack knowledge about the company's history and processes. In the first few months after an implementation, forecasters and planners may find the system will need to be tuned to become effective and that the first interchanges of information may not be perfect.

Supply Chain Management Technologies and Methodologies

Specific technologies and methodologies are instrumental to enabling SCM. Among these are:

- Radio Frequency Identification

- Vendor Managed Inventory

- Electronic Data Interchange

Not only do these technologies and methodologies support an efficient supply chain, but they also enable smooth-running processes such as Order to Cash and Purchase to Pay.

Radio Frequency Identification Data

Tiny computer chips or tags can be embedded in products and packaging that allows them to be tracked via wireless networks using wireless technology. These chips or tags are called **Radio Frequency Identification Data (RFID)**. This technology enables the chips or tags to be tracked from a supplier's factory floor to the retailer's store shelves. Currently, the most common application of RFID technology is for tracking goods in the supply chain from manufacturing, shipment, and customer delivery, tracking assets, and tracking parts from a manufacturing production line. By providing real-time visibility into inventories and supporting a perpetual inventory system, RFID enables companies to maintain and control optimum product levels to save costs and ensure better customer service.

One of the major advantages of using RFID for tracking inventory is now that instead of using FIFO or LIFO assumptions, RFID can track units on an individual basis. Each item can have a tag, and each tag can transmit manufacturer codes, product codes, exact associated costs, data manufactured, length of time on the shelf and other useful information. In addition, unlike bar codes, RFID tags do not require "line of sight," technology. Barcodes must be scanned within a foot of the actual product, but RFID tags need only be within range of a reader to be read. A typical RFID system includes transceivers, tags and a computer system to process the information. There are two types of tags: active and passive. Active tags have an internal battery that constantly transmits data and permits them to be read from a greater distance. Passive tags do not have a battery and only transmit data when a transceiver activates them by coming within a certain range. Although active tags are more expensive, they have more potential applications. The information is stored, transmitted in real-time and shared with warehouse management, inventory management, financial and other enterprise systems. As technological advancements lead to even higher levels of data transmission—in addition to an inevitably lower cost—RFID technology will become ubiquitous within the supply chain industry and other industries, increasing overall efficiencies and significantly improving the ROI.

Customer	Supplier
Reduced inventory due to lower safety stock since supplier can control lead time better than customer.	Reduced inventory because supplier knows how much and when customer is going to buy.
Reduced stock-outs because supplier keeps track of inventory movement and takes over responsibility for product availability.	Better forecasting because of real-time demand information from customer.
Increased customer satisfaction due to less stock-out.	Reduced purchase order errors and purchase returns by customer because of fewer mistakes.
Reduced forecasting and purchasing activities.	Improvements in service level agreement since supplier knows the need for item and thus orders right product and right time. Leads to supply chain cooperation.
Increased sales due to less stock outs.	Increased sales due to increased customer sales.

Figure 10 – 2: Benefits of Electronic Data Interchange

Source: 1EDISource Inc.

Electronic Data Interchange

The use of computerized communication to exchange business event data between companies, called **trading partners** is known as **Electronic Data Interchange (EDI)**. Generally used for high volume transactions running in batch mode, or in situations where critical just-in-time information is required between trading partners, EDI allows organizations to create electronic documents (such as purchase orders and invoices), transmit them over private networks or the Internet to their customers' and suppliers' computers, and receive electronic acknowledgements in return.

There are estimates that manual order entry can result in errors in as much as 50% of all documents and nearly 70% of all computer output becomes computer input. The goal of EDI is to reduce the amount of data capture and transcription activities, thereby saving time and reducing the chance of data entry errors for all documents that need to be transmitted between trading partners. Areas such as inventory management, transportation and distribution, administration and cash management all benefit from EDI.

EDI transmissions must be in a standardized format (common language) to be read by an organization's supplier and customer information systems. The recognized standard for EDI transmissions is **ANSIX12**, a format developed by the **American National Standards Institute (ANSI)**. Data for an EDI exchange originates from an ERP system. Major ERP vendors provide this technology as part of Core or will partner with a third party to provide this feature. Third party EDI providers are known as Value Added Networks. The outsourcing of this service relieves the outsourcer (and the ERP Vendor that must develop the technology) of setting up the security and transmission infrastructure necessary for conducting EDI. Figure 10 - 2 presents benefits of EDI to the customer and supplier.

Customer	Supplier
Lower inventory levels: purchase order takes less time to transmit.	Personnel reductions: There are estimates that as much as 70% of all computer output becomes computer input. With EDI, the supplier is relieved of the process of re-keying orders and verification of orders.
Quicker order acknowledgment: customer can find an alternative supplier if current supplier cannot provide the desired product (and when needed).	Elimination of problems and delays caused by customer order entry errors. Errors in order entry mean missed ship dates, shipment of wrong items or quantity, and lower customer satisfaction.
Reduced time spent matching supplier invoices to purchase orders and entering Accounts Payable information.	Improved Cash Flow: Time taken out of the invoicing/payment cycle improves the cash flow of the supplier.
No Back-Orders or Out-of-Stock.	Inventory reductions.

Figure 10 – 3: Benefits of Vendor Managed Inventory

Source: Tata Consulting Services.

Vendor Managed Inventory

Outsourcing the replenishment of inventory to suppliers, a form of business process outsourcing, is known as **Vendor Managed Inventory (VMI)**. In VMI, the supplier creates purchase orders based on the demand information exchanged by the retailer. The supplier assumes responsibility of inventory management for the customer. Because the supplier is now in charge of replenishment for the customer, theoretically both the customer and the supplier can maintain lower inventory levels due to better forecasting and replenishment. This approach amounts to outsourcing inventory management functions. Since the supplier is taking on that function, it is able to forecast more accurately based on sales information and can create the necessary purchase orders to optimize the customer's inventory. This is a backward replenishment model where the supplier determines the demand and then meets it. VMI was first applied in the grocery industry between companies like Procter and Gamble, a supplier, which began VMI efforts at and Wal-Mart, a distributor. Figure 10 - 3 presents benefits of VMI to the customer and supplier.

More SCM Technologies

Various other software solutions that can be integrated with ERP and improve supply chain efficiency include:

- Point of Sale (POS) systems to capture accurate sales data.

- Radio Frequency terminals to capture accurate inventory receipts and improve the accuracy of physical inventories.

- Warehouse management systems.

- Global data repositories to help improve product identification and reduce errors.

- Vendor portals to facilitate collaboration.

- Transportation planning and management systems.

Summary

This chapter discusses production, inventory management, supply chain and related technologies that enable the efficiency, reliability, and performance of manufacturing companies. Modules that are integral to operations are production planning and inventory management. Bolt-ons to core manufacturing modules include applications such as plant maintenance and service management. Technologies and methods that enable the SCM include RFID, EDI, VMI and Lean Manufacturing. The overall goal of these technologies and methodologies is to make the processes of acquiring materials, producing goods and delivery to customers through the supply chain as efficient as possible. ERP is the battering ram that integrates all that information together in a single application, and SCM applications benefit from having a single authoritative source to go to for real-time information.

Keywords

American National Standards Institute (ANSI)

ANSIX12

Bill of Material (BOM)

Capacity Requirements Planning (CRP)

Closed Loop MRP

Cost accounting

Economic Order Quantity (EOQ)

Electronic Data Interchange (EDI)

Engineering BOM

Feedback loop

Inventory Management

Inventory Status File

Just-in-time manufacturing

Lean manufacturing

Lead time

Manufacturing BOM

Master Production Schedule (MPS)

Material Requirements Planning (MRP)

Motion

Move order

Plant Maintenance

Production Planning

Quality Management

Radio Frequency Identification Data (RFID)

Service Management

Supply Chain Management (SCM)

Trading partner

Vendor Managed Inventory (VMI)

Wait state

Warehouse Management System (WMS)

Quick Review

1. True/False: The immediate predecessor of ERP system is Material Requirements Planning systems.

2. True/False: The Bill of Material is a full list of all the necessary raw materials needed to produce a single item.

3. _____ module of an ERP system helps an organization by building quality tasks into the production process in all phases of a product, from planning through use.

4. The technology used to exchange business event data electronically between companies in a standardized format is called _____.

5. The outsourcing of inventory replenishment to suppliers, essentially a form of business process outsourcing, is called _____.

Questions to Consider

1. List and define each step in the evolution of ERP systems in manufacturing.

2. What are the three files that are integral to MRP systems? Define each.

3. What tasks need to interface with each other in manufacturing?

4. For manufacturing companies adopting an ERP system, what key modules should they look at? What does each do?

5. What are some benefits of RFID to companies?

6. List benefits of EDI to the customer and supplier.

7. List benefits of VMI to the customer and supplier.

References

123 EDI. (2007). *EDI Supplier Benefits*. Retrieved June 1, 2008, from http://www.123edi.com/edi-supplier-benefits-101.asp

1 EDI Source, Inc. (2003). *EDI 101: A Guide to EDI*. White Paper. Retrieved from http://www.1edisource.com/

Anonymous. (2008). *Materials requirements planning*. Retrieved from http://en.wikipedia.org/wiki/Material_Resource_Planning

Inman, R. (2007). *Manufacturing Resource Planning*. Retrieved June 1, 2008, from http://www.referenceforbusiness.com/management/Log-Mar/Manufacturing-Resources-Planning.html

Jutras, C. (2007). *The 2007 ERP in Manufacturing Benchmark Report*. Aberdeen Group White Paper. Retrieved from http://www.aberdeen.com/summary/report/benchmark/RA_ERP_CJ_3361.asp

QAD. http://www.qad.com/manufacturing-inventory-software.html.

Krotov, V. (2008). *RFID: Thinking Outside of the Supply Chain*. Retrieved June 1, 2008, from http://www.cio.com/article/174108/RFID_Thinking_Outside_of_the_Supply_Chain

Kumar, P., & Kumar, M. (2003). *Vendor Managed Inventory in Retail Industry*. Tata Consulting White Paper. Retrieved from http://www.tcs.com/resources/white_papers/ Pages/ VendorManagedInventoryinRetailIndustry.aspx

Martec International. (2004). *Smarter Supply Chain Utilization for the Retailer*. Microsoft White Paper Retrieved from http://download.microsoft.com/download/6/c/3/6c343a53-5e25-488b-9f00-2419fe255950/Smarter_Supply_Chain.pdf

Microsoft. (2004). *Microsoft and RFID*. Microsoft White Paper. Retrieved from http://whitepapers.silicon.com/0,39024759,60178323p,00.htm

Oracle. (2005). *JD Edwards EnterpriseOne Quality Management Data Sheet*. Retrieved May 2, 2008, from http://www.oracle.com/media/peoplesoft/en/pdf/datasheets/e1_scm_ds_qualitymgmt_5 1205.pdf

Oracle. (2007). *JD Edwards EnterpriseOne Preventive Maintenance Data Sheet*. Retrieved May 2, 2008, from http://www.oracle.com/media/peoplesoft/en/pdf/datasheets/e1_cam_ds_preventive_mai ntenance.pdf

Wailgum, T. (2008). *Supply Chain Spending On the Rise*. Retrieved May 2, 2008, from http://www.cio.com/article/168700/Supply_Chain_Spending_On_the_Rise

Worthen. B. (2008). *ABC: An Introduction to Supply Chain Management*. Retrieved November 8, 2008, from http://www.cio.com/article/40940

Womack, J., Jones, D., & Roos, D. (1990). *The Machine that Changed the World: The Story of Lean Production*. New York, NY: HarperCollins.

Chapter

11

Auditing ERP and Risk

Objectives

- Know the objectives of internal controls.

- Understand the Enterprise Risk Management Framework.

- Differentiate between IT General Controls and Application Controls.

- Recognize the types of IT General Controls and examples of Application Controls.

- Be familiar with the AICPA SAS 70 audit purpose and uses.

Introduction

In Chapter 8, we studied how ERP systems support financial and accounting processes. Among these processes, we discussed how financial accounting generated information in the form of statements and reports to stakeholders outside the business such as stockholders and regulators. In addition, we explored the ways businesses add value by making better use of the information generated by the activities in which they engage. Consequently, the ERP systems that generate and store this information must be reliable and secure. The reliability of these systems and accuracy of this information is best demonstrated by a comprehensive and structured audit process, while the security of this information is supported by a thorough approach to risk management. This chapter will look at risk management and ERP auditing objectives.

Internal Controls

The input and subsequent processing of data must be controlled to assure the accuracy of the output. Internal controls are set in place to reduce or eliminate the possibility that inaccurate, incomplete or unauthorized information is entered into the system and to ensure the information in the system is properly processed to produce reliable output. Internal controls can be dictated by company leadership such as its Board of Directors or management and, to the extent that the ERP technology is used to enforce those controls, they would be implemented and monitored by the system's support staff in such a way that their effectiveness is assured. Internal controls seek to meet objectives in:

- Effectiveness and efficiency of operations – Addresses an entity's basic business objectives, including performance and profitability goals and safeguarding of resources.

- Reliability of financial reporting – Relates to the preparation of reliable published financial statements, including interim and condensed financial statements and selected financial data derived from such statements, such as earnings releases, reported publicly.

- Compliance with applicable laws and regulations – Consists of complying with those laws and regulations to which the entity is subject.

For public companies, government entities, or those in a regulated industry in the United States, internal controls over information systems that process financial information must be audited annually. These audits often involve public accounting firms that are specialists in ERP systems and the audit process. As an objective third-party, these auditors have an interest in finding controls that are ineffective, are not enforced, or otherwise expose the system and its data to potentially risky circumstances. As auditors identify such issues, the company must move to remediate the control and demonstrate how the original objectives are now achieved. These audit reports are included in the entity's year-end financial statement publications. Additionally, because of a number of high profile corporate fraud cases such as Enron and WorldCom, regulators have imposed new requirements on publicly traded companies governing the effectiveness of their internal controls. **The Sarbanes-Oxley Act of 2002 (SOX)** is one example of regulatory attempts to spotlight internal controls. Pursuant to SOX Section 404, management at publicly-traded companies must:

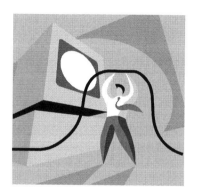

- Establish, document, and maintain internal controls and procedures over financial reporting.

- Audit the effectiveness of internal controls and procedures over financial reporting.

- Assess the deficiencies to determine the effectiveness of its internal controls over financial reporting.

The Public Committee Accounting Oversight Board (PCAOB) was created as a result of SOX as a private sector non-profit organization to oversee the auditors of public accounting firms. Recently they issued Auditing Standard No. 5 which states that the objective of an audit of internal control over financial reporting is "to express an opinion on the effectiveness of the company's internal control over financial reporting." The auditor must plan and perform the audit to "obtain competent evidence that is sufficient to obtain reasonable assurance about whether material weaknesses exist as of the date specified in management's assessment."

While these requirements are specifically targeted at publicly traded companies, many privately-held companies also seek to meet these requirements and undertake similar audits for various reasons.

For example, such an auditor's report may help a company as they seek financing; indeed, prospective lenders may require such an audit. In addition, taking steps toward acting like a public company, or becoming "SOX Ready," may make a company more attractive as a takeover target by lowering the risk for acquisition-minded companies and their underwriters.

Enterprise Risk Management

Internal controls are designed to prevent the introduction of inaccurate information into the system as well as to ensure the proper processing of that information and the generation of the system's output. These inaccuracies may arise accidentally, such as when a transaction is entered incorrectly by a poorly trained employee, or they may arise intentionally, such as when an employee seeks to alter data in a nefarious scheme to defraud the company. Companies routinely face both risks.

Generally speaking, a **risk** is the potential an event (or series of events) that can adversely affect the achievement of a company's objectives. While positive events can create opportunities and value for the organization, risks can prevent value creation or erode existing value. **Risk management** includes the activities that identify the threats the company faces as well as the subsequent actions taken to minimize the potential negative impacts that these threats may present. By implementing internal controls, companies are practicing risk management. In the context of a large company, **Enterprise Risk Management (ERM)** deals with risks and opportunities affecting value creation or preservation, and includes:

- Programs established by the company's board of directors often focused in the office of a formal Risk Manager.

- Gathering risk management input into all phases of the company's operations from corporate strategy to basic tasks.

- Exercises intended to identify potential events that may affect the entity.

- Risk management techniques to move the risk within the company's risk appetite.

- Providing reasonable assurance regarding the achievement of corporate objectives.

The fundamental concepts of this approach to ERM include:

- Risk management is an ongoing process.

- Risk management is affected by people at every level of the organization.

- Risks must be aggressively identified.

- Risks should be managed so that the risk falls within the company's risk appetite specifically in regard to both costs and benefits.

ERP and Risk

Earlier we discussed that the implementation of an ERP system is often the most significant information technology investment a company may ever make, in many cases costing millions of dollars. The scale of this effort and the intricate nature of these systems introduce a multitude of risks that must themselves be managed. A recent Gartner Study indicated that 20% of all new ERP systems implementations fail at a huge cost to companies and government agencies. Early involvement by IT Auditors can help reduce the chances of failures by timely identification of problems to Senior Management.

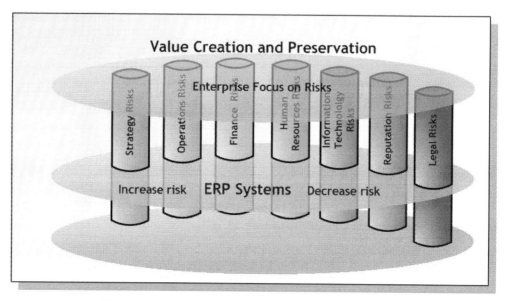

Figure 11 – 1: The Relationship between ERP and Risk

Each stage of the ERP life cycle involves risks from the planning phase to "go live." After implementation, an ERP system must be managed properly to minimize the negative impacts of risks. Figure 11 - 1 shows the many different types of risks that can impact an organization. It also shows that ERP systems cut across all of the risk categories. Since ERP systems are the central building block of a company's information systems, managing all of the company's business processes, transactions, and events, they can both decrease and increase firm risk. Figure 11 - 1 shows that ERP can create opportunities (positive impact) or create risk (negative impact.) For example, inadequate training on the ERP system or lay-offs during or after the ERP implementation can negatively impact both human capital risks and reputation risks. Lack of reengineering can increase operational risks. Failure to configure controls over user access to the system can increase IT risk.

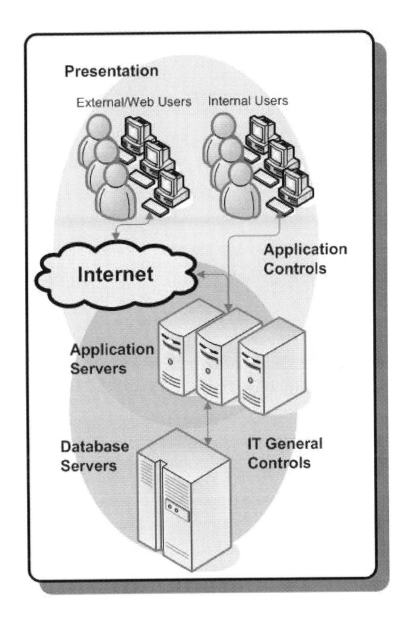

Figure 11 - 2: Three-Tier Architecture

As we know, ERP systems also create a host of opportunities for the company. Standardizing company-wide locations on common business processes and data integration can decrease operational risk. Centralizing data into one authoritative data source can decrease IT risk by reducing the number of individual systems that must be audited. Adopting the GRC module of Financials to assist with SOX compliance can decrease legal risks. Greater efficiencies can be attained through accelerated financial statement close processes, reducing the time needed to produce the financial statements and provide key information to Senior Management in real-time. While these are just a few examples, both positive and negative, ERP systems can impact risk in many ways. The next sections describe the types of controls and configurations that allow ERP systems to support these efforts to manage risks. These controls can be distinguished into one of two categories:

- **IT General Controls** – Support the technical environment in which ERP systems operate.

- **IT Application Controls** – Support the transactions within the ERP system assuring that the data that is entered and the processing and system output are accurate.

These controls must be in place for the **integrated audit**, a more holistic approach to auditing that entails more than just testing and verifying the accuracy of the amounts in the financial statements. The integrated audit places much greater emphasis on internal IT controls. Both corporate management and the financial statement auditors must attest that internal controls are in place throughout the organization. Management must have their own process in place to generate accurate financial statements and cannot simply rely on auditors and company management will have to remediate internal controls that perform inadequately. Figure 11 – 2 was also presented in Chapter 2, but we now show where IT General and IT Application controls are tested. Testing general controls means that the auditor attempts to gain an overall impression of the controls that are present in the environment surrounding the information systems. Application controls, which are built into the ERP system, enable and also limit the actions that a user can do through the interface and in the system. For auditor reliance that Application controls are working correctly as part of the year-end audit process, the auditor must first ascertain that the General IT controls are working properly. The reason for this is that changes to the applications must be performed in a controlled environment in order to ensure that none of the Application controls have been modified incorrectly.

IT General Controls

When processes and services are supported by information technology, logic rules can be embedded in the hardware and software to enforce business rules relating to access to information, authentication of users, and permissions of groups of users to execute groups of tasks. These controls are known as IT General Controls (ITGC) and are embedded in IT processes and services. They surround all the company's hardware and software applications and work to both secure and validate the information supported within an effective functioning ERP system. IT general controls include the following three types of control and are shown in Figure 11 – 3 as the pillars that support the application controls embedded in business processes.

- **Change Controls** – Changes to processes and data create an authoritative record of the people responsible for the change.

- **Information Security Controls** – Data can only be modified as defined by the business rules established for the processes the system supports.

- **Computer Operations Controls** – The hardware and software used to support business processes are protected from internal and external threats.

Here we see that the business processes for a typical inventory-intensive business such as a manufacturer across the top in red, are built on an ERP system that supports the objectives stacked in blue. These application controls, in turn, rely on the database, operating system, network and hardware resources which are supported by the ITGC change control, information security and computer operations. Let's study each of these pillars and identify the methods they use to support their role as IT general controls.

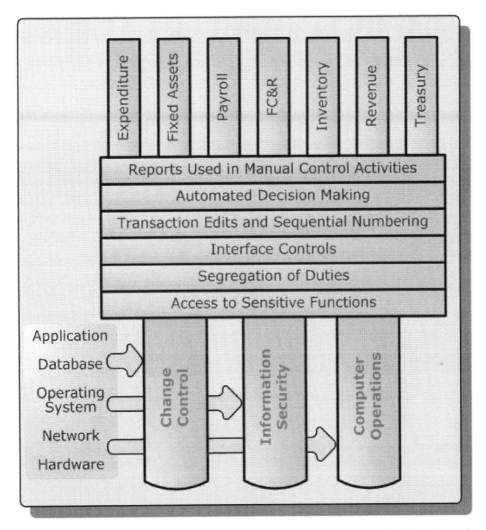

Figure 11 – 3: Relationship between IT General Controls and Application Controls

Source: Deloitte

Change Controls

The controls that govern the changes effected on the ERP system and the associated technical resources are called change controls. They seek to ensure that the development of and changes to these systems are properly designed, tested, validated and approved prior to moving their deployment in the live, **production system**. Deficiencies in change controls increase the potential for fraudulent and unauthorized changes, systematic transaction processing errors, and incorrect and unexpected application behavior and program logic.

Figure 11 - 4 depicts the stages through which programs should progress in a typical large IT environment to ensure that only authorized and tested programs are placed in production. Smaller companies may not have the resources to separate environments this way, and therefore other controls must be put in place to compensate for the lack of separation of duties.

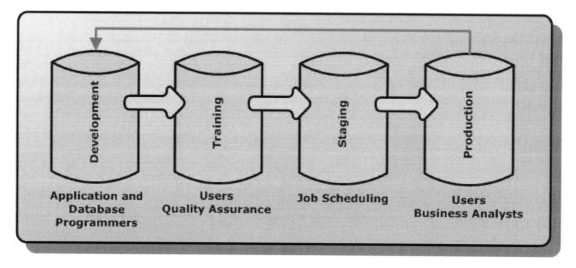

Figure 11 – 4: Change Controls

An important aspect of the approach in Figure 11 - 4 is that separate organizational entities are responsible for each stage in the change control process. This assures that the technical behavior of the systems used to support live operations meets expectations. Without these controls, the systems and software applications may be one on which:

- Program changes are not authorized by management prior to development.

- Changes are not tested prior to moving to production.

- There is improper segregation of duties among those involved in program change.

- Changes are not approved and/or accepted prior to implementation.

- Records regarding system changes do not reflect sufficient evidence of approvals and authorizations.

As modifications to databases and information systems are developed and deployed, the transitions from one business group to another should indicate that each modification meets objective criteria for promotion from one step to another. Specific change controls should be implemented to address deficiencies like the ones described earlier. In addition, each of these handoffs should be adequately documented to eliminate all doubt, from the auditor's point of view, that the change controls function properly. In smaller organizations, these levels of segregation may not always be available or possible. In these situations, auditors need to look for compensating controls that may reduce the risks and deficiencies noted. The deficiencies noted above may be resolved in an environment in which:

- Existing programs are not changed without a valid IT or business justification.

- Management in the business area requesting the change or IT Manager approves changes.

- Application programmers should make changes in a copy of production used for **development system** (also referred to as the "sandbox".)

- Once work is completed, application programmers place new programs in the testing area.

- Business users and other IT staff other than the developers test to make sure the environment applications respond suitably.

- After testing is complete, IT personnel not involved in the changes moves changes to either to production or to staging.

- Once testing is complete and sign-offs of quality have been obtained, an IT manager moves the programs into production.

Information Security Controls

These include both physical and logical controls that prevent unauthorized access to information system resources. Figure 11 - 5 shows the various resources exposed to risk, and that the most important asset to safeguard from risk is the application and the data it uses.

- Access to applications is not properly managed and rights are granted without adequate justification. Nor are these privileges monitored to assure that they remain current, complete and accurate.

- Improper segregation of duties allowed within programs such that users are able to circumvent controls exposing the system to unnecessary risks.

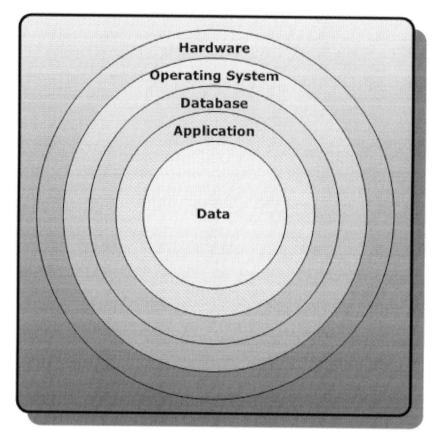

Figure 11 – 5: Information Resources Exposed to Risk

Some common deficiencies associated with information security controls are:

- Improper segregation of duties in setting up user accounts to access systems.

- Providing poor control over access privileges.

- Too many "administrators" or "super users" with unnecessary or essentially unfettered access.

- Authorizations for access are not evident, not adequately archived or not retained.

- Changes in users' roles not reflected in changes to system access; user access profiles can become obsolete quickly.

These deficiencies create increased potential for fraudulent transactions, the ability to override application controls, unauthorized changes to program calculations, and accidental changes to data and programs.

186

Information security controls would include those processes that may address deficiencies such as those noted. Such controls may be implemented such that:

- Users are required to have a unique user identifier in order to distinguish one user from another and establish accountability.

- Application owners authorize the nature and extent of user access privileges and such privileges are periodically reviewed by application owners to ensure access privileges remain appropriate.

- User access is controlled through passwords or other mechanisms. These are changed periodically.

- The IT security administrator is notified of employees who have changed roles and responsibilities, transferred, or been terminated. Access privileges of such individuals are immediately changed to reflect their new status.

- Roles and responsibilities related to IT security are defined and assigned to appropriate personnel.

- Use of privileged access such as administrators or "super users" is limited to appropriate personnel, and their access is logged and their necessity is periodically reviewed.

Computer Operations Controls

A review of the organization's data center is necessary to ensure that systems and programs run properly and timely and that appropriate infrastructure and environmental controls are in place. Computer Operations Controls are a critical element of ITGCs because they focus on the physical access to the systems that run the company. Because of the costs associated with protecting data from all types of attacks, companies must identify the potential risks facing their information systems and perform a cost-benefit analysis to determine the appropriate level of protection.

Common deficiencies related to the data center include:

- Poor job scheduling procedures.

- Insufficient system or data back-up.

- Poor physical security.

- Unmanaged third party service level agreements.

The first two deficiencies create increased potential for incomplete transaction and event processing, untimely or out of sequence system close, and the inability to recover lost data in the event of a system "crash." The last deficiency relates to outsourcing certain IT-related services to a service organization. Examples include application service providers, claims processing centers, Internet Service Providers, or other hosted data centers.

Controls to ensure that the above deficiencies over computer operations are minimized or eliminated include:

- Processing is monitored by management to ensure successful and timely completion, including a review and resolution of any exceptions.

- Automated scheduling tools have been implemented to ensure the authorization and completeness of the flow of processing.

- Automated data retention tools have been approved by management and implemented to manage the backup and retention data plan and schedule.

The physical assets of the company's IT platform are subject to risks. These risks reside in the data center, which must be designed to protect against both environmental and man-made hazards. The data center includes servers, workstations, and printers that support the systems and databases that generate the financial statements. Computer Operations (also known as Data Center) controls seek to address their exposure to risks arising from the tangible nature of these assets. These controls include:

- **Infrastructure and environmental controls** – An **uninterruptible power source (UPS)** or generator can protect against a power outage. A review should also check the adequacy of air conditioning (temperature, humidity), smoke detectors/fire suppression systems, a conducive clean and dust free environment, protection from floods and water seepage as well as neat and identifiable electrical and network cabling.

- **Redundant utilities and equipment** - A dual power source and water source should be used to ensure that computer systems will keep running in the event of a power outage. Lines should also be underground for extra protection.

- **Entry and exit** – Generally, entry points should include a main entrance and an exit which are locked. Both entry and exit points should be monitored with surveillance cameras and visitors to the data center should be logged. Security guards at the entry point add extra protection.

- **Authentication** – Authorized individuals should confirm their identity to enter the data center. Oftentimes employees will have to scan their employee badge for entry. For highly sensitive data centers, **two-factor identification** may be used whereby a badge must be accompanied by entering a password. **Biometrics** is the highest level of authentication and may be used to provide greater access controls.

Effective IT general controls help ensure that application controls function effectively over time. If IT general controls are ineffective, application controls may still operate successfully, but this fact will still affect both financial statement and internal control audit strategy. An IT general control deficiency does not directly result in a misstatement in the financial records. However, IT general controls should be evaluated in relation to their effect on the underlying application control. Classification of the IT general control will generally mirror the classification of the deficiency in the underlying application control. Meaning, if application controls are deficient, oftentimes IT general controls are found to be deficient as well. The following qualitative factors need to be considered when evaluating IT general control deficiencies:

- Nature and significance

- Pervasiveness of deficiency

- Complexity of systems environment

- Proximity of control to applications and data

- Transactional or systematic in nature

- Susceptibility to fraud

- Cause and frequency of known exceptions

- History of misstatements

- Competency of management and IT management

Application Controls

Application software, such as an ERP system, is the software that processes business transactions. The application comprehends data with reference to their business context. The rules pertaining to the business processes are integrated in the application software. Most users interact with the IT systems through application software, which enables and also limits the actions that the user can do. It is very important to subject application software to a thorough and detailed audit because the business processes and transactions involving money, material and services flow through the application.

The objectives of **application controls** are to ensure the completeness and accuracy of the records and the validity of the entries made therein. The first question that must be answered is "what does this application do?" In this regard, it is necessary for the IT auditor to have business knowledge and not just technical knowledge. Hence, the first step in reviewing application software is to understand the business function/activity that the software serves. This can be done through the study of the operating/work procedures of the organization or other reference material. Another alternative is to interview key personnel such as the controller, internal auditor, accounts receivable supervisor, accounts payable supervisor, and HR manager.

Examples of Application Controls	
Purchase to Pay	
On-line approval of documents	Sequential numbering of documents
On-line edit checks of data entry	Three-way match of purchase order, receiving report and vendor invoice
Duplicate payments	Integration with Electronic Data Interchange
Financial Closing & Reporting	
On-line edit checks of data entry	Automated roll-up of financial statements
On-line approvals of entries	Integration with other ERP modules
Fixed Assets	
Depreciation calculation	Gain/loss on fixed asset sale calculations
Payroll	
Integrated timekeeping with payroll inventory	Payroll/deduction calculations
Monitoring of inventory levels	Match of receipt to purchase orders
On-line edit checks data entry	Integration of inventory with shipping
Order to Cash	
Credit Checking	Automated pricing of orders
Integration with Electronic Data Interchange	Sequential numbering of documents
Integration of orders with shipping	Invoice and discount calculations
On-line approval of AR adjustments	On-line edit checks for data entry

Figure 11 - 6: Application Controls over Business Processes

Once this is done, it is necessary to identify the potential risks associated with the business activity/function served by the application (what can go wrong?) and to see how these risks are handled by the software (what controls it?).

Application controls can be programmed or **IT dependent manual controls**. **Programmed controls** are automated controls within the application such as data entry validation. IT dependent manual controls are procedures that are reliant on output from information systems. An example of the latter could be a manual calculation of accrual of revenue made from reports showing percentage of completion calculations on projects. Figure 11 - 6 shows common application controls over business processes including order to cash and purchase to pay.

Controls over Outsourcing Business and IT Functions

It has become commonplace for an enterprise to outsource some -or even all - of their information systems and management of business processes. For example, a company may use NetSuite to host their ERP system. This is known as **application outsourcing** and was discussed in Chapter 7. A company could also outsource the management and processing of payroll to a third party such as ADP discussed in Chapter 9. This type of outsourcing is known as **business process outsourcing (BPO)**, in which the service provider *performs* the function for the company. In both cases, the IT general and application controls over the function still must be tested to assure their proper operation. The Statement on Auditing Standards #70 (SAS 70), issued by the American Institute of Certified Public Accountants (AICPA) is the authoritative source for service organizations and mandates that they disclose their internal control activities and processes to their customers and their customers' auditors in a uniform reporting format. The SAS 70 exam covers controls over service organizations and must be part of the customer's financial statement audit.

The AICPA SAS 70

A **SAS 70** examination and certification signifies that a service organization has had its control objectives and control activities examined by an independent public accounting firm. The audit, which is performed by the service organization's public accounting firm, does not necessarily have to encompass the entire organization. The areas that need to be audited include those systems that process transactions or provide data processing services to customers.

The report, issued by the public accounting firm, can be adjusted to specifically identify the applicable data centers, operating environments, and applications that are covered in the audit. Since the purpose of a SAS 70 audit is to provide information concerning the service organization's internal control environment, control elements at the organizational level will be included in the engagement.

At the conclusion of a SAS 70 engagement, a **Service Auditor's Report** will be issued to the service organization for distribution to its customers who request it for auditing purposes. However, the user organization is accountable for obtaining the audit report and passing it along to their auditors. This process should be formally communicated by both parties through an engagement letter.

There are two types of reports that can be issued to these service organizations, **Type I** and **Type II**. A Type I report describes the service organization's description of controls at a specific point in time. This report includes the service auditor's opinion on the fairness of the presentation of the service organization's description of controls that had been placed in operation and the suitability of the design of the controls to achieve the specified control objectives. This report does not present an opinion on the operating effectiveness of the controls and therefore has limited reliance by the external auditors, who often are required to perform additional tests to ascertain controls at the third-party service provider.

A Type II report not only includes the service organization's description of controls, but also includes detailed testing of the service organization's controls over a minimum six month period. The testing then is a basis for the Type II Service Auditor's Report, which includes the service auditor's opinion on whether the specific controls were operating effectively during the period under review. Auditors of the company using the services of the service organization highly prefer the Type II as it can serve as first hand testing in conjunction with the financial statement audit. The Type I cannot be used for this purpose.

Non-SAS 70 Factors

A SAS 70 audit provides assurance to consumers of third party services. The information provided in these reports may not include everything a user organization should know. Here are few other things an organization should consider:

- Familiarity with what is being outsourced to understand the level of risk management that should be extended.

- Understanding of the risks and dependencies, regulations and compliance controls.

- Review of service provider's risk management level. Know key policies, procedures and audit findings found from a SAS 70 report.

- Inquire of employee training and background checks.

- Ensure data is protected appropriately.

- Request transparency for monitoring and controlling data and services housed at the service organization.

- Create a clear and explicit **Service Level Agreement (SLA)** and have it reviewed by an attorney.

IT Certifications

In today's complex business environment, which demands optimal utilization of information technology in the midst of mounting security threats and expanding government regulations, opportunities exist for accounting professionals who can leverage their core competencies with knowledge of information systems. The market for systems-related engagements has expanded, and the accounting profession has seized opportunities to redefine and rethink its practices. Fueled by the explosion of IT-related services, IT audit professionals are in great demand and in many cases are commanding higher salaries than their financial statement audit counterparts.

Accounting professionals in IT audit or whose jobs require knowledge of the IT infrastructure of a firm use a wide variety of skills ranging from managerial to highly technical in carrying out this professional function. Certification in IT-related fields gives accountants a "stamp of approval" among systems professionals. Along with business experience, certifications can imbue in accountants the competence and proficiency they need to excel in this highly technical world.

A number of IT/IS certifications help differentiate professionals in the marketplace. Some of these certifications have been around for many years; others have been developed more recently. For an accounting professional, choosing the most appropriate certification depends on many factors, including level of technical expertise, business experience, education, and desired career path. The following are brief descriptions of IT/IS certifications, including criteria for certification and status of the credential

Certified Information System Auditor

The **CISA** is the flagship certification of the **Information Systems Audit and Control Association (ISACA)** qualifying an individual as globally proficient in the areas of IS audit, control, and security. Established in 1978, the CISA title has been earned by more than 55,000 professionals in auditing, accounting, and IT security and governance. The CISA is becoming increasingly recognized by employers and professionals alike as the premier IT audit certification. The CISA cover six main areas of practice: IS audit process, IT governance, systems and infrastructure lifecycle management, IT service delivery and support, protection of information assets, and business continuity and disaster recovery.

Certified Information Security Manager

Offered by ISACA, the **CISM** is geared towards the changing role of the security manager and bridges the knowledge gap between business strategy and IT security. This certification is relevant for experienced information security managers, with its business-oriented focus, addressing enterprise-wide risk administration issues in the design, management, and assessment of information security. Since the CISM certification was introduced in 2002, it has since been earned by nearly 8,000 professionals.

Certified Information Technology Professional

Offered by the **American Institute of Certified Public Accountants (AICPA)**, the **CITP** certification recognizes a CPA's ability to bridge the gap between technology and business. In contrast to other IT certifications that require no previous credential, the CITP can only be obtained by licensed CPA's. Currently there are approximately 1700 CITP Credential Members.

Certified Information System Security Professional

Offered since 1995 by the **International Information Systems Security Certification Consortium (ISC)** the **CISSP** certification is emerging as one of the leading and most well known certifications for professionals in information security. As of June 23, 2008, the ISC reports certifying more than 58,800 information security professionals in over 130 countries. The CISSP exam tests a common body of knowledge fundamentally based on the information security and assurance tenets of confidentiality, integrity and availability , and attempts to balance the three across ten areas of interest, which are also called domains. Examples of domains include access controls, cryptography, business continuity and disaster recovery, and telecommunications and network security.

Certified in the Governance of Enterprise IT

ISACA's newest certification, the **CGEIT**, is designed to recognize the knowledge and application of IT governance principles and practices. **IT governance** is an important element of enterprise governance and consists of the leadership and organizational structures and processes that ensure that the organization's IT sustains and extends the organization's strategies and objectives. It allows professionals to effectively handle the needs of growing business demands that require a comprehensive IT governance program that defines responsibility and accountability across the entire enterprise. The CGEIT encompasses the five focus areas laid out in COBIT: IT governance-strategic alignment, resource management, risk management, performance measurement and value delivery-as well as on frameworks that support IT governance.

COBIT

The certifications discussed above are helpful for professionals performing IT related services; however, the organizations using these services need some form of guidance as well. The IT Governance Institute, created in 1998, designed and created the **Control Objectives for Information and related Technology (COBIT)** guidance. COBIT is increasingly becoming the internationally set of guidance materials for implementation of effective IT governance and controls and maximization of IT benefits throughout an enterprise. This guidance is the generally accepted internal control framework for IT. COBIT provides best practices across four domains including:

COBIT Mission

To research, develop, publicize and promote an authoritative, up-to-date, internationally accepted IT governance control framework for adoption by enterprises and day-to-day use by business managers, IT professionals and assurance professionals.

Source: ISACA

- Plan and Organize

- Acquire and Implement

- Deliver and Support

- Monitor and Evaluate

Each domain is further broken down into process objectives and then specific tests for those objectives. For instance, under Deliver and Support domain, one process is Manage Third Party Services. This would include obtaining a SAS 70 report for IT services that are outsourced to a service organization.

Summary

While the benefits of ERP systems have been widely discussed in this book, ERP systems can create a host of risks as well. Properly managing these risks in concert is essential to an ERM initiative. Two types of controls over IT include general and application controls. Classifications of IT general controls are change controls, information security controls and computer operations controls. Application controls are controls programmed into the ERP system and are only as good as the general controls that surround the system. General and application controls must be in place regardless of whether systems that support transaction processing (including ERP) are kept in-house or outsourced. The SAS 70 gives guidance on how these controls are tested, the scope of the testing, and the communication of findings to the outsourcer's auditors. Professionals interested in IT governance, security and audit can obtain certifications that differentiate them as technically competent. Most of these are issued by ISACA, which also developed COBIT as authoritative guidance for IT governance and conducting IT audits.

Keywords

American Institute of Certified Public Accountants (AICPA)

Application controls

Application outsourcing

Authentication

Biometrics

Business process outsourcing (BPO)

Certified Information Security Manager (CISM)

Certified Information System Auditor (CISA)

Certified Information System Security Professional (CISSP)

Certified Information Technology Professional (CITP)

Certified in the Governance of Enterprise IT (CGEIT)

Change Controls

Computer Operations Controls

Control Objectives for Information and related Technology (COBIT)

Development system

Enterprise Risk Management (ERM)

Information Security Controls

Information Systems Audit and Control Association (ISACA)

Integrated audit

International Information Systems Security Certification Consortium (ISC)

IT Application Controls

IT dependent manual controls

IT General Controls

IT governance

Production system

Programmed controls

Public Committee Accounting Oversight Board (PCAOB)

Risk

Risk management

Sarbanes-Oxley Act of 2002 (SOX)

SAS 70 Type I

SAS 70 Type II

Service Auditor's Report

Service Level Agreement (SLA)

Two-factor identification

Uninterruptible power source (UPS)

Quick Review

1. True/False: IT general controls include change controls and application controls.

2. True/False: The SAS 70 Type II audit is the preferred type of audit because it covers testing of controls.

3. _____ controls focus on the physical access to the systems that run the company.

4. Programmers should make changes to application software in the _____ environment.

5. The _____ certification qualifies an individual as globally proficient in the area of IS audit, control, and security

Questions to Consider

1. When conducting a review of IT General controls, which areas should the auditor examine?

2. Explain the difference between a SAS 70 Type I and Type II report.

3. What is the importance of COBIT?

4. List the IT-related certifications and the focus of each.

References

Bradford, M., & Houston, M. (2006). IT and the Accounting Profession: Using IT Certifications to Prove Your Worth. *Interim Report.*

ISACA. (2008). http://www.isaca.org/

ERP-Implementation-Resource.com. (2007). *ERP Implementation Risks.* Retrieved April 10, 2008, from http://www.erp-implementation-resource.com/erp-implementation-risks.php

Kelley, D. (2007). *7 Tips for Secure Outsourcing.* Retrieved April 10, 2008, from http://www.cio.com/article/104805/_Tips_for_Secure_Outsourcing_

Lainhart, J. (2008). *Certification Proves its Worth to IT Security Professionals and Employers.* Retrieved March 8, 2008, from http://gocertify.com/article/ISACA-Certifications2.shtml

Margolis, D. (2007). *(ISC)2 to Intensify Requirements for CISSP.* Retrieved March 8, 2008, from http://www.certmag.com/read.php?in=2851

SAS70Solutions.com. (2008). http://www.sas70solutions.com/services.php

Scalet, S. (2005). *19 Ways to Build Physical Security into a Data Center.* Retrieved March 19, 2008, from http://www.csoonline.com/article/220665/_Ways_to_Build_Physical_Security_into_a_Data_Center?contentId=220665&slug=www.csoonline.com&

ERP Bolt-Ons: Business Intelligence, Performance Management, and Knowledge Management

Objectives:

- Be familiar with the ERP bolt-ons discussed in this chapter.

- Understand types of functionality within each bolt-on.

Introduction

Companies generate information from routine business operations that is stored in databases and legacy systems throughout the company. Oftentimes, ERP and other systems are good at processing

events and transactions, but are weak at analyzing and reporting information. The data is often too granular for serious knowledge discovery but are a gold mine of knowledge waiting to be discovered. The competitive advantage of IT can often be gained from bolt-ons to ERP systems that use analytics to tease knowledge and intelligence out of the operational data. In addition to improving decision-making and cutting costs, the business case rationale for implementation of these bolt-ons would be a greater focus on company strategy and the identification of problem areas and new business opportunities. Since ERP systems may not have sufficient data analysis functionality, bolt-on tools are often needed to unlock the gems of information waiting to be discovered. Several bolt-ons are discussed in this chapter: Business Intelligence, Performance Management and Knowledge Management. These systems individually or collectively can enable businesses to use their data strategically rather than merely operationally.

Business Intelligence

Business Intelligence (BI) is an interactive process for exploring and analyzing structured, domain-specific, information looking for trends and patterns, thereby producing valuable knowledge that provides insights and helps draw conclusions. It is a collection of technologies used to analyze data extracted from various business systems and data sources in order to reveal meaningful knowledge. Usually, BI projects will focus on certain domains such as customers, service operations, suppliers, products and competitors. As BI systems have become more robust, technology has allowed for timelier data uploads of batches of data from daily or weekly updates. . This more frequent processing provides greater currency to the trends that are identified and provide for more timely analysis.

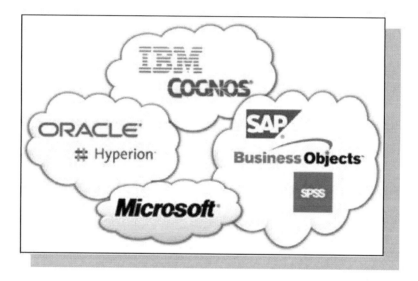

Figure 12 – 1: Business Intelligence Vendor Consolidation

Source: SAS Institute, Inc.

The process of BI includes:

- Start off with a business case of what analyzing the data should accomplish.

- Store data.

- Conduct studies.

- Solve problems/find opportunities/answer questions.

Many ERP systems include BI as a bolt-on. Best of breed vendors that have specialized in BI for a longer period of time also hold major market share. Figure 12 - 1 shows how the ERP giants have acquired leading BI/Analytics software vendors. SAS is not in the diagram because it remains the largest unaffiliated BI/Analytics software provider.

Type of Business Intelligence

BI is more than just corporate reporting or a set of tools to coax data out of enterprise systems. It is an umbrella term that includes many different tools. Some of these tools are rather basic and reactive in nature. Others are proactive and require more advanced statistical analysis for solving problems or finding opportunities.

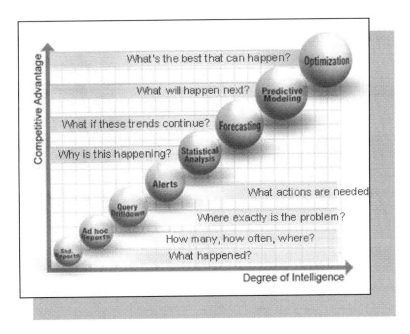

Figure 12 - 2: Reactive vs. Proactive Decision Making

Source: SAS Institute, Inc.

Figure 12 - 2 presents some of these tools on a graph showing the degree of intelligence. Green denotes common, low level functions of BI applications that generally provide little competitive advantage. Blue tools answer the "why" questions such as forecasting, optimization, and predictive modeling. These latter types of techniques are more apt to help companies gain a competitive advantage. The following sets of tools are included in many modern BI packages:

- **On-line Analytical Processing (OLAP)** - the fast analysis of shared multi-dimensional information (FASMI). At the core of an OLAP system is the OLAP cube, which consists of numerical facts called measures categorized by dimensions such as geography or type of product

- **Ad hoc Querying and Reporting** - using a query method (e.g., Query by Example, in which queries are built with menus, or using a query language such as Structured Query Language (SQL)) users can quickly get answers to their questions and develop their own reports and graphs.

- **Predefined Reports** - the reports, graphs and dashboards that come standard with a BI tool.

- **Scorecarding** and Dashboards- using color codes, such as Red, Yellow, Green, KPIs are able to quickly communicate when business performance is satisfactory or needs attention.

> Business Intelligence solutions are among CIO's top spending priorities for 2007 and beyond.
>
> *Source: CIO Magazine*

- **Alerts** - event notification to users based on predefined occurrences.

- **Extract, Transform, Load** - retrieving data from one or more sources within a company, transforming the data using data cleansing techniques, and loading the data into a data repository for BI analysis.

- **Data and Text Mining** - statistical analysis of large pools of historical data or text looking for correlations, trends, and patterns that may have escaped unnoticed. Data mining can be described as "what you didn't know you didn't know."

- **Analytics** - advanced statistical analysis including predictive modeling, optimization and forecasting.

Data Mining

Efforts that involve the statistical analysis of large quantities of data as a basis for sales forecasting, inventory management, or other applications is known as **data mining.** This involves sorting through data to identify patterns and establish relationships. Typically, data mining usually takes place outside the ERP system so that operational activity will not be slowed down. Also known as **knowledge discovery**, data mining may start with a hypothesis or research question, or users can allow the data to "tell its own story."

One of the more popular classes of data mining software is CRM, which can analyze customer sales histories, segment customers, and analyze salesperson performance.

Data mining has its roots in marketing and financial services. In marketing, data mining is used to understand customer buying behavior, understand hidden patterns of buying, make marketing efforts more targeted and identify opportunities that will move the company into position to gain greater market share. Some specific types of data mining activities in marketing include:

- **Profiling**: the process of using relevant information to describe characteristics of a group of customers and identify what discriminates them from other customers to determine drivers of their purchasing decisions. Example: Who are the better customers, and who are the high-risk customers?

- **Association**: sometimes certain events occur frequently together. Example: Grocery stores have learned that consumers that buy one product, such as diapers, will often buy another, such as beer. More detailed analysis revealed that the rule applied more strongly to men after 5:00 pm.

- **Market segmentation**: the process of dividing customers into mutually exclusive groups so that customers in one group are as similar as possible and customers in another group are as different as possible. Example: How do we market to females in their 30's that own their own home and live in a certain area of town?

- **Personalization**: often called one-to-one marketing, this is the process of marketing to the individual rather than to a segment. Example: Companies like Amazon and Expedia tailor their web pages to individual customers. By analyzing sales histories, they can determine the products and services that an individual customer might be interested in based on what has already been bought. The most profitable items can be pushed or sequenced to match expected norms derived from the historical data.

> "Every day, Walmart uploads 20 million point-of-sale transactions to a centralized database with 483 processors."
>
> *Source: Byte.com*

In financial services, data mining can be used to identify anomalies that may point to fraud or other security problems. Credit card companies have used data mining to develop models that can flag a transaction suspected of being fraudulent. One of these types of transactions is using a credit card at a gas station for a very small amount. Often, this could mean that a stolen credit card is being used for a small transaction to see if it is active. Insurance companies use data mining to determine if prospective or current customers are likely to create much higher payouts than others. One insurance company found that customers who drive red or black cars are more aggressive drivers than customers with white or yellow cars. Thus, color matters to this insurance company when pricing auto insurance.

Determinants to Using Business Intelligence Tools

Like any application adopted by an organization BI is only helpful if the end-users are actually using it. Research has determined the key factors that most influence the use of BI are:

- Perceived usefulness – potential users must be confident that the knowledge they gain from the tool will benefit their decision-making efforts.

- Ease of use – Users must be able to extract the desired knowledge without the need to navigate through a frustrating interface.

- Flexibility – The system must be able to respond to a wide range of requests for knowledge relevant to many different objectives.

Usefulness and ease of use are stronger determinants for usage, while flexibility has less of an impact. Regardless, BI can still provide a significant return and should be considered an important advantage. User training and help desk support can help boost the system's perception of usefulness and its ease of use and also work to ensure that the advantages of the system are attained quickly.

Data Stores for Business Intelligence

Data Warehouse

As data is gathered from the various domains and collected into a central data store, the storage facility begins to function as a **data warehouse**. The warehouse is a large relational database that combines pertinent data in an aggregate, summarized form suitable for enterprise wide data analysis, reporting, and management decision making. Data warehouses have the following characteristics, which are also presented in Figure 12 - 3:

- Subject oriented – The data are structured to retain the identity of the domain that generated it.

- Time variant – The activities that generate the data spans a certain range of time.

- Non-volatile – This is not active transaction data but data that remains after transactions are completed; once stored, the data are not changed except for a compelling reason.

- Integrated – The structure allows data arising from various domains, times and customers to be combined and compared.

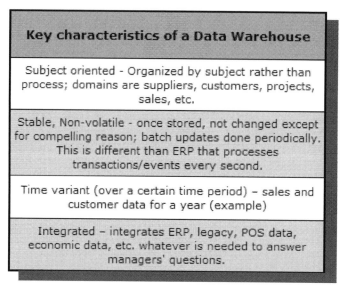

Figure 12 – 3: Key Characteristics of a Data Warehouse

Source: CIO Magazine

To populate a data warehouse, data is extracted from various sources such as ERP systems, legacy systems, and **point of sale (POS)** systems. It may be restructured and attributed to a domain and is stored in a large, efficient data management system specifically designed to support data warehouse and BI operations. Data from external sources such as competitor information, industry information, or public economic data can be combined with internal data. The process of supplementing data extracted with other pertinent data is known as **data enrichment**. Data from these systems are uploaded into the data warehouse using a batch process that adds data all at once from transactions closed over a specific period such as daily, weekly, or monthly.

Data Mart

A **data mart** is a subset of a data warehouse usually designed for a specific set of users. Whereas a data warehouse combines databases across an entire enterprise, data marts are usually smaller and focus on a particular subject or data context for a limited audience. An example would be a data mart designed for retail buyers or logistics managers. The key difference between a data mart and a data warehouse is that the creation of a data mart is predicated on a specific, predefined need for information to serve a target group of users. Any number of data marts might support different target groups within a single organization each one relevant to one or more business units for which it was designed. Data marts may or may not be dependent or related to other data marts in an organization.

Data Governance and Data Cleansing

Data lacking high quality is useless to an organization regardless of the supporting software in place. **Data governance** involves the creation and management of the organizational structures, policies, and processes needed to define, control, and ensure the quality of the enterprise data including criteria such as availability, usability, integrity, and security. A sound data governance program includes a data governance entity empowered by senior management, a defined set of procedures for data quality, and a plan to execute those procedures.

The creation of a data warehouse or mart to facilitate BI falls under the purview of data governance. Of course, the data warehouse implementation effort will include deploying the hardware and software that will make it an efficient system. In addition, the data that is moved into the data warehouse or mart from other data sources must be scrutinized to make sure it is an accurate reflection of the transactions and events. Not only must the records be checked for accuracy, but the relationships between records and tables must also be verified to assure that they can be used to provide new and meaningful insights into the historical record.

The central building block for BI is **data**, the raw facts and figures entered into an information system. In Chapter 2 we described how data is normalized into tables comprised of rows that represent a business record and columns that represent the data values related to that record. These records are the most fundamental component of any BI endeavor. The key to getting accurate insights from BI systems is standardizing data.

In order to provide the greatest meaning to the data in the data warehouse or mart, the data must be standardized, unambiguous, correct and complete. A process must be set in place by the data governance committee to make sure a data set will be consistent with other similar data sets in the system and the complications arising from errors or other inconsistencies in the creation of the original data records will be detected and resolved. This process, known as **data cleansing** or **data scrubbing,** must be applied to resolve these complications as they arise. The actual process of data cleansing may involve removing typos or validating and correcting values against a known list of entities. The validation may be **strict validation**, such as rejecting any address that does not have a valid ZIP code, or **fuzzy validation**, such as correcting records that partially match existing, known records.

Examples of data in need of cleansing include:

- J. Smith is found to be the same customer as John Smith in another system.

- A sale order date is recorded as 07/01/2008 in one system and 1 July 2008 in another.

- Inventory descriptions do not match many of the inventory numbers in one system.

- Some of the suppliers have no record of purchases made to them and thus the data to be stored on these suppliers is unnecessary.

Best Practices for Business Intelligence

A BI package can provide many benefits. However, there are a few consistent problems companies encounter during the process. The majority of the problems arise from inadequate planning, poor accounting of ROI, and people issues encountered during the process of implementing and beginning to use BI. Researchers have identified a number of best practices that will add value to the BI project:

- Clearly define business objectives and have a business case rationale prior to implementation.

- Cleanse data.

- Integrate all systems using the best data structuring alternatives available and avoid subsequent roadblocks resulting from poor data structure or fidelity or reliability.

- Train users both to shape the data as it is moved into the database as well as to manipulate the data to get the most meaningful and valuable answers.

- Deliver reports that provide the most value quickly and then tweak them. Do not spend too much time designing the perfect reports as needs change over time.

- Deploy BI with the idea that there are numbers out there that need to be found, and know roughly where they might be.

- Outline the specific benefits expected to be achieved, then do a reality check every quarter or six months.

Performance Management

While data mining may unlock valuable knowledge from historical records, **Performance Management (PM),** also known as **Business Performance Management (BPM),** tools are used to provide answers to the question "How well are we performing right now?" Examples of this kind of information include:

- A timer that indicates how long a call has been on hold.

- A counter that indicates the number of defects produced in a shift.

- A bar graph indicating the percentage of monthly sales projections currently reached for each region.

The subject of PM can be the company as a whole, division, region, department, employee, process or product. Regardless of the focus, PM tools help ensure that the company's objectives are consistently being followed in an effective and efficient manner. Software packages allow companies to automate PM using advanced presentation methodologies such as executive dashboards, scorecards, as well as advanced business intelligence and analytical applications. When properly implemented, PM bridges the gap between long-term strategies and day-to-day operations by aligning business measures with critical success factors identified by management. When BI tools are integrated with PM activities, companies are able to generate a set of KPIs designed to provide a clear and concise description of the company's health. Figure 12 – 4 presents ten characteristics of a good KPI.

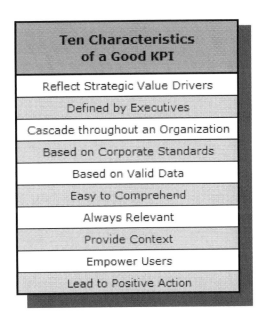

Figure 12 - 4: Ten Characteristics of a Good KPI

As organizations gather operational data, calculations using that data begin to provide meaningful measurements of performance. Oftentimes it may be difficult to figure out how to measure something like "increased data visibility" or "customer satisfaction." This is where a certain amount of ingenuity is required to construct a meaningful, accurate measure. For example:

- Dividing the number of orders delivered on time by the total number of order provides an "on time" ratio.

- Dividing the amount spent on labor in a month by the month's net sales provides the month's labor ratio.

- Dividing the number of satisfied customers by the total customer count provides a valid "customer satisfaction" ratio.

Calculations such as these, particularly when expressed as percentages, are known as **business metrics** and when viewed over time they provide meaningful measures of the company's performance. Historically, companies tended to focus more on financial metrics, such total sales, net profit, or ROI. While these provided accurate measurements, more recently, financial metrics have been criticized as backward-facing measures. More recently, as firms have embraced business process reengineering, the focus of their efforts tended more toward driving current and future performance. Consequently, while financial metrics are still important, other measure have been identified that supplement the financial perspective to provide a more meaningful, and balance

Business Intelligence (BI)	Business Performance Management (BPM)
Appeals to operations users and line-of-business (LOB) managers.	Appeals to financial applications users.
Embeds metrics analysis within internal processes to help users make timely business decisions, and to enable strategic or tactical planning.	Focuses on defined metrics to help users improve processes, and manage and increase performance.
Provides data needed to answer essential business issues and to plan and act based on the analysis of business problems.	Uses scorecarding and dashboarding to measure organizational metrics and to help organizations manage performance.

Figure 12 - 5: Business Intelligence versus Business Process Management

Source: Technology Evaluation Centers

Both BI and PM are focused on improving an organization's performance. However, some important differences should be noted (see Figure 12 - 5). The primary difference between BI and PM solutions is that while BI churns through historic transactional records to identify opportunities to gain an advantage, PM isolates specific data to indicate which process are currently operating at peak efficiency and which ones need immediate attention to avoid sub-optimal performance. The lines blur between these two tools as vendors offer packages that can perform a mixture of different functions.

The Balanced Scorecard

One popular type of performance management application is the **Balanced Scorecard**. In 1992, Drs. Robert Kaplan (Harvard Business School) and David Norton introduced the Balanced Scorecard as a type of performance management methodology building on prior methods for performance management such as Total Quality Management. The Balanced Scorecard is a structure around the way organizations measure how well they are functioning and how well they might do in the future. The concept entails mapping and translating complex business information into something that is understandable to everyone in the organization beginning with goals defined by the organization followed by scorecard measures. The measures generally include both corporate targets and business unit targets, which are then translated into individual measures and targets.

The central theme of the Balanced Scorecard methodology is that financial metrics are **lagging indicators**, providing knowledge of past activity; thus, financial metrics alone provide an incomplete picture of organizational performance. More strategic measures, **leading indicators**, are needed to "balance" financial metrics and set expectations for future activities. The concept behind the BS is that good performance in financial metrics does not necessarily indicate future success; poor performance in leading indicators may signal a future decline even though financials may look good. Following are explanations of the four perspectives of a Balanced Scorecard.

> "Oracle Balanced Scorecard is the preferred application to rapidly design, deploy and administer KPI-based custom performance management solutions. The Balanced Scorecard supports managers in closing the strategy-to-performance gap by helping them communicate strategic plans to their organizations, align their people and resources and focus them toward a set of common goals to manage the organization."
>
> *Source: Oracle*

Financial Perspective

From this perspective, the critical question is "*How do we look to shareholders*"? This perspective includes the traditional metrics that measure performance. Typical financial goals have to do with profitability, growth, and shareholder value.

Learning and Growth Perspective

From this perspective, the critical question is "*Can we continue to improve and create value?*" Metrics included in this perspective would capture the growth of the firm's human capital, the ability of employees to continue to improve long-term performance and the company's ability to move into and capture new markets.

Business Process Perspective

From this perspective, the critical question asks "*What can we do better than anyone else?*" Metrics based on this perspective tell managers how the business is running and whether or not products and services meet customer expectations. Companies should decide what processes and competencies they must excel at and specify measures for each. These metrics must be designed by those that know these processes most intimately.

Customer Perspective

From this perspective, the critical question asks "*How do our customers view us?*" Customers' concerns tend to fall into four categories: time, quality, service, and cost. Metrics in this perspective would focus on customer satisfaction as well as customer loyalty, market share, wallet capture and other customer focused metrics.

To put the balanced scorecard to work, companies should articulate goals for these aspects of their operation and then identify appropriate measures of performance toward those goals.

As the metrics are calculated, the scorecard takes shape reporting performance against these goals in the widely used format shown in Figure 12 - 6.

When the Balanced Scorecard was introduced it began to refocus companies that previously had relied on financial metrics to measure performance. Because of their tight focus on financial metrics, these performance measures often disregarded contemporary, value-creating opportunities and failed to identify or adequately assess the value-destroying threats facing the company.

ERP systems collect volumes of information, both financial and non-financial. And, as this information is integrated it is now easier to obtain a holistic view of cause and effect relationships. For instance, if customer satisfaction goes up over time we might see an increase in sales. This cause and effect relationship would be difficult to ascertain before ERP systems because these two metrics were in separate systems – marketing and accounting. In many cases, new software supported the collection of more information and this new information was manipulated to provide new, meaningful measures of performance that had never been contemplated. In many cases, processes were reengineered to allow the collection of information relevant to these new metrics and reduce many activities to a numerical form for collection, storage, display, and analysis.

Using the Balanced Scorecard

A sheet of paper with numbers on it can be created by one person and implemented by sheer force of authority. However, the point of a Balanced Scorecard is to:

- Align all members of an organization around common goals and strategies.

- Link initiatives to the strategy, making prioritization easier.

- Provide feedback to people on key issues, notably areas where they can have an impact.

- Provide an essential decision-making tool for everyone in the organization.

> "According to Bain & Co., 70% of organizations had at least partially implemented a balanced scorecard by 2006."
>
> *Source: CIO Magazine*

With these objectives in mind, the balanced scorecard enables management to identify the leading indicators that can predict future performance and gain additional insight into what drives performance. In a broader sense, the Balanced Scorecard is a *management system*, not merely a *measurement system*. It focuses attention on the company's most important goals first, and then makes sure that every action supports these goals. You justify the cost by virtue of the measurement itself and the results it presents. That's the ROI.

Example KPIs for a Balanced Scorecard	
Financial:	**Customer:**
Cash Flow	On-time Delivery Rate
ROI	Return Rate
Financial Result	Customer Satisfaction
Return on Capital Employed	Customer Retention
Return on Equity	Customer Growth
Internal Business Processes:	**Learning & Growth:**
Number of Activities	Investment Rate
Opportunity Success Rate	Absence Rate
Accident Ratios	Internal Promotion Rate
Defect Ratios	Employee Turnover
Inventory Turns	Average Training Hours

Figure 12 - 6: Example Balanced Scorecard KPIs

Balanced Scorecard Case Studies

Since its introduction in 1992, the BS has become a stable of management analysis. Many firms have embraced the Balanced Scorecard's call for focus on measures other than financial and have used it with remarkable results. Benefits of the Balanced Scorecard are shown in Figure 12 – 7. Below are notable real world case studies highlighting these benefits:

- **Nike Inc.:** This global athletic apparel company uses a balanced scorecard when evaluating suppliers. It looks at labor code compliance along with measures such as price, quality, and delivery time. Nike uses the tool to streamline its design methods and supply chain. Most importantly, it has helped manage workforces at foreign factories by developing more efficient production techniques. By reducing bottlenecks, Nike hopes to cut the amount of overtime required in Chinese factories and eliminate a major source of labor unease. "If you improve efficiency and innovation, it changes the cost equation", says Eric D. Sprunk, Nike's vice-president for global footwear operations

- **UMB Financial:** This Midwestern banking operation used the BS to differentiate between which metrics really drive the business and which are interesting, but irrelevant to the success of the company. As these metrics became more apparent through use of the BS, UMB was able to identify the markets and products the garnered the greatest ROI. More importantly, the company was able to identify the teams and the leaders of the teams that outperformed their coworkers and then leverage their expertise into their training and mentoring efforts.

As their metrics were refined, they were to support daily updates for their metrics and tie executive compensation to unit performance based on scorecard performance. Following the implementation, executives have become more focused on leading indicators and have found that their financial performance has improved dramatically.

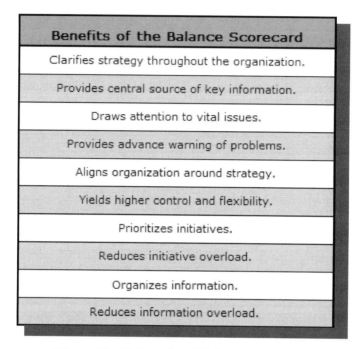

Figure 12 – 7: Benefits of Balanced Scorecard

Limitations of the Balanced Scorecard

The Balanced Scorecard can help companies identify targeted metrics within each of the four perspectives, but management must make sure they have followed through with all actions necessary to convert these measures to operational performance improvements that positively impact the bottom line. For example, if a company manages to achieve production efficiency, but does not know how to handle the excess human capacity, they will not see any cost savings, even though they may have met desired performance measures. Also, implementing the Balanced Scorecard will not add value to the organization if the company's initial strategy is not a profitable one. Companies must have a winning long-term strategy and performance measures that help them achieve this. Organizations must also recognize that the business environment is dynamic. Therefore, they should alter their mission, vision, and performance measures in the face of changing customer preferences, competition, and other market forces. Finally, each scorecard must have an owner. That owner makes the personal commitment to do everything possible to assure that the scorecard's goals are achieved and is held accountable for that commitment. In some cases, that may require an hour a month of effort, in other cases, it will be a full time job. On average, it's probably in the range of 10-20% of their time. Furthermore, every metric on their scorecard also needs to have an owner who is willing and able to make this very same commitment. A scorecard without an owner is nothing more than a report.

Knowledge Management

Knowledge is the information gained through experience, association, or having familiarity with something. Such knowledge includes who the company expert is on a certain subject or the solution to a complex problem that is used over and over again in various contexts. This knowledge must not be ignored or lost, but must be used by the company in order to improve operations. This is where Knowledge Management comes in. **Knowledge Management (KM)** is a directed process of figuring out what information a company has that could benefit others in the company (or shared with business partners), then devising ways of making it easily available. Put simply, KM is defined as "we don't know what we know." Knowledge suitable for managing in a company includes:

- Skills and knowledge that a company has developed about how to make its goods or services;

- Individual employees or groups of employees whose knowledge is deemed critical to a company's continued success; and

- A company's aggregation of documents about processes, customers, research results, and other information that might have value for a competitor (and which is not common knowledge.)

Explicit versus Tacit Knowledge

Knowledge can come in either explicit form or tacit form. **Explicit knowledge** is information that can be easily documented and codified. It includes such items as trademarks, legal agreements, customer lists, and patents. **Tacit knowledge** is contained in peoples' heads. It is what people know gleaned from years and years of working in a particular industry and/or for a particular company. Put simply, "It is the way things are done around here." Tacit knowledge is also considered intellectual capital, which is the brain-power of humans that can be put to work in the organization creating more power than if it was only possessed and used by its owner. As Andrew Carnegie once said "The only irreplaceable capital an organization has is its knowledge and its people." Both types of knowledge, when captured, become **organizational knowledge**, knowledge that has accumulated since inception of an organization.

> "75% of a company's worth may soon reside in its intellectual property."
>
> *Source: PriceWaterhouseCoopers*

What Knowledge is Useful?

According to the American Productivity and Quality Council (APQC), a nonprofit organization that helps companies learn from others' best practices, a formal audit is needed in which companies try and identify what knowledge they desire and where it may be located. This involves answering five questions:

- What processes in our organization have the biggest impact on the bottom line?

- What knowledge, if we had it, would make those processes work more effectively?

- Is this knowledge something we have inside the company but don't get it to the right places at the right times?

- Who would use the knowledge?

- How do we start bringing knowledge to people?

Reasons for Implementation of Knowledge Management Systems

KM has become a hot topic in business in recent years. Managers turn to KM for a number of reasons including:

- Sharing of best practices - Companies save millions a year by taking the knowledge from their best performers and applying it to similar situations elsewhere.

- Restructuring, downsizing, and outsourcing – Without effective mechanisms in place to capture knowledge of experienced employees, organizations make costly mistakes or have to pay again for knowledge they once had on tap.

- Knowledge can command a premium price in the market – Applied know-hose can enhance the value (and hence the price) of products and services.

- Globalization and competition – Many organizations rely on knowledge to create their strategic advantage. With available knowledge widely dispersed and fragmented organizations often waste valuable time and resources in reinventing the wheel or failing to access the highest quality knowledge and expertise that is available.

- Successful innovation – Companies applying knowledge management methods have found that through knowledge networking they can create new products and services faster and better.

- Supply chain integration – As companies turn toward their up-stream and down-stream supply chains for tighter process integration, the ability to transfer knowledge about the products and processes among supply chain partners becomes more critical.

In light of these forces in the modern business environment, companies have turned to KM to convert the knowledge in their employees' heads to knowledge that is accessible to the entire organization. Aggressively managing this knowledge enhances organizational learning as knowledge is shared across the enterprise and possibly the extended enterprise including customers and suppliers.

Creating a Knowledge Management System

With other applications and initiatives, a KM system should be a strategic business initiative, complimenting existing organizational objectives and a solid business case should be in place before proceeding. Creating a knowledge management system is a multi-step process involves the following steps.

- Recognize what employees know that is valuable and is not currently being shared.

- Create formal procedures to implement the system. This includes creation of a knowledge leader to promote the agenda and knowledge teams that include people from all disciplines to develop the methods and skills.

- Create a knowledgebase including best practices, expertise directories, market intelligence etc.

- Set up an enterprise portal that gives access to explicit as well as connections to experts (tacit knowledge).

- Give employees incentives for both sharing their knowledge as well as using others' knowledge.

> "80% of corporate knowledge flows through informal groupings – these are normally networks that businesses have little awareness of and zero control over."
>
> *Source: Lotus/IBM*

Without the aforementioned steps, knowledge is never discovered or passed along. Workers must constantly be reinventing the wheel. Creating incentives for knowledge sharing is a critical component of knowledge management. A company's KM initiative should be an enterprise-wide effort, lead by C-level executives. The CIO should provide insight to the KM program, but should not lead the initiative. This is because knowledge management should be centered on achieving corporate objectives and should not merely be a technological solution.

Texas Instruments (TI), when implementing their knowledge management system, had to change their incentive system to reward employees based on their collective efforts, rather than individual efforts. Their KM system allowed them to disseminate best practices throughout their semiconductor plants. Ultimately KM at Texas Instrument enabled them to respond more quickly to market demands and save over $1 billion.

Organizations that Benefit Most from Knowledge Management

Organizational size, company culture, and employee turnover are three important factors that influence the impact KM has on an organization. Smaller companies, or companies with one office, tend to be more aware of what is going on in the organization, and what person should be contacted for what issue. Larger organizations with hundreds of employees in geographically disbursed offices would benefit most from a formal KM program. In addition, some organizations have a culture that supports knowledge sharing more than others. Sometimes a formal knowledge management system is not needed if the company has a strong informal network of individuals who readily share information with others. Finally, a formal KM system would greatly benefit those organizations that have high turnover. Without a formal KM system, valuable knowledge is lost as soon as that employee leaves the company.

Benefits of Knowledge Management

Benefits of KM can not only improve organizational efficiency, but also cut costs and increase earnings. An effective knowledge management system allows companies to achieve one or more of the following benefits:

- Foster innovation by encouraging the free flow of ideas.

- Improve customer service by streamlining response time. This is where CRM and possible using a knowledgebase (frequently asked questions (FAQs) are an example) rather than over the phone.

- Boost revenues by getting projects and services to market faster.

- Enhance employee retention rates by recognizing the value of employees' knowledge and rewarding them for it.

- Streamline operations and reduce costs by eliminating redundant or unnecessary processes.

Obstacles to Successful Knowledge Management

The biggest challenge reported by practitioners is that of changing the culture from "knowledge is power" to "knowledge sharing is power." Other common obstacles are:

- Starting too big - Companies that seek to implement KM systems should start small. Piloting a knowledge sharing program in a small department or business unit for six to nine months would be beneficial before the program is rolled out company-wide.

- Relying on technological shortcuts - A KM system should not merely entail storing data in a large database. Data needs to be organized in such a way that people know where to find it. The information that is retained should only be useful information. Information that is considered a company 'best practice' should be documented in the policy or procedure manuals and/or incorporated in training programs.

- Not modeling the behavior - Managers, too, need to incorporate KM into their own behavior. They should understand how existing knowledge is leveraged and how to share knowledge gained on past projects. Companies should also establish metrics that define what they want to achieve from KM and when.

- Treating KM as a one-off project or quick-win – KM is a commitment to the long term – the organization's future prosperity.

- Ignoring the power of rewards - Employees have a natural reluctance to share knowledge because it means they are giving up an advantage they have over others in the organizations that do not possess this knowledge. After all, it is often the knowledge gained from experience that enables employees to move up the company ladder. Rewards can come in various forms. Buckman Laboratories, a chemical magnate, has used monetary compensation as a reward. Giant Eagle, a grocery retailer and distributor, uses peer recognition and embed use into its formal yearly evaluations. Because knowledge sharing is an unnatural act, linking KM directly to job performance, creating a safe climate for people to share, recognizing people who contribute is an essential component to an effective KM program.

- Ongoing maintenance - A KM system is not something that can be implemented once and ignored. It must be continually maintained to ensure that only relevant knowledge is retained. Companies want to avoid knowledge obsolescence by constantly amending, updating, and deleting data within the KM program. Appointing a formal **Knowledge Coordinator**, who will oversee these processes, is considered a best practice for KM.

- Not finding the time – With so many initiatives vying for attention, it is easy to sideline more challenging issues like KM.

- Individual disciplines or "turf wars" – KM goes beyond the remit of any single function.

Measuring the Value from Knowledge Management a System

One of the main objectives for a KM system is to reduce time and costs associated with solving problems and answering questions and to give proven, consistent and accurate answers. These objectives of efficiency and effectiveness are the "low hanging fruit" and goals and measures can easily be developed to and monitored post go-live to make sure the system is a success. Efficiency has to do with leveraging knowledge-based assets to improve processes. Metrics for efficiency could include:

- Diagnostic resource use - the percentage of times that a customers and support representatives leverage existing tools and knowledge resources to diagnose and resolve issues. >67%

- Talk time - The time it takes to convey an answer to a customer by phone. 13.2 minutes.

Effectiveness refers to the impact the KM system has on providing accurate, timely, and complete information to users. Example metrics include:

- Topic Coverage - Topic coverage describes the rate at which sought topics are available within the knowledge-base. 60% of topics covered.

- Customer Success - The rate that customers indicate they were successful in finding useful information. 52% success rate.

Once efficiency and effectiveness goals begin to be achieved, it's the opportunities that become more exciting. The KM system could result in freeing up managers and/or account teams to provide high-touch services for key accounts. More time could be spent on enhancing the knowledgebase content to cover more difficult and time-consuming topics, since the first knowledge that will go into the KM system will no doubt be the easier types of questions. This will further increase the savings associated with the system. A third opportunity is to reduce case backlog, which is one of the main reasons for customer dissatisfaction. Allocating additional resources to expediting closure rates can increase customer satisfaction. Finally, the KM system can free up time to visit top accounts, focus resources on service contract renewals, and proactively identify potential issues before they become service requests.

Technologies that Support Knowledge Management

Knowledge management solutions range from small software packages for individual use, such as brainstorming software, to highly specialized enterprise software suitable for use by teams, as with most groupware applications, or by hundreds of employees, as with some customer service KM software programs. Technologies that support knowledge management include: knowledge repositories, expertise access tools, E-learning applications, discussion and chat technologies, synchronous interaction tools, and search and data mining tools. Generally, organizations implementing a KM system already have a data center so they are not just building a knowledge database, but are also integrating it into their existing technical environment – their customer service system, **Interactive Voice Response (IVR)** system, email, remote diagnostics and other support systems. Experts suggest selecting a KM system that has open architectures and proven integrations into a variety of systems including help desk in order to ensure a successful implementation. A certain amount of reengineering will take place as processes will be affected requiring change in measurement and reporting.

Summary

ERP systems are great at processing events and transactions and gathering data. Yet, in many cases, their reporting tools are not dynamic enough to associate the data with that from other modules or other systems. In addition, the data may be granular and include too many irrelevant details or sub transactions. To gain valuable insights, often the data must be combined with other sources. BI Systems can consolidate data from multiple systems, ERP plus other disparate systems. In fact, most data warehousing projects include efforts to gather the data from as many relevant systems as possible. As it is gathered and written into the data warehouse, it may be transformed in several ways to make the data warehouse more efficient. Ideally, a company seeking to adopt a Balanced Scorecard would identify the processes and competencies that provide it with its greatest advantage and, then, identify the metrics that reflect its performance in these areas accordingly. As the company identifies these metrics, they would then establish the goals that would indicate success in meeting these objectives. Knowledge management helps capture knowledge that flows through informal groups – networks that businesses have little awareness of and zero control over. This knowledge can then be used by others in the organization that need it and don't know where to find it. All of these bolt-ons help to save time, money and energy in the organization, while finding new opportunities and identifying problem areas. These bolt-ons should work seamlessly with an ERP system in the overall context of the enterprise systems infrastructure.

Keywords

Ad hoc querying and reporting

Alerts

Analytics

Association

Balanced Scorecard

Business Intelligence (BI)

Business metric

Business Performance Management (BPM)

Data cleansing

Data enrichment

Data governance

Data Mining

Data scrubbing

Data warehouse

Explicit knowledge

Extraction

Fuzzy validation

Interactive Voice Response (IVR)

Knowledge Coordinator

Knowledge discovery

Knowledge Management

Lagging indicator

Leading indicator

Market segmentation

On-line Analytical Processing (OLAP)

Organizational knowledge

Performance Management

Personalization

Point of sale (POS)

Predefined report

Profiling

Scorecarding

Strict validation

Tacit knowledge

Quick Review

1. True/False: Whereas a data mart combines databases across an entire enterprise, data warehouses are usually smaller and focus on a particular subject or department.

2.   True/False: Tacit knowledge is knowledge gleaned from years and years of working in a particular industry and/or for a particular company.

3.   _____ is an interactive process for exploring and analyzing structured, domain-specific, information to discern trends or patterns, thereby deriving insights and drawing conclusions.

4.   _____ include activities to ensure that goals are consistently being met in an effective and efficient manner.

5.   _____ can be defined as the process through which organizations generate value from their intellectual and knowledge-based assets.

Questions to Consider

1.   List examples of higher-level business intelligence and lower-lower business intelligence.

2.   What are the four characteristics of a data warehouse?

3.   List the four perspectives of the Balanced Scorecard and explain.

4.   What is the difference between leading and lagging measures?

5.   What are the two types of knowledge, and which one is harder to extract?

6.   What are the steps to create a knowledge management system?

References

Arveson, P. (1998). *What is the Balanced Scorecard?* Retrieved November 26, 2007, from http://www.balancedscorecard.org/basics/bsc1.html

Compton, J. (2004). *Knowledge Management Plays A Key Role In CRM Success.* Retrieved November 26, 2007, from http://destinationcrm.com/print/default.asp?ArticleID=4532

David Skyrme Associates. (2008). Knowledge Management: making sense of an oxymoron. Retrieved August 1, 2008, from http://www.skyrme.com/insights/22km.htm

Dragoon, A. (2003). *Business Intelligence Gets Smart(er).* Retrieved May 3, 2008, from http://www.cio.com/article/29699/Business_Intelligence_Gets_Smart_er_

Eckerson, W. (2008). *Ten Characteristics of a Good KPI.* Retrieved December 2, 2007, from http://www.tdwi.org/publications/display.aspx?ID=7114

Glaser, J., & Stone, J. (2008). Effective Use of Business Intelligence. *Healthcare Financial Management*, *62*(2), 68-72.

Goeke, R. & Faley, R. (2007). Leveraging the Flexibility of Your Data Warehouse. *Communications of the ACM*, *50*(10), 107-111.

Markelevich, A. & Bell, R. (2006). RFID: The Changes It Will Bring. *Strategic Finance.* (August), 46-49.

Glossary

Account Payable Aging Report – A report used to group vouchers by due date in 30 day increments providing focus on those payable items that are oldest. (Ch. 8)

Account Payable Subsidiary Ledger – Also known as the Accounts Payable subsystem identifies the balances owed to every vendor calculated from purchases, returns to the vendor, allowances from the vendor and purchase discounts. (Ch. 8)

Accounts Receivable Aging Report – It is a report used to group receivables into 30 day increments that supports cash flow projections and provides focus on those balances that are the oldest. (Ch. 8)

Account Receivable Subsidiary Ledger – Also known as the Accounts Receivable subsystem identifies the balances every customer owes to the firm and is calculated from sales, less sales returns and allowances and sales discounts. (Ch. 8)

Activity – A step, or event, in a process. (Ch. 4)

Activity Based Costing (ABC) –ERP functionality that delivers business intelligence that supports strategic and operational decision-making by tracing overhead based on the cause and effect of relevant cost drivers to more objectively assign costs. (Ch. 8)

Ad hoc querying and reporting – Using a query method to allow users to quickly answer questions and develop their own reports and graphs. (Ch. 12)

Alert – Event notification to users based on predefined occurrences. These can be color coded, which would indicate scorecarding. (Ch. 12)

American Institute of Certified Public Accountants (AICPA) – National professional organization for CPAs that offers the CITP. (Ch. 11)

American National Standards Institute (ANSI) – Organization that helps to enhance both the global competitiveness of U.S. business and the U.S. quality of life by promoting and facilitating voluntary consensus standards and conformity assessment systems, and safeguarding their integrity. (Ch. 10)

Analytics – A type of business intelligence that uses advanced statistical analysis including predictive modeling, optimization and forecasting. (Ch. 12)

ANSIX12 – The recognized standard format for EDI transmissions that was developed by the American National Standards Institute (ANSI). (Ch. 10)

Application controls - Program controls embedded in business software that maintains segregation of duties and tracks activity in order to provide adequate security and maintain the integrity of the data the system supports. (Ch. 1 & 11)

Application outsourcing – A form of IT outsourcing in which the host maintains the software on their servers and licenses it to many different companies on a subscription basis over the Internet. (Ch. 7 & 11)

Application server – Hardware that runs business application software. (Ch. 2)

Application Service Provider (ASP) – A company that owns and manages data centers and provides hardware, software and network connectivity resources to its customers that have chosen to outsource those operations. (Ch. 7)

Appropriation request – A formal request for budget assignment and approval. (Ch. 8)

As Is – How work is currently being conducted in the organization. (Ch. 4)

Asset Management – The structured approach to controlling and tracking physical assets and costs of dispersed assets for capital intensive companies. In an ERP system, its basic function is to track financial and non-financial information about property, plant and equipment. (Ch. 8)

Asset Management Life Cycle – The steps to managing the life of capital assets: planning, approval, budgeting, implementation, settlement and capitalization, maintenance and use, retirement, and replacement investment. (Ch. 8)

Association – When certain events occur frequently together. Can be discovered during data mining. (Ch. 12)

Attributes – Fields that define the data in a database such as "Customer Name" or "Zip Code." (Ch. 2)

Authentication – The process of verifying the identity of users. Can be accomplished with passwords and User IDs. (Ch. 11)

Authoritative data source – The business logic between the application and database is programmed to maintain verifiable and valid data that is current, complete, and accurate. (Ch. 2)

Back office - Historical use of ERP systems. Includes financials, operations, and human resources functionality. (Ch. 2)

Back office systems – Traditional ERP systems that support transactional processing and operational support for activities that were not visible to the customer including accounting, human resources, and operations. (Ch. 7)

Balanced Scorecard - Performance management technique developed in 1992 by Robert Norton and Kaplan. Its premise is that to evaluate the health of an organization using four perspectives: customer, financial, business process and learning and growth. (Ch. 12)

Baseline performance measures – Performance measures taken before the ERP system is implemented. (Ch. 7)

Benchmarking - Comparing the firm's processes and performance to industry best practices and standards. (Ch. 3)

Benefit Administration– ERP functionality that permits HR professionals to administer and track employee participation in benefits programs. (Ch. 9)

Best practice - Certain techniques, processes and methodologies that have become generally recognized as more effective, efficient in an industry as it matures. (Ch. 1)

Big Bang Approach – The more aggressive approach to ERP implementation, in which the entire scope of the project is addressed at once across the organization. Also called the direct cutover approach. (Ch. 6)

Bill of Materials (BOM) – Defines the complete set of physical elements required to produce one unit of finished goods. (Ch. 10)

Biometrics - The highest level of authentication for systems. May be used to provide greater access control. (Ch. 11)

Bolt-on software – Third party software that is "bolted on" to the Core ERP system. Bolt-on software can be provided by the core system vendors or purchased from third party vendors. (Ch. 2, 6, & 7)

Bottlenecks – When a number of flows lead to a single role, the process may be hindered by insufficient resources dedicated to the roles and events downstream. (Ch. 4 & 10)

Business Intelligence (BI) - An interactive process for exploring and analyzing structured, domain-specific, information to discern trends or patterns, thereby deriving insights and drawing conclusions. (Ch. 12)

Business metrics - The accepted ratios and algorithms used by the financial and business community to judge the performance of a business. (Ch. 12)

Business Performance Management (BPM) – See performance management. (Ch. 12)

Business process - A collection of activities that together add value to the customer. (Ch. 1)

Business process improvement - Redesign of business processes in an incremental, methodical way. (Ch. 3)

Business Process Management (BPM) - Constant effort to improve business processes and help employees with process changes.

Business process outsourcing (BPO) – Outsourcing in which the service organization performs a business function for another organization (the outsourcer) (Ch. 11)

Business process reengineering (BPR) – The methods used to develop changes to processes, implement them, and gain efficiencies and new values. It is the fundamental, radical redesign in business processes to achieve dramatic improvements in key measures of performance, such as cost, quality, speed, and service. (Ch. 3)

Capacity Requirements Planning (CRP) – A method that uses the planned manufacturing schedule to analyze the requirements placed on manufacturing work centers. (Ch. 10)

Cash Journal – The journal that interfaces with AP and AR and can be kept in separate currencies and company codes. (Ch. 8)

Certified in the Governance of Enterprise IT (CGEIT) - The newest certification administered by ISACA. Designed to recognize the knowledge and application of IT governance principles and practices. (Ch. 11)

Certified Information Security Manager (CISM) - Certification offered by ISACA geared toward the changing role of the security manager, and bridges the knowledge gap between business strategy and IT security. (Ch. 11)

Certified Information System Auditor (CISA) - Flagship certification of ISACA qualifying an individual as globally proficient in the area of IS audit, control, and security. (Ch. 11)

Certified Information System Security Professional (CISSP) – Security certification offered since 1995 by the International Information Systems Security Certification Consortium. (Ch. 11)

Certified Information Technology Professional (CITP) - IT certification offered by the American Institute of Certified Public Accountants. (Ch. 11)

Change agents – Consultants that assist in organizational transformation. (Ch. 1 & 6)

Change controls - The controls that govern program changes. (Ch. 11)

Change management – The systematic approach to dealing with change, both from the perspective of an organization and on the individual level. (Ch. 1& 6)

Chart of Accounts – Listing of all accounts and their numbers tracked by the accounting system. (Ch. 8)

Clean slate reengineering - Involves starting from scratch, essentially a blank slate, and overhauling a process design. (Ch. 3)

Client server – Software architecture model that reduces network traffic by providing a query response rather than total file transfer. (Ch. 2)

Close probability – The percentage chance that an opportunity will be closed to a sale order. (Ch. 7)

Closed Loop MRP – MRP systems that were expanded to address other production capacities of the organization such as the availability of production personnel, machines, space and warehouse capacity. (Ch. 10)

Compliance – The tactical action to mitigate risk. (Ch. 8)

Computer operations controls - Controls that help ensure that the operational procedures over systems and programs in the company's data center run properly and timely. Protects hardware and software used to support business processes from internal and external threats. (Ch. 11)

Conference Room Pilot (CRP) – The cornerstone of systems testing where employees can execute real, duplicate, or model transactions in the new system. (Ch. 6)

Configuration - When the ERP system is tailored to fit the business by allowing system administrators to choose from a number of different options. (Ch. 2 & 6)

Constrained reengineering - Another term for technology-enabled reengineering because of the constraints imposed on the resulting business operations. (Ch. 3)

Contact –Engaging the customer and gathering information in an effort to match his/her needs with the company's capabilities. (Ch. 7)

Contact to Contract to Cash – Composed of the following activities: contact to contract, quote to cash, and order to cash. It is also known as the sales or revenue cycle. (Ch. 7)

Control Objectives for Information and related Technology (COBIT) – Guidance that is the generally accepted internal control framework for IT. (Ch. 11)

Core competency – The process that a company employs that transform generic inputs into uniquely developed products or services that provide the company with the competitive advantage. (Ch. 3)

Core ERP - Traditional ERP that includes HR, finance and operations. (Ch. 1 & 7)

Corporate governance – The structure and relationships that dictate how a corporation is directed, administered and controlled. (Ch. 8)

Cost accounting – Type of management accounting that tracks the cost of manufacturing and relates those costs to established cost standards. (Ch. 8 & 10)

Cost center – Organizational departments or functions that do not produce revenue but add to the cost of running an organization. (Ch. 8)

Cost center accounting – Type of management accounting that helps determine a cost center's costs. (Ch. 8)

Cost-benefit analysis – Comparing the cost and benefits of multiple alternatives and deriving the best ERP solution for an organization. (Ch. 3 & 5)

Create, read, update, delete (CRUD) – Defines user access and privileges to certain data. (Ch. 2)

Credit Management – Included in ERP financials. Supports the automatic update of AR balances so that credit analysts have up-to-date information on customer balances and credit limits. (Ch. 8)

Cross-functional flowchart – Widely used to diagram business processes involved in initiatives such as ERP implementations, business process reengineering and business process improvement. It is also referred to as a Process Map. (Ch. 4)

Cross-sell – The strategy of pushing new products to current customers based on their past purchases. (Ch. 7)

Customization - When programmers rewrite the underlying ERP code or develop extra code to make the software perform in ways the software vendor had not originally intended. (Ch. 2 & 6)

Customer order – The document that begins the fulfillment process of pick, pack and ship. (Ch. 7)

Customer Relationship Management (CRM) – Software that focuses on customers and potential customers allowing the company to drive revenue growth and reduce sales-related expenses. (Ch. 7)

Cycle time – The time consumed during process flow. Can provide a suitable subject for performance measurement, providing focus on the length of time it takes from the start to the end of the process. (Ch. 4)

Dashboard – Graphical user interface that includes graphs, charts, reminders, and KPIs. (Ch. 2)

Data – Raw facts and figures entered into an information system. (Ch. 12)

Data cleansing - The act of detecting and correcting (or removing) corrupt or inaccurate records from a record set. It is also known as data scrubbing. (Ch. 12)

Data duplication – Flows that point to and from information systems can be analyzed, to identify the extent to which the necessary data and the activities that create or use that data can be shared among the organization's many processes. (Ch. 4)

Data enrichment – The process of supplementing data extracted with other pertinent data. (Ch. 12)

Data governance – The creation and management of the organizational structures, policies, and processes needed to define, control, and ensure the quality of the enterprise data including criteria such as availability, usability, integrity, and security. (Ch. 12)

Data mart - A subset of a data repository usually designed for a specific set of users. (Ch. 12)

Data mining – The statistical analysis of large pools of historical data looking for correlations, trends, and patterns that may have escaped unnoticed. It is also known as knowledge discovery. (Ch. 12)

Data scrubbing - The act of detecting and correcting (or removing) corrupt or inaccurate records from a record set. Also known as data cleansing. (Ch. 12)

Data store – Information systems that support a business process. (Ch. 4)

Data symmetry - With a single data entry point errors are eliminated and users share a common view of the data. (Ch. 2)

Data warehouse - A large relational database that combines pertinent data in an aggregate, summarized form suitable for enterprise wide data analysis, reporting, and management decision making. (Ch. 12)

Database normalization – Sophisticated process by which database designers structure tables. (Ch. 2)

Database server - Computers optimized for database operation and can provide for data input and output from any number of application servers. (Ch. 2)

Decision point – A point in a process where a choice has to be made. Depicted as a diamond in process maps. (Ch. 4)

Development system – The database in which application programmers make changes to a system. (Ch. 11)

Direct Cutover Approach – The more aggressive approach to implementation, in which the entire scope of the project is addressed at once across the organization. It is also called the big bang approach. (Ch. 6)

Economic Order Quantity (EOQ) – Calculation where items in the stock are analyzed for their ordering and carrying costs to get the optimal ordering quantity to minimize both of these variable costs. (Ch. 10)

Electronic Data Interchange (EDI) – The use of computerized communication to exchange business event data between companies. (Ch. 10)

Employee Performance Management – ERP functionality that helps to streamlines employee appraisal from goal planning and coaching to performance assessments and rewards. (Ch. 9)

Employee Self Service - Allows employees to enter and update work-specific information by providing access to system interfaces tailored to the employee's role, experience, work content, language, and information needs. (Ch. 9)

Engineering BOM – The necessary raw materials calculated to determine what must be on hand as production begins in order to get a desired quantity of finished products. (Ch. 10)

Enterprise application integration (EAI) – The process of combining information from any number of sources. A form of middleware that connects applications together. (Ch. 2)

Enterprise Learning - ERP functionality that includes employee training profiles, courses, sessions, instructors, and course evaluations. (Ch. 9)

Enterprise Resource Planning (ERP) - Systems that serve as the most important part of an enterprise's systems because they support the information associated with the organization's primary inputs of materials and labor, its production and value-adding processes, and its distribution and sales. (Ch. 1)

Enterprise Risk Management (ERM) – Framework that addresses risks and opportunities affecting value creation or preservation. (Ch. 4 & 11)

Enterprise Systems (ES) – Includes ERP. Any business system used throughout the organization. (Ch. 1)

Environment, Health and Safety - ERP functionality that provides the tools to administer compliance with the health and safety regulations that arise from local, state and federal agencies. (Ch. 9)

Event - A step in a business process. (Ch. 4)

Event monitoring – When certain events happen, CRM users are notified. For instance, when a customer's purchases reach a certain amount, gift cards are mailed to the customer as a reward. (Ch. 7).

Explicit knowledge - Information that can be easily documented and codified and stored in a knowledge management system. (Ch. 12)

Extraction – The retrieval of data from one or more sources within a company. It involves combining data from several sources into one. (Ch. 12)

Fat-client – A PC in a client server environment that provides rich functionality independent of the server. (Ch. 2)

Feedback loop – Information provided from capacity requirements planning to the master production schedule if there is not enough capacity available to produce the desired quantity of a product. (Ch. 10)

File server – A computer attached to a network that has the primary purpose of providing a location for the shared storage of computer files (e.g., such as documents, sound files, photographs, movies, images, databases) that can be accessed by the workstations that are attached to the computer network. (Ch. 2)

File sharing - Allows users to download a file and the personal computer software to use its computational power to perform a job. (Ch. 2)

Financial Accounting – The type of accounting aimed at external users, such as shareholders, governmental agencies, the work force and the general public. Its primary purpose is to produce financial statements such as the Income Statement, Statement of Retained Earnings, Balance Sheet, and Statement of Cash Flows. (Ch. 8)

Financials – The module of ERP systems which include a suite of integrated applications that encompass all financial activity including accounting, finance and asset management. (Ch. 8)

First Tier ERP Vendors - Fortune 500 companies and other companies whose sales are over $250 million including large government and other national operations and with employees over 1,000. (Ch. 1)

Flow time – Time between process events that can be measured to identify substantial contributors to delays and underutilization. (Ch. 4)

Forecasting – Using sales information and purchase histories including who sold what, when, when promised, who serviced, what were the incident reports and customer service overhead. (Ch. 7)

Foreign key – A key that points to a primary key in a different or "foreign" table. (Ch. 2)

Front office – A resource system that support activities that more directly involve customers. (Ch. 2)

Front office systems – Software, such as CRM, that supports activities that directly involve the organization's customer interface. (Ch. 7)

Full time equivalents (FTE) – The total internal cost of labor that can be calculated by multiplying the percentage of team members' time dedicated to the project, the length of their commitment to the project and the team headcount. (Ch. 5)

Functional configuration – Selecting from various options in ERP software to enable, disable, or otherwise modify the way processes behave. (Ch. 2)

Fuzzy validation – The correction of records that partially match existing, known records. (Ch. 12)

Gap-fit analysis – A methodology used to quantify the comparison of system functionality to system requirements. (Ch. 5)

Generally Accepted Accounting Principles (GAAP) – Standards and conventions US-based companies follow in recording and summarizing transactions and preparing financial statements. (Ch. 8)

General Ledger (GL) – The backbone of financial accounting, which includes the balance of every account within the chart of accounts. (Ch. 8)

Governance – Manages the strategic directives a company wants to follow. (Ch. 8)

Governance, Risk, and Compliance (GRC) – Functionality that supports controls for enterprise applications such as enforcing proper segregation of duties in enterprise applications, reducing fraud with continuous monitoring of business transactions, and providing defensible evidence of a proper control environment. (Ch. 8)

Graphical user interface (GUI) – An interface between the user and the information system. (Ch. 2)

Handoffs – Processes that involve departmental interaction or the transfer of responsibility from one role to another. These can provide opportunities for mistakes, miscommunication, or delay. (Ch. 4)

Homepage - A web page is intended to provide a starting point used to navigate to the information and applications needed by a group or team of employees, it can be considered a homepage. (Ch. 2)

Human capital – The employees, executives, contractors and the other people that participate in and contribute to the organization's objectives. (Ch. 8)

Human Capital Management (HCM) - The administration of employees, executives, contractors and the other people that participate in and contribute to the organization's objectives; and the strategies embraced to optimize the value of these assets. (Ch. 9)

Human Resources (HR) – The department in a company involved in hiring and employing employees. (Ch. 9)

Human Resources Management – In ERP terms, the software solutions used by the Human Resource (HR) department. (Ch. 9)

Incremental approach – A slower approach to deployment in which the ERP system is rolled out by function (module by module) or geographical area. It is also referred to as a phased approach. (Ch. 6)

Information flows – In process maps, the movement of information across the organization. (Ch. 4)

Information security controls – Controls that require that data only be modified as defined by the business rules established for the processes the system supports. (Ch. 11)

Information Systems Audit and Control Association (ISACA) – Global organization for information governance, control, security and audit professionals. Offers the CISA, CISM, and CGEIT certifications. (Ch. 11)

Instance – An installation of ERP software and related components and defined by the boundaries set on the business process it supports. (Ch. 2)

Integrated Audit – A newer type of audit that entails more than just testing and verifying the accuracy of the amounts in the financial statements; there is and a much greater emphasis is placed on internal controls. (Ch. 11)

Internal controls – Checks and balances put in place in the system to reduce or eliminate the possibility that inaccurate, incomplete or unauthorized information is entered into the system and to ensure the information in the system is properly processed to produce reliable output. (Ch. 4 & 11)

International Information Systems Security Certification Consortium (ISC) – The organization that offers the Certified Information System Security Professional (CISSP) certification. (Ch. 12)

Inventory Management – Refers to ERP functionality that supports activities such as the tracking and control of raw material, stocked items, WIP and finished products in a single integrated inventory control environment. (Ch. 10)

Inventory status file – A file that maintains a record of inventory on hand. (Ch. 10)

Investment Management – ERP functionality that provides the tools for pre-investment analysis. (Ch. 8)

IT application controls – Controls that support the transactions within the ERP system, assuring that the data that is entered and the processing and system output are accurate. (Ch. 11)

IT dependent manual controls - Procedures that are reliant on output from information systems. (Ch. 11)

IT general controls – Controls that support the technical environment in which ERP systems operate. (Ch. 11)

IT Governance- Refers to the leadership and organizational structures and processes that ensure that the organization's IT sustains and extends the organization's strategies and objectives. (Ch. 11)

Just-in-Time (JIT) – Inventory methodology that allows companies to minimize inventory while still having product on hand when needed to fulfill sales orders. (Ch. 10)

Knowledge Coordinator – The person in an organization responsible for implementation of a knowledge management system. (Ch. 12).

Knowledge discovery - The statistical analysis of large pools of historical data looking for correlations, trends, and patterns that may have escaped unnoticed. It is also known as data mining. (Ch. 12)

Knowledge Management (KM) - A formal, directed process of figuring out what information a company has that could benefit others in the company then devising ways of making it easily available. (Ch. 12)

Lagging indicator – Refers to financial metrics, which provide knowledge of past activities. (Ch. 12)

Lead time – The time that elapses between placing an order and actually receiving it. (Ch. 10)

Leading indicator – Refers to other metrics besides financial that set expectations for future activities. (Ch. 12)

Lean Manufacturing – A manufacturing strategy that seeks to produce a high level of throughput with a minimum of inventory. (Ch. 10)

Learning Management – ERP module that includes employee training profiles, courses, sessions, instructors, and course evaluations. It is also referred to as Enterprise Learning. (Ch. 9)

Legacy system - An older, stand-alone system that does not connect or share data with other systems. (Ch. 1)

Liquidity forecast – ERP functionality that integrates anticipated cash inflows and outflows from financial accounting, purchasing and sales in order to show mid- to long-term cash flow trends. (Ch. 8)

Local Area Networks (LANS) – A computer network covering a small geographic area, like a home, office, or group of buildings. (Ch. 2)

Mainframe architecture - All computing intelligence is within the central host computer. (Ch. 2)

Managerial Accounting – Type of accounting aimed at internal users, which are those information consumers that act inside the company to further the firm's objectives. (Ch. 8)

Manager Self-Service – ERP functionality that provides managers an insight into their staff and their budget, two areas most pressing for managers. (Ch. 9)

Manufacturing BOM – A description of what to do with the materials, what equipment to use, and how to go about making the product, and the stated amount of output when making a product. (Ch. 10)

Manufacturing Requirements Planning II (MRP II) – Systems developed in the 1970s to address issues such as frequent changes in sales forecasts which require continual readjustments in production. (Ch. 1)

Many-to-many – Technically, a very complicated relationship where any number of key values may be associated with any number of attribute values. (Ch. 2)

Many-to-one – This is essentially the reverse of the "One-to-Many" case. (Ch. 2)

Market of one – When products are marketed to specific individuals versus segments. (Ch. 7)

Market segmentation – The process of dividing customers into mutually exclusive groups so that customers in one group are as similar as possible and customers in another group are as different as possible from the other groups. (Ch. 12)

Master file – Relatively permanent data files of records that reflect current status of business items such as inventory, fixed assets, customers and employees. (Ch. 2)

Master Production Schedule (MPS) –The production plan for finished goods based off the sales forecast. (Ch. 10)

Material Requirement Planning (MRP) – A method of an ordering system that uses a bill of materials (BOM) and explodes it based on the master production schedule (MPS) to determine materials requirements. (Ch. 10)

Materials Management (MM) – ERP functionality that supports materials management functions and processes in day-to-day business operations. (Ch. 10)

Material Requirements Planning (MRP) – A software-based production planning and inventory control system used to manage manufacturing processes. (Ch. 10)

Middleware – Software that connects software components or applications. (Ch. 2)

Modules - Separate software components, grouped into certain business functions, of an ERP system; one module may support financials, while others would support production planning, materials or vendor management. (Ch. 1 & 2)

Motion – The ergonomic issues of the production process and include such things as repetitive lifting, bending, and reaching in a work place. (Ch. 10)

Move order – Transfers the standard cost of raw materials to the plant and updates WIP. (Ch. 10)

Multi-tier architecture – Systems architecture in which a middle tier (application) is added between the user system interface client environment and the database server environment. (Ch. 2)

Occupation Safety and Health Administration (OSHA) – Federal regulatory agency charged with the regulation of the health and safety of employees. (Ch. 9)

Off-Balance Sheet financing – Expensing payment for services such as software instead of capitalizing on the Balance Sheet as assets. (Ch. 7)

Off-page Connector – A process mapping symbol used to indicate that the process continues onto another page. (Ch. 4)

On Demand – A fast, inexpensive method of implementing software in which the software is hosted by a third party. (Ch. 7)

On-page Connector – A process mapping symbol used to indicate that the process continues at another point on the same page. (Ch. 4)

On Premise – Traditional method of implementing software on the company's own servers. (Ch. 7)

On-line Analytical Processing (OLAP) – The fast analysis of shared multi-dimensional information. (Ch. 12)

One-to-Many – A relationship between two entitles where one table is one (1) and the relationship with another tables is many. (Ch. 2)

One-to-One – The primary key is associated with an attribute that will have only a single value. (Ch. 2)

Opportunity –Potential sales by salesperson. (Ch. 7)

Order Management – Functionality to capture and track customer orders through fulfillments, billing and payment. (Ch. 7)

Order to Cash – Activities that presume a quoted price and begins when the customers place their orders. (Ch. 7)

Organizational knowledge – Explicit and tacit knowledge that has been captured and accumulated since the inception of an organization. (Ch. 12)

Overhead costing – Management accounting that helps with planning, allocating and controlling overhead in a company. (Ch. 8)

Overhead costs – Indirect costs that cannot be assigned to a specific cost product. (Ch. 8)

Parallel Accounting – Functionality in ERP Accounting module that enables a company to keep several General Ledgers simultaneously according to different accounting principles to ensure that local and international reporting requirements are met. (Ch. 8)

Partner Portal - An interface that manages all correspondence related to partners, customer support and marketing campaigns. (Ch. 7)

Payroll– ERP functionality that automates accounting and preparation of payroll checks for employee salaries, wages and bonuses, calculation of various taxes and benefit deductions, and the generation of periodic payroll checks as well as the various local, state and federal tax information and forms. (Ch. 9)

Performance Management – Bolt-on to ERP that provides answers to the question, "How well are we performing right now?" It includes activities to ensure that goals are consistently being met in an effective and efficient manner. (Ch. 12)

Personalization – The ability to sell to the market-of-one based on data collected such as buying history and market or personal demographics. (Ch. 7 & 12)

Personnel Management – ERP functionality that covers all HR aspects from recruiting to retirement. (Ch. 9)

Phased approach – A slower approach to deployment in which the ERP system is rolled out by function (module by module) or geographical area. It is also called an incremental approach. (Ch. 6)

Plant Maintenance – ERP functionality that helps an organization increase the availability of machinery and other fixed assets, reduce the number of breakdowns through preventive maintenance, coordinate and employ human resources to fulfill specific maintenance orders, and reduce costs of inspections and preventive and planned maintenance. (Ch. 10)

Point of sale (POS) – The hardware and software used for checkouts and is the equivalent of an electronic cash register. (Ch. 12)

Portal – The user's homepage. (Ch. 2)

Predefined report – The reports, graphs and dashboards that come standard with a BI tool. (Ch. 12)

Pre-hire-to-retire employee lifecycle – The HR process from recruitment to retire. (Ch. 9)

Primary key – An attribute in a table that uniquely identifies the data in a row of a table. (Ch. 2)

Process map – Systems diagramming technique widely used to flowchart business processes involved in initiatives such as ERP implementations, business process reengineering and business process improvement. It is also referred to as a Cross-Functional Flowchart. (Ch. 4)

Product configurator - An automated software application that guides a prospect through the various options and generate the specifications necessary to generate an accurate quote by checking to make sure that different components of a product will work together .(Ch. 7)

Product costing – A component of managerial accounting used for managing manufacturing costs and providing services. (Ch. 8)

Production Planning (PP) – ERP functionality that enables the production planner to create realistic production plans across the different manufacturing locations, including subcontractors, to fulfill demand in a timely manner and according to standards expected by the customer. (Ch. 10)

Production system – The system that represents the "live" deployment of an ERP system. (Ch. 11)

Profiling – The process of using relevant information to describe characteristics of a group of customers and identify what discriminates them from other customers to determine drivers of their purchasing decisions. (Ch. 12)

Profit center – A department or other business unit responsible for both revenues and costs of the center. (Ch. 8)

Profit center accounting – The type of accounting focused on determining the operating profit of a center (such as a department or division). (Ch. 8)

Profitability analysis – The method of management accounting that considers segments of the organization and determines the profit they generate. (Ch. 8)

Profitability segment – Can be the intersection of any number of entities such as products, customers, activities, or organizational units. (Ch. 8)

Programmed controls - Automated controls within the software application such as data entry validation. (Ch. 11)

Public Committee Accounting Oversight Board (PCAOB) – A board created by SOX as a private sector non-profit organization to oversee the auditors of public accounting firms. (Ch. 11)

Qualification – The step that occurs after engaging the prospect, in which the sales representative will determine if the prospect meets certain criteria: applicability, affordability, and authority. (Ch. 7)

Quality controls – Controls that are implemented to reduce error rate in manufacturing. (Ch. 3)

Quality Management – Functionality in an ERP system that helps an organization by building quality tasks into the production processes in all phases of a product – from the planning phase through the implementation and use phases. (Ch. 10)

Quote – A dollar amount of an estimate of costs and usually includes an expiration date. (Ch. 7)

Quote to Cash - Activities that begin when a price is quoted and continue until the account is paid. (Ch. 7)

Radio Frequency Identification (RFID) – Tiny computer chips or tags embedded in products and packaging that allows them to be tracked over wireless networks using wireless technology. (Ch. 10)

Real-time - Responding to input immediately. (Ch. 1)

Records – An instance of the data in a database such as all attributes of a customer. Records are the rows in a database. (Ch. 2)

Recruit-to-Retire Process – The process used to recruit an employee and continuing to the time the employee retires. It is also known as the pre-hire-to-retire employee lifecycle. (Ch. 9)

Recruitment Management– This module typically supports the opening components of the employee life-cycle including: attracting potential applicants, evaluating their suitability as an employee, analyzing the skills necessary to support various functions in the organization, articulating job descriptions for those functions, and matching potential new-hires with job descriptions. (Ch. 9)

Reengineering Principles – Managerial techniques thought to make companies world-class. In his book, Reengineering the Corporation, Hammer expands on these principles. (Ch. 3)

Relational database – A type of database where data is stored in tables (or relations) connected with attributes in common. (Ch. 2)

Request for Information (RFI) - is an invitation for vendors to submit information about themselves and the ability for the solution to support the functional requirements identified as critical to the business. (Ch. 5)

Requirements analysis – The detailed analysis companies go through to determine all the functionalities they need and desire from an ERP system. (Ch. 5)

Return on Investment (ROI) – The economic advantages of the project are weighed against the cost. (Ch. 5)

Rework – Remediating inventory or other work because of error. (Ch. 4)

Risk – The potential an event (or series of events) can adversely affect the achievement of a company's objectives. (Ch. 11)

Risk Management – Assesses the areas of exposure and potential impacts. It also includes the activities that identify the threats the company faces as well as the subsequent actions taken to minimize the potential negative impacts that these threats may present. (Ch. 8 & 11)

Role ambiguity – Process maps can firmly identify which participants are responsible for filling which roles, thereby eliminating confusion among the participants in the process. (Ch. 4)

Roles – Functional units in a process. (Ch. 4)

Sales Cycle – All of the steps included in earning revenue. (Ch. 7)

Sales Force Automation (SFA) – Provides functionality that reduces the burden typically associated with sales efforts. (Ch. 7)

Sales Order – A customer order of merchandise or services. (Ch. 7)

Sarbanes-Oxley Act of 2002 (SOX) – A congressional act passed in 2002 for the purpose of spotlighting internal controls over financial reporting for publicly-traded companies. (Ch. 4 & 11)

SAS 70 – The examination and certification that signifies that a service organization has had its control objectives and control activities examined by an independent public accounting firm. (Ch. 11)

SAS 70 Type I – The simplest SAS 70 report that only describes the service organization's description of controls at a specific point in time. (Ch. 11)

SAS 70 Type II - includes not only the service organization's description of controls, but also includes detailed testing of the service organization's controls over a minimum six month period. (Ch. 11)

Scorecarding – Using color codes to monitor metrics on a dashboard. (Ch. 12)

Second Tier ERP Vendors - Medium sized companies with sales from $2-$250 million with most of the companies between $5 and $50 million. Employees range between 100 and 999. (Ch. 1)

Segmentation – Grouping customers according to certain attributes such as region, age, gender, or purchasing power allowing for more effective targeted marketing. (Ch. 7)

Service Auditor's Report – The title of the SAS 70 report that is issued to a service organization's customers. (Ch. 11)

Service Level Agreement (SLA) – A document that defines the responsibilities of both parties such as payment by the client and minimum level of availability by the provider. (Ch. 7)

Service Management – ERP functionality that manages the lifecycle changes to existing services or installed products after the initial order is fulfilled. (Ch. 10)

Small-to-medium sized enterprises (SME) – it is made up of the second and third tiers in the ERP market. (Ch. 1)

Software as a Service (SaaS) – Licensing applications over the Internet for a fee. (Ch. 7)

Strict validation – Method of data cleansing that rejects any incomplete information or entries. (Ch. 12)

Super-user – A person in a functional area that is trained by the trainer then relays information and knowledge to the rest of the team. (Ch. 6)

Supply Chain Management (SCM) – Considered a bolt-on to core ERP, as well as the technologies that support an efficient and smooth flow of materials to and from the enterprise. (Ch. 10)

Swim lanes – The roles in the process indicated with vertical or horizontal rows across or down the page. (Ch. 4)

System Diagrams (SD) – Type of information systems documentation that provides a graphical representation of the flow of the process and the interactions between employees and the information generated by work they accomplish. (Ch. 4)

Tacit knowledge - This type of knowledge is contained in peoples' heads and is what people know. It is knowledge gleaned from years and years of working in a particular industry and/or for a particular company. (Ch. 12)

Talent Management - Works with Recruitment Management to analyze personnel usage within an organization and help retain good employees. (Ch. 9)

Technical configuration - These settings allow the software to operate on the company's hardware and network, and to gain access to the data and other resources available. (Ch. 2)

Technology-enabled reengineering – Involves the use of technology to facilitate the reengineering process; the company's processes are reengineered to match best practices in the software. (Ch. 3)

Termination – The end of a process. (Ch. 4)

Thin-client – PCs that connect or browse to web pages supporting any number of software applications. (Ch. 2)

Third Tier ERP Vendors – Smaller companies with sales under $2,000,000 and under 100 employees, and other smaller organizations such as government, non-profits and academic institutions. (Ch. 1)

Three-tier architecture – Technical architecture that includes a middle tier between the user system interface client environment and the database server environment. It is also known as multi-tier architecture. (Ch. 2)

Time and Labor Management Module – ERP functionality that allows workers to submit timecard data online and supervisors to review and approve. (Ch. 9)

To Be – Improved or reengineered processes. (Ch. 4)

Total Cost of Ownership (TCO) – The total amount that will likely be incurred throughout the system's life cycle. (Ch. 5)

Total Quality Management (TQM) – Processes are studied in an attempt to identify opportunities to effect minor, small-scale changes leading to small improvements that are expected to accumulate and build on one another over time. (Ch. 3)

Two-factor identification - Authentication to information systems that require the combination of two forms of ID. (Ch. 11)

Trading partner – Companies that exchange EDI communications with each other. (Ch. 10)

Train-the-trainer – A training technique in which someone in a functional area becomes a super-user by attending in-depth training conducted by the vendor, consultant, or implementation partner and then trains their coworkers. (Ch. 6)

Transaction – A business event that has an impact on the financial statements

Treasury Operations – ERP functionality that includes cash management, cash flow analysis in any currency and in multiple time periods and capital budgeting. (Ch. 8)

Trending – Providing data to operations managers to highlight potential shortfalls or excesses in stock levels allowing for accommodations to mitigate the effects of otherwise unforeseeable market activity. (Ch. 7)

Trigger event – The activity that begins a business process begins. (Ch. 4)

Type I – see SAS 70 Type I.

Type II – see SAS 70 Type II.

Uninterruptible power source (UPS) – A generator that protects servers against a power outage. (Ch. 11)

Up-sell – Marketing additional items to the customer or items that are more profitable or otherwise preferable for the seller instead of the original sale. (Ch. 7)

Vanilla Implementation – The acceptance of all the defaults with which the ERP package is shipped, thereby eliminating all customization and configuration requirements, relying explicitly on the ERP software vendor's prescribed methodology. (Ch. 2 & 6)

Vendor Managed Inventory (VMI) – A type of business process outsourcing in which the supplier creates the PO based on the demand information exchanged by the retailer/customer. (Ch. 10)

Vertical solution – A business system that is targeted to a single, specific industry. (Ch. 1)

Voucher system – The matching of the purchase order, receiving report and vendor invoice prior to payment. (Ch. 8)

Wait state – In a manufacturing environment, the time where production is stalled, usually due to bottlenecks, long production runs, and poor synchronization. (Ch. 10)

Warehouse Management System (WMS) – Controls the activities of movements into, out of, and through a warehouse by using real-time information about the status of inventory supply and demand. (Ch. 10)

Web browser – A graphical user interface that allows users to interact with application servers via the Internet or through a company intranet. (Ch. 2)

Workforce Analytics - Allows the organization to measure the effectiveness of their HR strategies and programs and measure their workforce's contributions to the bottom line. (Ch. 9)

Workforce Management – In ERP terms, the software solutions used by the Human Resource (HR) department. Also known as Human Resources Management. (Ch. 9)

Index

D

E

5156957R2